VAGRANCY IN LAW AND PRACTICE UNDER THE OLD POOR LAW

Vagrancy in Law and Practice under the Old Poor Law

AUDREY ECCLES

Routledge
Taylor & Francis Group
LONDON AND NEW YORK

First published 2012 by Ashgate Publishing

Published 2016 by Routledge
2 Park Square, Milton Park, Abingdon, Oxon OX14 4RN
711 Third Avenue, New York, NY 10017, USA

First issued in paperback 2017

Routledge is an imprint of the Taylor & Francis Group, an informa business

British Library Cataloguing in Publication Data
Eccles, Audrey.
Vagrancy in law and practice under the old poor law.
1. Vagrancy – England – History – 18th century. 2. Poor laws – England – History – 18th century.
I. Title
345.4'20248-dc23

Library of Congress Cataloging-in-Publication Data
Eccles, Audrey.
Vagrancy in law and practice under the old poor law / Audrey Eccles.
p. cm.
Includes bibliographical references and index.
ISBN 978-1-4094-0487-3 (hardcover) 1. Vagrancy – Great Britain – History – 18th century. 2. Contraventions (Criminal law) – Great Britain – History – 18th century. 3. Poor laws – Great Britain – History – 18th century. I. Title.
KD8079.E23 2012
345.42'024809033 – dc23

ISBN 13: 978-1-138-10873-8 (pbk)
ISBN 13: 978-1-4094-0487-3 (hbk)

Contents

List of Plates

Acknowledgements

I began this research over thirty years ago, when I was an archivist at Kendal Record Office and completing a PhD on the history of obstetrics, and was lured into the study of vagrancy by the fortunate coincidence that the Westmorland Quarter Sessions rolls contain an unusual number of vagrant women giving birth on the road. Since then I have continued the research in five other counties, chosen for no more scientific reason than that I happened to live there for a time.

Over these years I have accumulated many debts of gratitude to archivists and librarians, many of whose names I never knew. Among those I did know I must first mention my old friend and former colleague the late Sheila MacPherson, who during my time as her senior assistant at the Kendal office gave me the ongoing task of calendaring the Westmorland Quarter Sessions records and thus introduced me to the vagrants, some of whose stories appear in this book; likewise my predecessor at the office Richard Samways for much hospitality and many stimulating discussions over the years. Jacqui Halewood and the searchroom staff at Dorset have contributed their local knowledge, while Sally Bevan and the searchroom staff at London Metropolitan Archives and Joy Caisley, law librarian at Southampton University, have been most helpful, as have the staff at my local library Lockswood.

Although this work has been done as an independent scholar I had the good fortune to meet Joanna Innes about two years ago, whose encouragement and generous sharing of her expertise have played a large part in bringing the work to fruition. Others at the same conference have since given me the benefit of their experience, especially Pete King on certain legal points. Any errors that remain are of course my own. I also wish to thank my grandson Matt Orton for reading the bulk of the book in draft and asking useful questions during his time reading history at Magdalen College Oxford. And last but a long way from least I thank my husband for endless support and encouragement, and patient sorting out of IT issues.

Audrey Eccles

Preface

Historians have addressed the concerns of government to control the wandering poor, both in the sixteenth and seventeenth centuries and after the New Poor Law in 1834. In the former period disbanded retainers, former soldiers, gypsies and Irish immigrants were the focus of concern, in the latter tramps of all sorts, again including the Irish, but also the drunk and disorderly and a ragbag of petty offenders. In both periods there was a persistent belief on the part of propagandists and legislators that vagrancy was caused not by unsatisfactory conditions of employment or by any actions of governments but by moral failings on the part of the 'inferior classes'.

However, there has so far been remarkably little attention paid to vagrancy in the intervening period, although this assumption that vagrancy was the fault of the feckless poor continued, despite a few dissenting voices. Nevertheless vagrancy law changed considerably in the first half of the eighteenth century by a process of repeated adjustments as the system was revised to take account of flaws emerging in practice. This evolutionary process from the crucial 1700 Vagrant Removal Costs Act to the 1744 Vagrant Act is addressed in detail in this book for the first time, and forms the background to the case studies of those dealt with under vagrancy law by the justices of the peace and parishes in the second half of the century.

In working on the Quarter Sessions records left by the application of vagrancy law by county magistrates it emerged that the justices were manipulating the law to plug gaps in government provision, notably for servicemen and their families and the mobile poor in general, and to deal with a mass of minor offences. In this it supports the work of Peter King on the justices' remaking of the law at local level. It became clear also that vagrancy was not exactly the same thing in Middlesex as it was in Dorset or Westmorland, and I suspect other counties than the six I have explored would yield further insights.

Between 1744 and 1792 no further changes to vagrancy law took place, but in the first quarter of the nineteenth century there was a further period of revision as a response to a changing demographic situation and changes in the economy. Population growth put pressure on an economy only just beginning to industrialize, and an even worse economic situation in Ireland greatly increased in-migration both temporary and permanent. Inflation and the food shortages of the 1790s, partly caused by import difficulties during the wars against France, increasing rural unemployment but growing industrial demand for labour, provoked a good deal of social dislocation and movement from place to place.

A further phase of adjustment to vagrancy law followed to deal with these problems and the increasing burden on the ratepayers from the support, however minimal, of the poor, especially the mobile poor, for whom no provision had ever legally been made. Indeed both settlement law and the 1792 Vagrant Act were intended to inhibit such movement without official permission. Many were dealt with as vagrants for want of a better system, and the increase in 'casual poor' in the early nineteenth century caused the system so painstakingly established in the first half of the previous century to collapse under the strain.

By 1824 much of the old system had been dismantled or quietly allowed to lapse. In some counties vagrant offices where the mobile poor could obtain a night's lodging and a simple supper attempted to facilitate the movement of workers from places of serious unemployment, mostly rural, to the new industrialized towns, and to make begging unnecessary. Arguably these offices served as models for the casual wards of the post-1834 period, beyond the scope of this book.

Chapter 1
The History of Vagrancy Law

Vagrancy law before the eighteenth century

Vagrancy was first made a criminal offence in the reign of Edward III. In the late fourteenth century attempts to restrict the movements of labourers were prompted by the shortage of labour caused by the high mortality of the Black Death, which opened up an opportunity for labourers to move from the manor where they belonged to others where the dire need for hands might induce lords of the manor to offer better terms. By the early sixteenth century, as the feudal system broke down, discarded retainers were the problem: lacking a patron and often a craft, they posed a potential threat roaming in search of a livelihood. Later in the century groups of disbanded soldiers were much feared: on discharge they were allowed to keep their arms and uniform, and although parishes were supposed to support them there was little or no legal obligation for them to do so, hence they were alleged to be wandering about wresting what they needed from a terrorized public (Beier 1985; Slack 1974). Indeed, the almost complete failure of subsequent governments to provide financial support for discharged soldiers and seamen and their dependants remained a prominent cause of vagrancy even in the Victorian period (Trustram 1984; Brereton 1986, 8–9).

In 1572 previous vagrancy acts were repealed but fresh ferocious measures were enacted against vagrants: beggars over the age of fourteen could be committed and if found guilty at the next sessions 'grievously whipped and burned through the gristle of the right ear with a hot iron of the compass of an inch across' unless a householder would take them into service and they served a whole year. A third offence by anyone over the age of eighteen was felony without benefit of clergy (14 Eliz. c. 5 1572). Although these extreme punishments were rare, they were occasionally inflicted (Leonard 1900, 70). It was simply assumed that work was always available and that anybody wandering and begging must be wilfully idle. The same act, anticipating that the addition of vagrants would greatly increase the number of prisoners sent to gaol, enacted that the justices in sessions should assess a reasonable sum in each parish towards the relief of such prisoners.[1]

A list of idle and suspicious characters was supplied in this act, most of whom reappeared in eighteenth-century legislation. Harbouring vagabonds was made punishable by a fine of 20s, rescuing them £5. Exceptions were made for soldiers and sailors with a licence from two justices, harvest workers, honest servants whose masters had died or turned them away, and victims of highway robbery. Licences were only valid within one county, and had to be renewed in the next. Fines were imposed on constables neglecting to apprehend vagrants. Poor refusing to do work they were capable of doing were to be whipped or set in the stocks for a first refusal, then to be rogues and vagabonds within the act.

More positively the bones of a settlement system and statutory provision for poor relief were established by the same act, administered by the justices, who were supposed to register aged and impotent poor who had been resident in their district for three years and give them an allowance, and to appoint overseers of the poor. Poor other than the leprous and bedridden were to be removed to their place of birth or where they had last lived for three years.

This act was further developed four years later (18 Eliz. c. 3 1576): reciting that, whereas by the former act vagrants were ordered to be sent to gaol at the charge of the parish where they were apprehended, and that to avoid the charge 'many are suffered to pass and winked at', the constables were now to pass them from one constable to the next, the cost to be shared by each parish through which they passed en route to the gaol. It may be doubted whether this was any more effective, and the system was changed again in 1700.

A very important and long-lasting innovation under this act was the establishment of houses of correction or bridewells, on the model of the London Bridewell, to be set up in every county and paid for by a county tax collected by officers appointed by the justices in Quarter Sessions, who were also directed to appoint the governors or keepers. Hitherto there had only been county gaols run by gaolers under the sheriff in the king's name, and various private prisons; the houses of correction were the first prisons under direct county control, combining punishment and setting the poor to work. Parish officers faced with poor who would not work or spoiled and embezzled materials they were given were empowered to commit them. Individuals were allowed to make gifts and bequests towards the cost of houses of correction and for providing stocks of materials for the poor to work on; from the very start bridewells were intended to deal with both local poor and wandering rogues. Paupers were expected

[1] This clause was still in force in 1764 and formed the authority for the relief of prisoners, although by then prisoners were a county charge (Burn 1764, 38).

to manage on whatever relief they were given; if they begged they were to be whipped, and to be punished as rogues and vagabonds for a second offence. There was no appeal process.

Around the turn of the century, notably in 1597 (39 Eliz. c. 3) and 1601 (43 Eliz. c. 2), new laws further developed the embryo poor law provision. By the 1597 act impotent poor might beg for food in their own parish by permission of the parish officers, and discharged soldiers and mariners with passes might beg notwithstanding the general ban on begging of the same act (39 Eliz. c. 3 ss 10 and 15). Measures against the idle and disorderly and vagrants (chiefly 39 Eliz. c. 4 1597 and 7 James I c. 4 1609) were enacted in parallel to deal with disorderly and wandering poor.

In 1656 the Cromwellian parliament enacted measures authorizing a justice to punish as rogues and vagabonds wandering persons who in his opinion had no good reason for doing so, even if they were not begging, and any person making music, offering to make music, or entreating persons to hear them make music in any inn, alehouse or tavern (Burn 1764, 46, 126). Although all acts of the interregnum were held to be invalid on the restoration of Charles II, it is possible that the first of these laid the foundation for the power of justices to convict a person as a rogue and vagabond 'on his own view' and for the notorious 'sus' clauses of later vagrancy legislation, and the second may have been occasionally used against itinerant fiddlers.

The 1662 Settlement Act (13 & 14 Charles II c. 12) assumed forty days' residence as grounds for settlement 'either as a Native, Housholder, Sojourner, Apprentice or Servant' and subsequent amendments enabled more people to gain settlements, such as yearly hired servants and apprentices. Case law established the settlement of others: for example, married women were held to take the husband's settlement, although no statute existed to that effect (Burn 1755 vol. 2, 220). The 1662 act also instituted a reward of 2s for the apprehension of vagrants, authorized the raising of a parish rate to pay vagrancy charges, and made incorrigible rogues punishable by transportation.

By these measures the framework of the Old Poor Law was constructed and remained in force until 1834, when the New Poor Law replaced almost the entire system (4 & 5 William IV c. 76). Vagrancy laws were enacted to control disorderly poor, ensure the able bodied all worked, and keep them in their place, in every sense of the word; often the same statute combined measures to help the deserving settled poor and to punish undeserving settled poor and wandering poor. In the eighteenth century the management of vagrancy shifted from the parishes to the counties and became separate from the poor law, although linked to it by issues such as settlement and the provisions for dealing with the idle and disorderly.

The poor law and settlement law together persuaded successive governments and many contemporary writers that nobody need beg, and that therefore beggars were all dissolute, wicked and deserving of punishment, and the vagrancy laws continued to be updated well into the nineteenth century. Unhappily, attempts to set the poor on work were notoriously unsuccessful, except in a few places and in the short run, partly because there was not enough work available; other obstacles arose from the protectionist policies of trade guilds and corporations and the reluctance of parishes to fund stocks of materials and carry out supervisory tasks.

Development of vagrancy law during the eighteenth century

By 1662 therefore, a system existed whereby, theoretically, every individual had a settlement in some parish, and that parish had an obligation to relieve any settled parishioner whose circumstances required it. In practice there were a number of gaps in this provision, some of which came to be plugged using vagrancy law. Vagrancy law, like the houses of correction, was at this period squarely aimed at controlling the movements and activities of the poor; it was the stick counterbalancing the carrot of poor law and settlement law.

Often there was alternative legislation to deal with the same sorts of misbehaviour by those with means, who tended to be fined and required to find sureties and give recognizances. For example, whereas the poor deserting their families were dealt with under vagrancy law, those able to pay but refusing to do so were forced to comply by orders of distraint on their property (5 Geo. I c. 8 1718).

The 1700 Vagrant Act

By the first vagrancy legislation of the eighteenth century, the Vagrant Removal Costs Act of 1700 (11 & 12 William III c. 18), the cost of conveying vagrants with passes was no longer to be paid by the parish but by the county, out of the gaol money or a special rate. It was not clear whether the 1700 act also applied to vagrants apprehended within the county, and an amending act swiftly followed extending it to all vagrants (1 Anne stat. 2 c. 13). The aim of the act was to stop the vagrancy by returning the vagrant to his settlement, which had a duty either to put him to work or to relieve him, and to increase the likelihood that vagrants would be apprehended and punished, since the county, not the parish, would now have to pay for conveying them to the bridewell and to their settlements.

The act also initiated a system for paying constables reasonable expenses for their time and trouble: the justice was to make out a certificate noting how many were to be conveyed, where to, and whether on foot, by horse or by cart. He noted this allowance on the back, and the constable claimed the money from the chief constable on producing the certificate. He in his turn gave the chief constable a receipt to serve as his authority for claiming the money from the county treasurer.

Passes now had to be checked by a local justice in each county through which the vagrant was conveyed. This was intended to prevent the use of counterfeit passes, clearly because the exemptions of previous acts for those with passes had supplied a loophole against apprehension and punishment for vagrancy. Evidently counterfeit passes came into circulation as soon as passes were allowed for certain groups, and remained a problem in the nineteenth century.

An unintended downside of the 1700 act was that parishes, in order to transfer the cost to the county, began to treat as vagrants travelling poor and non-settled residents falling sick, lying in, or otherwise costing the parish money for looking after them. Whether this was done extensively or not, and whether the act achieved its purpose of increasing the apprehension rate, the cost of conveying vagrants was soon found to be greater than the gaol money could cover, and an act of 1706 (5 Anne c. 32) re-enacted the clause authorizing the raising of a county rate for the purpose, and also set up a procedure for appeal to Quarter Sessions against disputed constables' expenses claims. From 1739 the cost of poor prisoners in both gaols and houses of correction was included in the general county rate and not raised by a separate rate as previously (12 Geo. II c. 29).

The 1714 Vagrant Act

The 1714 Vagrant Act (12 Anne stat. 2 c. 23 in *Statutes at Large*, 13 Anne c. 26 in *Statutes of the Realm*) repealed the acts then in force (39 Eliz. c. 4, 1 James I c. 7, and the part of 7 James I c. 4 relating to privy searches) and, developing the provisions of the 1700 act, set up the system that, with some later modifications, governed the mode of dealing with vagrants that remained in place for the rest of the century and well into the next. To address the concern that counties were oppressed by the conveyance as vagrants of persons who ought not to be, this act provided a detailed definition, largely based on Elizabethan vagrancy legislation, of those who were to be dealt with under vagrancy law. This definition included idle and disorderly poor, whether in their own parishes or wandering outside them, and a long list of frauds and unlawful entertainers.

Persons wandering and begging; all persons pretending to be patent gatherers[2] – that is, asking charity by brief or letters patent for some worthy cause or because of some personal disaster – or collectors for prisons, gaols or hospitals wandering abroad for that purpose; all fencers, bearwards, common players of interludes, minstrels, jugglers; all persons pretending to have skill in physiognomy, palmistry or like crafty science or to tell fortunes; those using any subtle craft, games or plays; all able-bodied persons deserting their families who, having no other source of income, loitered and refused to work for usual and common wages; and all other idle persons wandering abroad and begging, were defined as rogues and vagabonds. From 1 August 1714 when the act came into effect all these could be apprehended and taken before a justice of the peace. An exception was again made for soldiers and mariners licensed by some testimonial or writing under the hand and seal of a justice of the peace, setting down the time and place of their landing and the place to which they were to pass and limiting the time of their journey, while they continued in the direct way and during the limited time.

The same act enabled the justice to make a discretionary order for 2s reward to any person apprehending a vagrant, payable by the constable of the last parish where the vagrant was begging unapprehended. This seems to have been intended as a spur to constables since they had to pay the reward, which could be levied by distraint on the constable's property if he did not. For the same reason any constable failing to apprehend a vagrant on a justice's order could be fined 10s. It set up quarterly privy searches,[3] laid down a model form of pass, and required the vagrant to be examined by the justice and the examination filed at Quarter Sessions. The pass itself went with the vagrant. Rogues and vagabonds might be whipped or sent to the house of correction and then passed. The act directed vagrants to be passed to their settlement, if they had gained one, or place of birth; crucially this clause enabled those without settlements, primarily the Irish and Scotch, irremovable under settlement law, to be removed as vagrants. The 1714 act introduced considerable confusion by making procedural distinctions between vagrants with and without settlements; these differences acknowledged that those with settlements had access to poor law support unavailable to those without. All those apprehended were to be examined by any justice and the examination filed at Quarter Sessions. But those with settlements were to be removed 'by such Order and in such Manner as ... Persons likely to be chargeable

[2] As in the eighteenth century 'pretend' could mean 'claim' in general, the 1740 act clarified the meaning by adding the word 'falsely', dropped again in 1744.

[3] Not for the first time, 7 James I c. 4 had instituted privy searches.

to the Parish are to be sent' – that is by a pauper removal order signed by two justices – yet the cost was to be paid by the county as for other vagrants. Those without settlements were to be passed on the order of the examining justice to their place of birth, or if that was unknown back to the parish where they had last begged unapprehended. This last instruction was rarely followed but was not changed until 1744. An order of William Freke Esq. 4 May 1741 passed John and William Raynolds, apprehended in Lydlinch, to Sturminster Newton as the last parish where they begged unapprehended, because their settlement could not be known.[4] The act also empowered the justice at his discretion to order the vagrant publicly whipped and passed forthwith or sent to the bridewell to hard labour (s. 5).

If the justice thought the vagrant dangerous and unlikely to be reformed he could commit him to hard labour either in the bridewell or gaol (ignoring the lack of provision for hard labour in gaols) until next sessions. If then a majority of the justices found him an incorrigible rogue, he could be publicly whipped on three successive market days and afterwards kept to hard labour 'during such time as they in their Discretion shall think meet', thus permitting a potentially unlimited term of imprisonment. Persons escaping from the house of correction or gaol were to be felons; the act did not specify whether within clergy or not, but the case was to be heard in the county where the runaway was apprehended, not where the escape happened. In 1752 (25 Geo. II c. 36) persons taken up during a general privy search and suspected of other crimes might be held six days and advertised in the newspapers.

Justices were forbidden to pass any vagrant without taking a settlement examination, or to pass anyone to his place of birth if he had gained any settlement since, on pain of £5 and costs to any person who sued for it in one of the Westminster courts of record. This clause provided some redress to an aggrieved parish, but protection of justices against such actions enacted in 1751 (24 Geo. II c. 44) meant that henceforth only the Lord Chancellor could deal with errant magistrates. There was no way in which an individual wrongly punished as a vagrant could obtain redress, not least because any punishment had already been inflicted. Any vagrant refusing to be examined or knowingly giving false information about his settlement might be summarily convicted by one justice and punished as a dangerous and incorrigible rogue, but he had to be warned of the punishment at the time of examination.

Building on the basic rules of the 1700 Vagrant Removal Costs Act, improvements to the passing system and financial control were made. Rates for maintaining vagrants and mileage allowances to constables were to be settled

4 DRO QDV box 1 bundle 2.

not by individual justices but by the justices in sessions, who were empowered to make any other rules they thought necessary to ensure regular proceedings under the act. The 1714 Vagrant Act, unlike the 1700 act, did not state that these rates were to include an element for time and trouble. Financial control was tightened: the constable must now have his certificate receipted by the receiving constable, to ensure he could not simply release vagrants and then claim for conveying them.

If the vagrant had crossed the county boundary the receiving constable took him with his pass to a local justice to get a new certificate for passing him on the next stage and claiming his expenses. This justice had the vagrant either whipped or sent to the house of correction for two or three days and passed on again, although there was a humane exemption from punishment for pregnant women and vagrants certified by a justice unable to endure it,[5] as well as the usual exemption for those with passes.

The county treasurer now had to produce to Quarter Sessions along with his accounts all the certificates and receipts given to him by the high constables to be checked and paid out of the county rate. Forgery or alteration of financial documents was punishable by a fine of £20 plus the amount fraudulently obtained, half to the informer and half to the use of the poor of the parish where the offence was committed. A justice could examine a constable on oath about his conveyance of a vagrant and if he refused to be examined or it appeared he had neglected his duty he forfeited the allowance and could be fined 20s; persons hindering the execution of the act or rescuing or abetting the rescue of an apprehended vagrant were liable to the same penalty.

On arrival at his settlement the vagrant was to be handed over to the overseers or churchwardens and set to work or otherwise provided for, but they need not receive a vagrant who had not been whipped or imprisoned. To prevent settlements neglecting to provide for vagrants and simply hustling them on again the settlement was made responsible for preventing the vagrant from escaping from the workhouse or poorhouse or wandering again, and could be charged any expenses another parish might be caused by their failure to control the vagrant even if in another county – a provision later dropped and probably impractical.[6]

Special provision was made for vagrants coming from Ireland, the isles of Man, Guernsey, Jersey and Scilly, or from foreign plantations, a particular problem since they were not included in the law of settlement. The masters of vessels bringing such persons 'likely to live by begging' could be fined £5 for each one they brought plus the constable's charges for apprehending, maintaining,

---

[5] 1714 Vagrant Act s. 11.

[6] Ibid., s. 17.

and putting him back on board. The beggar himself if caught was to be whipped and sent back. The money could be levied by distress and sale of the vessel or any goods in it, and if the ship had already sailed the case could be removed by *certiorari* to Queen's Bench where it could proceed by writs of *capias*, *fieri fecit* or *elegit*. The ship's master was free to traverse the order if aggrieved, giving £50 security to appear and answer the charge. It may be doubted whether this clause was ever of the slightest use in controlling the influx of vagrants. The reluctance of ships' masters to take vagrants back to these destinations was dealt with by making it legal for the justices to compel their compliance by warrant and set the rates to be paid. The constable was to pay the master on embarking the vagrant and claim the money back against a receipt in the same way as if conveying the vagrant by land to another constable.

A further measure was directed at those found to be dangerous and incorrigible rogues, persons who had gained no settlement since birth and had offended against the act, or anyone with a settlement who had lived as a beggar for the last two years. In such a case, proved by confession or the oath of one or more credible witnesses, the justice was empowered to commit him for seven years into the power of the informer, or to any body politic or corporate willing to receive him as a servant or apprentice, either in Britain or in a British plantation overseas, taking a recognizance in £40 of the master or mistress to provide properly for the servant and to release him at the end of the term or sooner. An appeal lay to Quarter Sessions and the vagrant could not be transported before it was heard and determined, but he might be held in prison in the meantime.

Two or more inhabitants could complain to the peace officers about any street beggar 'blind, lame or pretending to be so' and have him removed, and if he refused or was found begging again the constable or another officer was obliged to whip him, or forfeit 10s to the poor if he refused or neglected to do so; the act did not say he needed a justice's warrant.[7] The rarity of such charges suggests few inhabitants did complain.

Lunatics with little or no estate 'furiously mad and dangerous to be permitted to go abroad' could be apprehended by warrant of two or more justices and locked up securely, chained if necessary, but only until they recovered. If settled elsewhere they could be passed in the same way as vagrants but were not to be whipped. Any money the lunatic had over and above necessary maintenance for his dependants was to be applied to his maintenance while under restraint, but if there was no money the parish was obliged to support him. Crown prerogatives over wealthy lunatics were naturally not to be affected by this provision.

7 Ibid., s.21.

The 1740 Vagrant Act

The impressively comprehensive 1714 act, not entirely new but certainly paying more attention to the mechanisms whereby it was to be enforced than any previous legislation, albeit demanding time-consuming paperwork, remained in force until 1740, when it was substantially re-enacted but with some modifications. The new act was probably a knee-jerk reaction to complaints by members of parliament about crowds of beggars blocking their access to the House in the exceptionally hard winter, and proved short lived. The 1740 Vagrant Act (13 Geo. II c. 24) further systematized the definition of vagrants into three categories – idle and disorderly, rogue and vagabond, incorrigible rogue, with an ascending scale of penalties –, made certain new provisions, and clarified some matters that had been disputed. It also dropped certain clauses, probably because most had proved unenforceable, but including the clause exempting pregnant women and the physically unfit from punishment.

The first category, the idle and disorderly, were 'settled' vagrants, namely the disorderly poor formerly dealt with under poor law legislation and under the 1714 Vagrant Act, but under the 1740 Vagrant Act it became possible to be a vagrant without setting foot outside one's own house, by merely threatening to run away and leave one's dependants on the parish – an expansion of the 1714 act, which had applied only to those actually doing so. Possibly this was a common threat designed to force relief from unwilling overseers. As in the 1714 act the idle and disorderly included anyone begging door to door or in the street, and whereas the 1714 act had referred to those 'wandering and begging' and could be construed to apply only to vagrants from outside the parish, the new act made it clear that it applied also to 'settled' vagrants begging in their own parish. Such idle and disorderly poor could be convicted before a single justice on the oath of one or more credible witnesses, usually a parish officer or the person from whom the individual had begged. There was no mention of exemption for poor wearing the parish badge, although this sort of licensed begging continued (Hitchcock 2001, 433–40; Hindle 2004, 67–9).

The reward payable by the parish for apprehending a beggar was raised from 2s to 5s, for apprehending a rogue and vagabond 10s payable by the constable (and reimbursed by the county, although this was not made clear in the act). Clauses were added enabling a justice to compel an overseer ordered to pay the 5s reward for apprehending a beggar but who refused or neglected to do so to pay out of his own pocket, probably because overseers often had refused, and similarly for 20s penalty against any petty constable not paying the 10s reward to a person apprehending a rogue and vagabond. Yet only chief constables had county funds in hand. Persons returning from their settlement without bringing a settlement certificate after being legally passed there were now added to the idle and disorderly group.

The second category was rogues and vagabonds, and included the wandering beggars out of their settlements and the frauds and illegal entertainers listed in the 1714 act, with several additions or clarifications. Patent gatherers were now defined as persons collecting alms under *false* pretence of losses by fire or other casualty; the loose wording of the 1714 act might be taken to include those begging with genuine documents. Additions included unlicensed hawkers and pedlars, persons wandering abroad and lodging in barns and outhouses not giving a good account of themselves, and persons wandering abroad and begging pretending to be soldiers, mariners, seafaring men or harvest workers – again, 'falsely' was intended and the usual exception for those with genuine licences was included. Persons going to work at any time of year were exempt provided they carried certificates from the minister and a parish officer of the place where they lived (but did not necessarily have a settlement). The Elizabethan legislation (39 Eliz. c. 4 1597) making gypsies and persons going about in the form and habit of Egyptians rogues and vagabonds was revived. Persons wandering abroad and begging and persons deserting their dependants now moved from the idle and disorderly category to rogues and vagabonds. The exemption from punishment for pregnant women and the sick was dropped, possibly because of county complaints that travelling poor and pregnant women had been frequently passed as vagrants instead of being relieved in the parish as casual poor.

The third category of the 1740 act was incorrigible rogues. These were partly those so described in the 1714 act, partly additions. They were defined as persons apprehended as rogues and vagabonds and escaping, or refusing to go before a justice to be examined on oath, or knowingly giving a false account of themselves on such examination after warning given them of their punishment, or breaking out of the house of correction before the expiration of the term for which they were committed by virtue of the act. Added to this category were persons previously punished as rogues and vagabonds who committed any of the vagrancy offences again, and end gatherers made incorrigible rogues by an act of 1727 (13 Geo. I c. 23). In practice this mainly affected persons illegally returning after being passed.

One alteration, possibly unintended and certainly promptly reversed, was the change from discretionary passing of vagrants taken up by a privy search to mandatory passing. Another clause that quickly proved impracticable was a change in the mode of passing where the vagrant was to be passed out of the county: instead of being passed from constable to constable, they were to be conveyed via the houses of correction. This somewhat baffling clause – they had to be conveyed there by the constable and often the house of correction was even further than the county boundary – was repealed four years later. The intention was probably to ensure punishment, but locally the expense was seen as more important.

The power of sessions to order potentially unlimited imprisonment for incorrigible rogues was now restricted to a maximum six months, but it was made clear that an incorrigible rogue escaping from prison could be transported for up to seven years and if he returned he was not only a felon but a felon without benefit of clergy. The penalty for forging or altering orders for constables' expenses was raised from £20 to £50, and the penalty of £20 on parish officers for refusing or neglecting to convey or receive a vagrant was now payable also for refusing to give a receipt for a vagrant. High constables were liable to a penalty of double distress for refusing or neglecting to pay petty constables. The clauses allowing parishes to refuse to receive vagrants who had not been punished by whipping or imprisonment, and permitting parishes to claim from the settlement any expenses for dealing with vagrants they had allowed to wander again were omitted, no doubt because they had proved unworkable. Such measures were particularly difficult to enforce across county boundaries.

The new act also incorporated some minor legislation passed since 1714, such as an act of 1737 (10 Geo. II c. 28) relating to players of interludes that further defined players subject to the vagrancy laws as persons who for hire gain or reward act, represent, perform, or cause to be acted, represented or performed any interlude, tragedy, comedy, opera, play, farce or other entertainment for the stage, or any part or parts therein, not having a legal settlement where the same is acted represented or performed, and without authority by royal letters patent. This 1737 act also provided that they could be exempt from the punishments of the vagrancy law on paying a fine of £50, a clause not included in the 1740 Vagrant Act.

A significant addition to the 1714 act was a clause making anybody permitting a vagrant to lodge in his house or outbuildings and not apprehending him liable to pay any charges brought on the parish plus a fine of between 10s and 40s, payable half to the informer and half to the parish. If the fine could not be met then the offender had to be committed to hard labour for up to three months. This clause, which might be seen as a serious deterrent to charity, claimed to be motivated by the expense allegedly brought on parishes by such vagrants falling sick, but in the same breath parishes were permitted to provide lodging and relief to any persons too sick to be removed. Hospitals too could give any relief allowed under their foundation rules. Clearly at this date the parish and not the county was expected to support sick travellers, at least any not previously apprehended and convicted as vagrants, although the complaints about parishes passing sick travellers as vagrants suggest they often did no such thing.

A further clause was added to enable the justices to improve or build houses of correction, appoint and dismiss keepers, make rules and inspect them. The expense of these bridewells and for maintaining and conveying vagrants was to be raised on the county rate according to an act of the previous parliamentary session (12 Geo. II c. 29 1739). Justices could now sentence anybody to hard labour until next sessions or until discharged by course of law for any offence within their powers for which the law did not set down a particular penalty. The act came into force 1 June 1740 and repealed the 1714 act.

The 1744 Vagrant Act

The 1740 act was both short lived and poorly drafted, but much was incorporated in the 1744 Vagrant Act (17 Geo. II c. 5), which repealed the 1740 act and its predecessors, and remained in force for nearly fifty years. The 1744 act may be seen as the culmination of a period of trial and error since 1700: measures that had been found useful were re-enacted, others dropped or modified, and a few added. Most of the changes of 1744 were aimed at making the law tougher, minimizing the cost to the county, or stopping up loopholes.

The financial control system remained, as did the passing system, except that passing became discretionary and the requirement of 1740 to pass vagrants via houses of correction where the vagrant was to be conveyed a long way was dropped in favour of passing constable to constable in all cases (unless the vagrant had actually been committed), no doubt because of protests from counties such as Dorset where this would often have involved an expensive detour. A power was added to order the bundles of a suspect to be searched, and any money or effects used to defray the cost of passing the vagrant. The clauses relating to lunatics were amended to allow any friend or relative to take care of them, evidently a simple omission in former acts and also designed to save expense.

The powers of the justice were unobtrusively but considerably extended by allowing him to convict a vagrant and commit him to hard labour for up to one month 'on his own view' – he need not even have the oath of one credible witness.[8] Control of the justices over bridewells was enhanced: two justices were to visit at least twice per year and supervise management, and bridewell keepers could no longer appeal against dismissal by removing the matter to King's Bench by *certiorari*.

---

8 The potential for oppressive use of this power was exploited by Henry Fielding, himself a magistrate, in *Joseph Andrews*.

A justice was now 'required' to order the vagrant publicly whipped or sent to the house of correction. If he decided to pass the vagrant he had to file a duplicate pass at Quarter Sessions in addition to the duplicate examination, to serve as evidence in any future court proceedings. Sentences were extended: sessions could now sentence a rogue and vagabond up to six months, an incorrigible rogue to not less than six months or more than two years, and both could be whipped as often, however, whenever and wherever the court chose. Vagrants could be passed on discharge, but they did not have to be. Incorrigible rogues escaping could be transported and male incorrigible rogues over twelve could be sent into the army or navy at any time during their sentence.

The clause dropped in 1740 exempting pregnant women and sick people from these punishments was not reinstated. Indeed an iniquitous clause (s. 25) was added allowing parishes to take any woman who lay in on the road and thereby became chargeable to a justice, who was then required to examine and commit her until the next sessions, when the court might order her publicly whipped and further detained. This clause applied to army wives as much as to bastard bearers, but the normal rule that a bastard was settled in his place of birth was altered – a bastard born on the road was to take the mother's settlement.

A new power was added enabling the justices in sessions to remove any child over seven committed with a vagrant and place the child out as an apprentice or servant for any period they saw fit or until the age of twenty-one (s. 24). The justification for this clause was the protection of the children and the prevention of future delinquency, persons offending against this act often 'having Children with them whom they bring up in a dissolute Course of Life, destructive to such Children, and prejudicial to the Kingdom, in which a Race of disorderly Persons will increase, if such Children are suffered to remain with such Offenders'. If the vagrant was found again with a child so placed out he became an incorrigible rogue.[9] The clause against lodging in houses and outbuildings was extended to include lodging in alehouses or sleeping rough; alehouses throughout the eighteenth century were much condemned as vagrants' haunts. Soldiers' and mariners' passes were now supposed to include a list of the chief towns along the route. Anybody refusing to be conveyed by pass was added to the list of incorrigible rogues, and in addition to the quarterly privy searches justices were now required to issue a search warrant at any time on information that vagrants were in the area.

The law relating to vagrants with no known settlement was altered by dropping the clause of the 1714 act making them the responsibility of the parish

---

[9] I have found no children taken away and apprenticed under s. 24, but *orphans* of vagrants certainly were apprenticed by order of sessions.

where they had last passed unapprehended, retained in 1740 but probably unenforceable. Instead the power of the court to place them out as servants and apprentices was extended to include keeping them in the house of correction at hard labour indefinitely 'until they can provide for themselves' or sending them, if male and over twelve, into the army or navy (s. 28). To stop parishes fraudulently refusing to receive vagrants by claiming the examination was false, a new measure was introduced: the case must now be heard in sessions, and if the examination was indeed false the vagrant could (after punishment as an incorrigible rogue if the court thought proper) be removed by two justices as a pauper (s. 11).

Developing the 1744 act

The scope of the 1744 Vagrant Act was subsequently increased at various times by the inclusion, as had already been done in the case of end gatherers, of assorted offenders whose crimes did not seem sufficiently heinous for inclusion in the 'bloody code'. In 1783 an act was passed (23 Geo. III c. 88) to bring a new category of offenders 'within the intent and meaning' of the 1744 Vagrant Act. Mainly aimed at urban criminals, it explained that hitherto the justices' powers to demand sureties of the peace for good behaviour had not been adequate to deal with these people and therefore from 1 August 1783 any person found with

> any Picklock Key, Crow, Jack, Bit, or other implement, with an Intent feloniously to break and enter into any Dwelling-house, Warehouse, Coach-house, Stable or Outhouse, or shall have upon him, her or them any Pistol, Hangar, Cutlass, Bludgeon, or other offensive Weapon, with Intent feloniously to assault any Person or Persons, or shall be found in or upon any Dwelling-house, Warehouse, Coach-house, Stable or Outhouse, or in any inclosed Yard or Garden or Area belonging to any House, with an Intent to steal any Goods or Chattels

was a rogue and vagabond within the meaning of the 1744 Vagrant Act. Like much other legislation this codified and made statutory a longstanding practice of county benches, which had been using the vagrancy law to cope with suspicious persons for decades.

Again in 1787 (27 Geo. III c.11) offenders against the lottery laws were brought within vagrancy law, after previous attempts to deal with them by a licensing system and fines failed; they were not to be judged summarily, however, but in court. By then the vagrancy laws were interpreted by the justices to cover any sort of game, whatever its name, that gave rise to a complaint of cheating, fraud or theft (Eccles 2008).

The 1792 Vagrant Act

Prompted largely by soaring county rates and the cost to the county of dealing with vagrants, a new Vagrant Act was passed in 1792 (32 Geo. III c. 45). There had been complaints that the laws were not enforced, and calls for new tough measures, notably from the Proclamation Society. These arguments made the complacent assumption that the existing provision for the poor was perfectly adequate; in fact the vagrancy laws were not enforced precisely because they had been widely used to compensate for gaps in the provisions for the poor, notably for travel by military personnel and their families, for poor travellers falling sick, and for Irish and Scotch immigrant poor. They also took no account of other heavy financial demands on the counties imposed by recent legislation.

There were indeed a handful of contemporaries who could see that the problem was not entirely the fault of the poor, and that the disruption of repeated wars, the rising price of food, and the unemployment caused by a population growing faster than job opportunities were largely to blame. They claimed the laws were already too severe and their very severity was partly the reason why they were not systematically applied. They did not however offer any alternative solution – indeed, in the state of late eighteenth-century England no solution was politically or economically feasible and their voices cried in the wilderness in vain.

The 1792 Vagrant Act was therefore more of the same, tweaked here and there to include the post-1744 extensions to the 1744 act and to make certain other modifications. Its chief purpose was stated in the preamble, 'great Abuses are committed in conveying, from one Place to another by Passes, Persons who are not Rogues or Vagabonds, or in conveying such Persons who are Rogues and Vagabonds without complying with the Directions of the Act' – that is, by first publicly whipping or committing them; it therefore enacted that, whenever a justice made out a pass, he must certify in it that the person so passed had been whipped, or imprisoned for a minimum seven days, and had genuinely committed an act of vagrancy within the true intent and purpose of the act. The passing system was retained, and the authorities were also empowered to pass in the same way as vagrants any persons acquitted or discharged in court who applied to be passed, without taking any fee for it, and noting the fact in the pass. The passing system was modified to give justices a choice of passing vagrants constable to constable or via the houses of correction. This was intended to deal with the misconduct and negligence of constables; clearly the old system of fining them had not been satisfactory.

Distinctly illiberal was a clause withdrawing the exemption from vagrancy penalties for begging of soldiers and mariners with licences. This permission to beg was now declared 'highly improper'; they were to be treated as rogues and vagabonds, although no other funding was made available to them. This clause was reversed in 1803 (43 Geo. III c. 20), by which time no alternative way for them to travel had yet been put in place and it was admitted that some had indeed been punished under the 1792 act. The clause against refusing to work and support dependants or deserting them was expanded by including among the idle and disorderly those who wasted their money in alehouses or in any other improper manner so that their families became chargeable. Their case was not to be heard by a single justice however but two.

Most of this was aimed at tightening the law; the 1792 Vagrant Act did however contain the sole relaxation of the vagrancy laws throughout the century: not only did it tacitly repeal the clause about whipping lying-in women, but it forbade the whipping of any female vagrant whatsoever, even incorrigible rogues, and whether ordered by a justice or by the court in sessions. Possibly this surprisingly liberal reform was prompted by an awareness of the unpopularity of such a clause if applied to army wives, deserted women and recent widows, how high a proportion they formed of those passed as vagrants, and how rarely justices saw fit to inflict the letter of the law. Women could of course still be whipped for larceny and so forth until 1818. There are ample signs that whipping was no longer much used even for male vagrants: after this act was passed, when it certainly seems to have been obeyed, at least for some time, the seven-day prison sentence was virtually always the option certified as having been used.

Vagrancy law beyond the 1792 Vagrant Act

No further Vagrant Act as such was passed until 1822, but several other acts had considerable bearing on the way vagrancy was dealt with in practice. Although there is some debate about how widespread restrictive settlement practices were, it had always been legal under settlement law for a parish to obtain a removal order from two justices and send non-settled poor who might possibly become chargeable back to their settlements.[10] In 1795 an important poor law reform act was passed (35 Geo. III c. 101) to prevent the removal of poor persons until they became actually chargeable, and to enable the parish where such persons fell ill,

10 This debate is usefully summarized in Wells 1993.

whether travelling poor or non-settled residents, to claim the expense of looking after them from their settlement. It did not however address the problem caused by those without settlements. Pregnant single women were to be deemed actually chargeable and therefore removable, but not in circumstances that endangered their lives. This act further developed a provision of 1782 (22 Geo. III c. 83 s. 38) that for the first time enabled one parish to claim the expense of looking after sick poor from another, but only if both parishes lay in the same county; previously this had only been done in the adjudication of settlement cases. There was also provision for the justices to modify unfair claims for expenditure.

The chief aim of the 1795 act, which admitted that the old settlement certificate system had not served the purpose, was to allow more labour mobility, prompted by changing patterns of industry. The practice of giving out-relief to settled parishioners resident elsewhere, particularly in the industrializing northern counties, was encouraged by this reform (Sokoll 1997; Taylor 1997). The same act also provided for the suspension of a vagrant pass during a person's sickness, a much-needed clause that went some way to preventing the previously common occurrence of vagrants dying or giving birth under a pass.

In 1803, in addition to the act already mentioned restoring the exemption from the penalties of the vagrancy laws of discharged soldiers and mariners with licences, another act (43 Geo. III c. 61) extended the giving of certificates – licences to beg by another name – to the wives and children of soldiers left behind when the men embarked, another measure legalizing a practice that justices had been using extra-legally for decades.

A poor law act of 1819 (59 Geo. III c. 12) at long last legitimated the practice of passing poor persons with no settlement in England, previously irremovable under the poor law, as vagrants – precisely the practice that the insistence of the 1792 Vagrant Act on punishment of all persons passed as vagrants was meant to stop. Section 34 of the 1819 act read,

> And Whereas poor Persons born in Scotland and Ireland, and in the Isles of Man, Jersey and Guernsey frequently become chargeable to Parishes in England and no Provision is made for the Removal of any such poor Person, unless he or she shall have committed some Act of Vagrancy, and shall be adjudged to be a Rogue and Vagabond; and no Person so adjudged can be lawfully removed without having been first publicly whipped or imprisoned in the House of Correction: And Whereas it is expedient to authorise the Removal of such poor Persons, although they may not have committed any Act of Vagrancy

and went on to require two justices, on complaint of the parish officers that such a person or his family had become chargeable, to examine the person on oath as to his place of birth and to remove him and such of his family as had not gained a settlement, in the same way as vagrants were conveyed under the 1744 Vagrant Act but without punishment.

This clause therefore enabled parishes, immediately Irish or Scotch vagrants applied for relief and thus became actually chargeable, to get rid of them at county expense, as they had been doing illegally for decades. Those who had committed an act of vagrancy were still supposed to be whipped or imprisoned seven days as before, but even more surprisingly s. 34 authorized any justice at his discretion to order persons so born and convicted to be passed under this act without punishment, so placing them in a more favourable position than beggars with a settlement in England. Probably by this time the urge of 1792 to punish all vagrants had waned and punishment was again widely neglected, and indeed the anomaly was rectified by the 1822 Vagrant Act (s. 6), which extended the same provision to those with settlements.

The last vagrant acts before the enactment of the 1834 New Poor Law were passed in 1822 and 1824. The 1822 Vagrant Act (3 Geo. IV c. 40), enacted temporarily until 1 September 1824, repealed all previous vagrancy acts except for the 1819 act for passing Irish and Scotch poor and the 1737 act (10 Geo. II c. 28) relating to players, but re-enacted large parts with additions. Idle and disorderly persons now specifically included common prostitutes and nightwalkers, legitimating another very longstanding use of vagrancy law to deal with a group where other laws had proved unsatisfactory, but no mention was made of whipping the idle and disorderly, although they could still be committed to hard labour for one month by any justice 'on his own view'. The list of rogues and vagabonds was extended by adding persons lodging in tents, carts or wagons, but it did not mention gypsies as such.[11] It added persons exposing in public any indecent exhibition, exposing wounds or deformities with intent to gather alms, causing a child to beg, and very controversially indecent exposure.

The list of offensive weapons added guns, and the places where people might be apprehended for lurking with intent were stretched to include any navigable waterway, dock, basin or quay. Fraud was neatly encompassed in 'all Persons imposing or endeavouring to impose on any Churchwarden or Overseer of the Poor, or upon a Charitable Institution or Private Individual, by any false or fraudulent Representation, either Verbally or in Writing, with a View to obtain Money or some other Advantage or Benefit'. This clause was partly directed at writers of begging letters, who had become an increasing problem but were not

[11] The Elizabethan penal laws against gypsies had been repealed in 1783 (23 Geo. III c. 51).

thought to be covered by previous vagrancy law.[12] Persons charged under the act and bound by recognizance to appear in court but failing to do so became incorrigible rogues. It also became legal for anyone apprehending a person under the act to use the offender's own animal or vehicle to take him before a justice.

The reward for apprehending a vagrant was cut to 5s and was discretionary, but the penalty for not doing so was unchanged and was mandatory. A penalty of 10s was imposed on persons defacing or destroying notices put up in pursuance of the act, but the act did not repeat the former method of claiming, paying and accounting for such rewards and fines, nor did it repeat the rules for conveying vagrants and claiming the cost, or set up any alternative, although it did say the justices in sessions were to pay the expense of executing the act out of the county rate.

The provision of the 1819 act for a justice to waive punishment if he saw fit in the case of Irish and Scotch vagrants was now applicable to all vagrants, even if an act of vagrancy had been proved. The 1744 provision was revived for the justice to order baggage searched and money or property found to be used for paying the cost of apprehending and maintaining the vagrant. Sessions might order rogues and vagabonds and incorrigible rogues, if male, to be whipped, and impose sentences of hard labour up to six months on rogues and vagabonds, and twelve months on incorrigible rogues. No licences to beg were permitted except under the 1803 act (43 Geo. III c. 61) to military personnel.

The novel inclusion of indecent exposure raised a furious controversy: alarming pictures were painted of elderly respectable gentlemen suddenly taken short by a call of nature and run in by officious constables. It was claimed such a clause infringed civil liberties and opened the way to blackmail and extortion. For the first time it raised the spectre of well-to-do people coming within the scope of the vagrancy laws – laws that had hitherto been used almost exclusively against the poor, whose civil liberties were obviously of far less importance. The clause had its defenders, who, also playing the class card, drew similar pictures of pure-minded young ladies shocked and horrified by a glimpse of male anatomy (Adolphus 1824; Roberts 1988). Following a vigorous press campaign Home Secretary Peel himself gave notice of his intention to move for amendment and even before the term of the 1822 act was over a new act was passed. The 1824 Vagrant Act (5 Geo. IV c. 83) revised the contentious clause to read anyone 'wilfully, openly, lewdly and obscenely' exposing himself 'with Intent to insult a Female', which presumably automatically excluded elderly respectable gentlemen, even those caught *in flagrante* with a prostitute. It also qualified 'common

12 1815 Mendicity report, 19.

Prostitute' by adding 'wandering in the public Streets or public Highways, or in any place of public Resort, and behaving in a riotous or indecent Manner'.

Either intentionally or by an oversight the punishment of whipping was now further limited to male incorrigible rogues. The act also gave a power to the justices to fine a master for ill treatment of an apprentice, which had in fact already been authorized by an act of 1793 (33 Geo. III c. 55). Certificates to beg under the 1803 act (43 Geo. III c. 61) were retained and extended to persons discharged from prison and given a licence by the justices, but the power of the court given by the 1792 act to pass acquitted persons was abolished. The entire thrust of the new act was to drop the universal mandatory punishment of vagrants but also to minimize the cost of enforcing the law against them. Probably the mendicity reports of 1815 and 1816, which highlighted the ineffectiveness of punishing people whose circumstances gave them little choice but to beg, had been influential in this change of emphasis.

Although one of the principal motives for passing the 1822 Vagrant Act in the first place had been complaints about fraud and abuse of the passing system (Roberts 1988, 288), this objective seems to have been somewhat derailed by the unexpected sound and fury over the indecent exposure clause. Neither the act of 1822 nor of 1824 explicitly abolished the passing system,[13] nor did either include any other provision for conveying vagrants to their settlements. Yet both acts 'retained' the 1819 provision for conveying Scotch and Irish poor 'in the same way' as vagrants and also the clause relating to lunatics, although the acts establishing the passing system and relating to lunatics had been repealed in 1822. These two laws were so ambiguously drafted that it was by no means clear whether the old system of conveying vagrants was intended to continue or not. Although Burn stated categorically that a repealing act reinstated any acts repealed by it (Burn 1793 vol. 1, xx), this seems never to have been universally accepted, and justices felt free to accept or reject previous laws as they thought fit.

Middlesex, which had its own reasons for wanting the passing system changed, was sufficiently baffled by the import of s. 20 of the 1824 act to take counsel's opinion in December 1825. Mr Samuel Marryat declared that 'the power of the justices to contract for the removal of vagrants, not being given by the only Vagrant Act in force no longer subsists'.[14] This opinion rather disingenuously ignored the fact that no previous Vagrant Act had given any such power either – Jacob Ilive, describing the ways in which vagrant contractors milked the system,

13 Some historians assert that it was abolished, for example Rogers 1991, 128, although he points out at p. 147 that in practice it did not end completely, and Hastings 1981, 156, but also at p. 158 that hundreds of vagrants were being removed at county expense in the 1840s.

14 LMA MJ/O/C/021, 383–4.

declared the contractor 'a new-created officer, as yet altogether unconstitutional' (Ilive 1759, 11) – and yet many, probably most, counties, had employed vagrant contractors, now re-titled pass-masters. The Middlesex bench, acting on this opinion, promptly terminated the contract of Thomas Davis with effect from 26 January 1826.

Hampshire on the other hand continued passing vagrants and paying out large sums for doing so long after 1824.[15] Parliamentary reports continued to refer to Irish and Scotch poor as 'vagrants', and it is therefore difficult to determine whether any 'vagrants' passed after 1824 were vagrants in the old 'criminal' sense of having been convicted of an act of vagrancy, or poor passed under the 1819 legislation. The Kirkby Lonsdale Vagrant Register 1825–35 includes only a minority of Irish and Scotch, but it seems unlikely the others had all been convicted. In 1825 the third edition of Nolan's handbook for justices of the peace still included the 1744 Vagrant Act in the list of statutes in force, and even declared all male vagrants could be impressed under it (Nolan 1825 vol. 2, 274), although the 1824 act had dropped all mention of impressment.

Thus the passing system, having been retained for the repatriation of Irish and Scotch poor, did not end with a bang but petered out, probably as county benches found it suited their policies to stop passing vagrants. In his 1833 report on vagrancy Harrison Codd, assistant commissioner for the western division of the metropolis, stated that Scotch and Irish paupers could still be conveyed in carts under the care of pass-masters, and many of the witnesses who contributed to his report were pass-masters still operating the system to remove both vagrants and Irish and Scotch poor.[16] Indeed all the abuses of the pass system continued: for example, on 10 August 1832 Warrington passed John Smith and his two children, whose pass declared them to be Scotch, to Westmorland. On 27 August he reappeared with a pass under the name of John Watson but was recognized from a fortnight before. On close inspection the name was found to have been altered from 'Jane Watson', from whom he admitted he had obtained the pass in Warwickshire. He was tried and sentenced to six months' hard labour for defrauding the Warrington overseer of 2s 6d.[17]

As the 1744 act had done, the 1824 act became a convenient pigeonhole in which to slot other undesirables, in 1838 shopkeepers exposing obscene prints in their windows, and in 1898 men living on immoral earnings. Offenders against New Poor Law discipline were dealt with under vagrancy law just as offenders under Old Poor Law discipline had been, in 1842 workhouse inmates

15 HRO Q10/6/5 1833–47.

16 1834 Report on vagrancy by Harrison Codd PP vol. 38 Appendix E.

17 Ibid., p. 89.

refusing to perform work tasks or damaging workhouse property, and in 1848 applicants for relief giving false information about their means (Rose 1988, 13). The history of vagrancy law is largely an illustration of the dictum '*Plus ça change et plus c'est la même chose*'.[18]

[18] The more things change, the more they stay the same.

Chapter 2
Processing the Vagrants

Processing the vagrants: the role of constables

Those charged with implementing the vagrancy laws were primarily constables and justices of the peace. Each parish, tithing or hundred had a constable, also known as tithingman, headborough or borsholder in different counties, chosen annually by the ratepayers from among the more substantial inhabitants, who served without pay as a parish duty, although he did receive certain allowances. Constables were sworn in and their appointments ratified by the justices in sessions. Thomas Gilbert made the revolutionary suggestion in 1782 that they should be given salaries out of the parish rate, but it was a step too far at the time (Gilbert 1782, 48). Towns however might also have salaried beadles and watchmen who performed many of the same tasks, and the paid horse patrol and Bow Street runners of later eighteenth-century Middlesex pointed the way to a salaried police. By the late eighteenth century many constables were paid deputies who might serve much longer than those serving as an unpaid parish duty.

Constables were much criticized for failing to be as enthusiastic about apprehending and punishing vagrants as their superiors wished, complaints that certainly stretched back into the sixteenth century: at East Grinstead a headborough was presented at the assizes for punishing a vagrant 'very slenderly, as with a whip taken out of the hedge', and in 1590 another put four vagrants, who had begged and assaulted a gentleman's servants, in the stocks very reluctantly, moved the stocks into a barn when it rained, and let them out very soon (J.R. Kent 1986, 201–2). Constables were between a rock and a hard place – either blamed for the vagrancy problem because of 'negligence' or accused of profiteering by claiming more than their entitlement. In 1757 the Middlesex justices, lamenting the ineffectiveness of the 1744 Vagrant Act, declared that,

> notwithstanding the Reward directed to be paid as an Incitement to Constables and others to do their Duty in this Respect, and the Punishment directed to be inflicted upon Offenders against the said Act, yet, by the Negligence and

> Remissness of such Officers ... the Towns and Places in this County are greatly pestered with Numbers of Beggars.[1]

On the other hand Middlesex was very anxious to cut the amount paid out for rewards and urged justices to give no more than 2s, although the law allowed 10s. Wrightson points out that much negligence by constables was due to their invidious position (in Brewer and Styles 1986, 30). Nevertheless complaints about constables are easier to find than actual examples of negligence or fraud by them (Morgan and Rushton 1998, 29).

Such cases do occur however in all counties: for example, the constable of Scalthwaiterigg was fined 1s in 1772 for dumping Christopher Wallas and his family in Docker instead of conveying them to Orton as ordered;[2] in Cambridge the constable of Great Chesterford Essex was ordered to pay the expenses of keeping John Lewis his wife and daughter in the house of correction because he had allowed them to return to Newmarket after they were passed to Great Chesterford.[3] It is highly doubtful however that this could have been enforced unless the Essex magistrates were prepared to back the order, nor is it clear how he could have stopped them. In Hampshire George Biggs, constable of the hundred of New Forest and John Hockley, constable of the hundred of Crondall were fined in 1782, but they may have failed to return the rates or been remiss in some other way unconnected with vagrancy,[4] and in Middlesex the constable of South Mimms was admonished and his bill disallowed in 1760.[5] Dionis Acreman was bound over to the Shaftesbury midsummer sessions in 1748 for allowing a prisoner to escape his custody, but John Meech Esq. wrote to the clerk on his behalf because it was a very busy time of year 'and believing him to be an honest man'.[6] Despite the oft-repeated claims of negligence by constables, which may certainly have had some foundation, very few were actually prosecuted and still fewer fined anything like the £20 they could have been under the 1744 Vagrant Act. But it was so difficult to find suitable men prepared to serve as constable that it is possible only flagrant cases were pursued.

The office of parish constable was undoubtedly the most onerous and thankless of the parish offices, and many men attempted to avoid serving by pleading old age or infirmity, others by hiring a substitute, which was quite legal and had the advantage of continuity but might be contentious. The high

1 LMA MJ/SP/1757/04/11.

2 WRO WQSR 376a/5, 12–13.

3 CA Q/SO/6 12 January 1759.

4 HRO Q1/19 October 1782.

5 LMA MJ/O/C/007 11 January 1760.

6 DRO Midsummer 1748.

constable and parish officers of Finsbury objected to William Weaver serving as substitute for Timothy Smith, on the grounds that he did not live in the parish, had formerly kept a private lottery office, and had three sons, all reputed thieves, one of whom had a conviction for felony.[7] The justices were reluctant to see the office entrusted to alehouse- and inn-keepers, but were often obliged to agree for lack of any other man prepared to undertake the role. For the same reason they tended to impose very small penalties on delinquent constables, and to tolerate much suspected negligence (Cockburn 1963–66, 484). In 1762 the Middlesex bench heard that several deputies had been sworn in Islington who were of mean circumstances and unfit persons, and decided that no deputies should be sworn in Islington, and no victuallers if any other fit person could be located, 'many instances of partiality by victuallers having been found'.[8]

The office of constable was unpopular because apprehending offenders, especially felons, involved some personal risk, either from the offender, his accomplices or sympathetic bystanders (Allen 1821, 28; 1815 Mendicity report, 16). In a letter of thanks to the duke of Newcastle, one of the principal secretaries of state, for sending troops to help in a campaign against armed street robbers, the Middlesex justices pointed out that constables could not be expected to hazard their lives and risk the ruin of their families without a reward in proportion to the risk. For the same reason the bench also asked the duke for a reward of £50 for two constables who had helped apprehend the Black Boy Alley gang in 1745.[9]

The policing of fairs too could be dangerous – a constable was killed on duty at May Fair in the 1740s[10] – hence the frequent recourse to the military in riot situations or as extra guards in prisons: a military guard was posted at Clerkenwell Bridewell and New Prison for some months following the Gordon riots in 1780 while they held the felons normally kept in Newgate. The public whipping of offenders might also expose the constable to odium and danger, as might the taking up of seamen and deserters: William Doe, constable of Sutton Poyntz Dorset, laid an information on 10 April 1759 that the previous Saturday evening as he was about to press a sailor he was assaulted and obstructed in the execution of his office by John Waters and Joseph Hardy, two local labourers.[11] Constables were certainly much more often the victims of obstruction and assault than any other parish officer.

---

7 LMA MJ/O/C/012 July 1792.

8 LMA MJ/O/C/007 July 1762.

9 LMA MJ/O/C/005 October 1744, February 1745.

10 LMA MJ/O/C/005 8 May 1746.

11 DRO Easter 1759.

The office was also unpopular because of all the travelling the constable had to do, in all weathers. He had to escort offenders to the justice, who might not be available, involving another journey, and then to the gaol or bridewell or into the next county, and he had to attend Quarter Sessions, often at a considerable distance. He might also have to look after a sick vagrant until well enough to travel, or even a sick felon. In 1723 the tithingman of Binstead held in his house a wounded Waltham Black, certified by the surgeon as too sick to be moved, but later rescued from the constable's house by a gang of about twenty confederates (Thompson 1975, 148). The constable had to collect the county rates, impress wagons to carry the king's baggage, assist in billeting soldiers when the army was on the move, and take up straggling seamen and army deserters. Complaints against the constable might arise from any of these duties, none of which was popular with the public; in 1743 the constable of Cerne Abbas was summoned to attend the George coffee house in Dorchester to answer complaints about the billeting of soldiers.[12]

The constable was evidently normally expected to possess at least one horse, and possibly a cart, and had to neglect his own personal business to do all this traipsing about. In isolated rural parishes this might not amount to much despite the greater distances, but in towns, especially those lying on busy roads, it could become a heavy burden. The resort to vagrant contractors in most counties was motivated mainly by an attempt to cut costs and to control finance more closely, but a large component of the costs was the unpredictable amounts that might legitimately be claimed by constables for escort duties and for travel on necessary business such as journeys to take advice from a justice or to make enquiries after a suspect. Hannah Fisher's lying in at Myerscough in 1764 involved seven journeys to take advice and make enquiries.[13]

Constables, although they received no salary, did receive expenses for escorting vagrants and other offenders, and might receive a fee for whipping vagrants and felons. These allowances were meant to compensate the constable for his time and trouble. Intended to encourage constables to be diligent in apprehending vagrants, it was also legal for the justice to issue a discretionary order for a reward, a provision that led to much dispute and complaint, but that might add up to a considerable income. Constables who found the allowances and rewards for vagrant work paid well might remain in office for years at a time, effectively acting as vagrant contractors over a limited area, whereas most constables were only too anxious to hand over the role to someone else at the end of their year, as the many petitions to Quarter Sessions to give up the office demonstrate.

[12] DRO Easter 1743.

[13] LRO QSP 1856/13.

Constables were much suspected of fiddling their expenses, or colluding with offenders and neglecting to take them up, despite the fines that could be imposed on them for negligence; but they might also be the victims of parish parsimony. In 1748 the constable of Glasshouse Yard Liberty sent in a bill for £4 16s 8d spent on extraordinary relief of four vagrants in distress, which the parish refused to pay. Equally reluctant to pay, Middlesex justices ordered that vagrants falling sick while being conveyed must be maintained as casual poor until passed by the parish where they fell sick, 'the charge thereof is not to fall upon this county'. But in February 1749 they were sufficiently uneasy to take counsel's opinion about the legal position: they asked two questions – whether the county or the parish should pay, and whether, if he decided the parish should do so, the justices had any power to compel the parish officers to reimburse the constable. Sir John Strange's opinion was that,

> As it was plainly the Intention of the Act to lay the whole Charge of conveying Vagrants upon the County, and it speaks expressly of maintaining them in the way, I think the Parish in which a vagrant is taken sick upon the Road ought not to be burthened with the Expence but the same ought to be borne out of the County Rate.

but that considering the Vagrant Act and the County Rate Act the justices had a power to reimburse the constable in this case on the county treasurer's account, which they duly did.[14]

The role of justices of the peace

Justices of the peace also served unsalaried, though there was a 'wage' for attending sessions, which in most counties was either ignored or spent on dinners for the justices' meetings or sometimes on charitable objects. In order to perform judicial functions justices each had to take out a writ of *dedimus potestatem*, but some viewed their nomination in the commission of the peace as purely honorary and never did so. Justices acted within a division, singly or in pairs, and joined together at sessions for those judicial cases that were committed to sessions and to deal with county business such as fixing the county rate and constables' allowances, appointing officers, awarding contracts, licensing alehouses, dissenters' meeting houses and theatrical performances, and administrative matters such as the repair of county bridges and buildings.

14 LMA MJ/O/C/005 8 December 1748, 23 February 1749.

Quarter Sessions also acted as a court of appeal and arbitration in such matters as settlement disputes and appeals against apprenticeship indentures, parish rates and parish officers' expenditure.

As the eighteenth century wore on this business was increasingly dealt with by committees, often at adjourned sessions held in inns or private houses and in towns other than those where sessions were held. The justices had extremely wide powers, both of summary justice acting singly in their own residences, in pairs, and in sessions, and the office required a substantial property qualification, although they were not obliged to have any legal training. They also enjoyed a great deal of legal protection, further extended in 1751 (24 Geo. II c. 44), although in theory aggrieved persons could report them to King's Bench for malpractice (Hay 2002; Landau 2002). Some highly active justices employed clerks, who acted as scribes and might have some legal knowledge, and in sessions they had the advice of the clerk of the peace, who was always legally qualified. Clerks of the peace were not salaried but were paid fees for every piece of business transacted. Justices' clerks also were entitled, with certain statutory exceptions, to fees for each document, also fixed in sessions. Justices of the peace did most of the judicial business of the county, albeit referring capital felonies to the assizes, and all the administrative business above parish level.

In corporate towns the mayor was *ex officio* a justice of the peace as was the vice-chancellor of Cambridge University. Their ready accessibility compared with rural justices was a great advantage and most vagrants apprehended in towns were dealt with by the mayor. In Middlesex the so-called 'trading justices' sat regularly at the rotation offices from the mid century. Winchester had had a public office 'time out of mind' kept by the clerk of the peace and the justices ordered it continued in 1760, 'complaints having been made to this Court for want thereof'.[15]

The situation in Middlesex was somewhat different because most of the routine work out of sessions was done by the trading justices or 'justices of low estate', who relied on the fees permitted for each piece of business, a situation that arose because the higher gentry did not wish to be involved in the vast amount of petty business necessary in a relatively densely populated area, and preferred to concern themselves with county management, finance and policy. In Middlesex the system of rotation offices evolved from 1763 onwards, when divisional magistrates organized a rota sitting at some local centre, of which the most famous was Bow Street.[16] This system was confirmed by parliament in 1792 (32 Geo. III c. 53) when the public offices were established by statute and some justices received official salaries from the government for the first

15 HRO Q1/17 January 1760.

16 The same system evolved for the same reasons in the City: see Beattie 2001.

time. The government had however been paying unofficial sums to Bow Street magistrates for some time.

Out in the counties justices might be far less accessible. In Dorset Pentridge was obliged to keep a vagrant four days, 'there being no Justice of the Peace in all the neighbourhood to give us an order for removing her', but recouped the expense from the county.[17] Constables' bills sometimes included items of expenditure for fruitless journeys to justices who were not at home; Styles notes that the absence of an acting justice in the wapentake of Morley hindered policing of coining in Yorkshire (Brewer and Styles 1980, 207).

Apprehension and examination

Although anybody at all was required to apprehend a vagrant and take him before a justice of the peace, and occasionally members of the public did so, most vagrants were apprehended by constables; out of a sample of forty-two commitments to Tothill Fields Bridewell for loose, idle and disorderly behaviour where the prosecutor is known thirty-two were instigated by constables, four by justices and parish officers, and only six by private citizens (Hitchcock 2001, 171–2). Some vagrants indeed approached parish officers of their own accord for help, and were 'apprehended'.[18] The constable then took the vagrant before a justice of the peace to be examined. The justice examined both constable and suspect on oath to establish whether an act of vagrancy had been committed, which could be done 'on his own view', on the vagrant's own admission, or on the evidence of one credible witness – generally the constable. The burden of proof was thus virtually non-existent in vagrancy cases, and probably justices formed their own opinion or took the constable's word for it, although they might decide to pass the vagrant without punishment, if a genuine object of compassion.

Acquittals as such are very unusual in vagrancy cases but do occur: the constables of St Giles Cambridge apprehended one Taylor and his wife as vagrants at a common lodging house, possibly during a general privy search, but they were not charged with a particular offence and next day gave a satisfactory account of themselves so the court ordered the constables to see them out of Cambridge on their way home and then discharge them.[19] Vagrancy law presumed the guilt of vagrants from their conduct, and the onus was on them to explain themselves; even in felony cases there was no presumption of innocence

---

17 DRO Midsummer 1748. Letter from George Templeman to William Templeman.

18 See Chapters 4 and 5.

19 CA Q/SO/7 2 February 1776.

at this period, and none in vagrancy well into the nineteenth century (Rose 1988, 13; Beattie 2001, 263).

Idle and disorderly persons if convicted could be sent to the house of correction to hard labour for up to one month. But if the person before him was a rogue and vagabond the justice was 'required' to order the offender publicly whipped or committed to the house of correction. Nevertheless it seems clear that many vagrants deemed genuine objects of compassion were neither whipped nor committed but simply passed or even discharged, neither of which options was envisaged in the 1744 Vagrant Act. In fact it was not legal to pass persons who had not been convicted and punished as rogues and vagabonds, nor was the settlement obliged to receive them; the correct procedure in that case was to remove them as paupers by order of two justices, giving due notice to the alleged settlement, which had the option to appeal.[20]

The second purpose of the examination was to determine the vagrant's settlement; the original objective of vagrancy law was to stop people wandering and begging, and to send them to their settlement as the only place where they were legally entitled to poor relief. Some vagrants were committed to the next sessions precisely because the justice had problems deciding where to send them, and then might languish in bridewell for weeks for no other reason. After the unworkable idea of sending a vagrant back to the parish where he last begged unapprehended was dropped there was no provision for sending the vagrant anywhere but to his legal settlement, or if he had none to his place of birth, although as we shall see, necessity being the mother of invention, some creative bending of the rules developed as the century wore on.

When the vagrant finally arrived at his settlement, if he ever did, he was handed over to the overseers or churchwardens, who were then responsible for him as a settled pauper. From local knowledge they were in a position to check the examination that had accompanied him, for false statements, and take further action if warranted.

Paperwork

From the 1714 Vagrant Act onwards the whole system was extremely bureaucratic, despite being wholly implemented by unpaid local officials. Almost every step had to be recorded in writing, partly because of statutory requirements, partly for reasons of financial accountability (see Plates 2 to 5). The initial arrest of a beggar did not need a warrant, but warrants were issued by the justices in some

[20] But see pp. 55–62 on appeals.

cases: for example, for the arrest of persons reported by the overseers as idle and disorderly, or as having deserted their families. A search warrant might also be issued on a report of vagrants being present in some outbuilding or alehouse, and warrants were supposed to be issued at least quarterly for privy searches to take place all on the same night.

When a vagrant was taken before him the justice was legally obliged to record in writing the gist of the examination, and to make out a duplicate examination and pass for filing at Quarter Sessions. The purpose of these duplicates was to facilitate the detection of repeat offenders, but it seems unlikely that it was ever systematically done. Some justices were more methodical than others, and in Middlesex batches of duplicates occur forwarded by the same justice, usually one of the justices at the rotation offices, yet the bench found it necessary on more than one occasion to remind justices of their duty to return these duplicates. Like so much eighteenth-century legislation these rules had no teeth, and a justice who simply ignored writing out all these documents faced no penalties, although he might be criticized by other more meticulous justices.

Many did comply however, at least part of the time, and the duplicates filed at Quarter Sessions form a valuable, if incomplete, body of evidence. Having made out the two copies of the examination the justice then made out a warrant for committal to bridewell, either for a period he determined or until the next sessions for the court to decide what was to be done, or a pass to convey the vagrant to his settlement. In both cases he also made out a certificate specifying the mode of travel and the next place on the route both for the constable's directions and to enable him to claim his expenses. He might also make out an order for a reward to the constable or whoever had apprehended the vagrant. Where a vagrant contractor was employed there might be a further order for the conveyance of the vagrant by the contractor.

In the eighteenth century, especially in rural counties and earlier in the century, these documents were often totally written out by hand; apart from a brief heading the examination and its duplicate were always hand written, and vary from a lengthy life history to a couple of lines noting the settlement and the grounds of settlement, and possibly some statement admitting the offence, such as 'being destitute and in want forced to wander and beg and received relief',[21] or 'by her own confession found laying in the open air in a very weak condition and lost the use of her limbs'.[22] Dorcas Mitchell, apprehended in Shaftesbury in 1752, said she was thirty-six and had always lived with her father in Crowan Cornwall as part of his family, where he had a leasehold estate of £8 to £10. Probably the

21 DRO QDV box 5 bundle 4; p&e 11 February 1787 of Mary Robins.

22 LMA MJ/SP/V/01/009/01.

justice asked her questions about whether she had ever been married, a yearly hired servant or an apprentice, but if the answer was negative what she had been doing all her life was of no interest as long as it had not gained her a settlement.[23]

On the other hand, when a detailed examination was recorded and filed the information is often highly illuminating. The Bridport calendar 1776 included one John Wood, a rogue and vagabond apprehended wandering in Sherborne. There is no note of sentence or discharge and he does not appear in any subsequent calendar. He might have been any one of hundreds of poor strangers, but his examination was taken before William Toogood Esq. on 8 September and the copy filed tells a strange story. He was born at Hartlebury Worcestershire, moved from there with his parents to Stourbridge in the same county, and lived with them until Easter 1776 when he left and went travelling the country playing on a cymbal. At Wolverhampton he got into company with Hannah Collier, who was then pregnant, and they agreed to travel together. At Warminster Wiltshire she was brought to bed of a boy, and after four or five days there they travelled about in Wiltshire; in the town of New Sarum Wood was committed to prison as a vagabond. While he was in prison Hannah Collier absconded, leaving her child aged ten or eleven weeks at a lodging house in Sarum. The landlady brought the child to Wood in prison and the bridewell keeper made him take the child and discharged him from prison. He then went to Wilton carrying the baby with him, but not knowing what to do with the boy went back towards Sarum and at Fisherton he laid the child, wrapped up in a cloak, on the floor of a barn near to a farmhouse and left it there, then set off for Shaftesbury and had travelled in Dorset ever since. He had not seen or heard of the child since, but he had seen Hannah Collier and heard that she followed the dragoons to Shepton Mallett in Somerset, 'and further this examinant saith not'. Vagrants 'dropping' children are usually the mother – this may be a unique case of a man having a child not his own thrust on him, and shows as much about the reluctance of everybody else to help as it does about Wood.[24]

Printed forms were adopted quite early to spare the justice or his clerk the tedious effort of writing out a great deal of common form, although if not carefully completed they could lead to administrative errors. Administrative slips occur not infrequently in the documentation of vagrancy cases. The Middlesex vagrant contractor had problems to contend with caused by the bridewell keepers not doing their paperwork properly, by the justices themselves directing the passes wrongly, forgetting to sign them, omitting the name of a

---

23 DRO QDV box 3 bundle 7; p&e 4 June 1752.

24 DRO Michaelmas 1776.

vagrant, or being unavailable. Timothy Downing, suspected of travelling with a forged pass, was lucky in that the Dorset justices bothered to check his story, and that his examination turned up, accompanied by a letter from the justice's clerk: 'I should have sent you the Examination of Timothy Downing who was Committed by my Master some time ago but Gave it my Master soon after taken who hath Misslayed it so have sent you a Copy of it which I happened to have by me'.[25]

Quite apart from the usual problems caused by the phonetic spelling of personal and place names in eighteenth-century documents, and the use of aliases, it is not unusual for a vagrant to be given different Christian names in different documents, a different surname, or a different marital status, although clearly the same person. In most legal cases a canny lawyer would enter a plea of misnomer, but vagrants rarely had a lawyer and most of them could not read and were obliged to assume when they made their mark that the clerk had written down their examinations accurately. If he did not they had no redress, and might even be accused of giving false information, which under the 1744 Vagrant Act automatically made them liable to punishment as incorrigible rogues. Jane Millar's pass was made out to Whitford Cambridgeshire, although in her examination she said her husband was settled at Whitford Cheshire.[26] Susannah Conner was described as 'widow of Jeremiah Connelly now in the London Infirmary'.[27] Jane Kitchen's examination said her husband died eleven years ago, which was crossed out and 'nine years' substituted, and went on to say she was married nine years ago, but the confusion might have arisen either from Jane or the clerk.[28] Mary Robins was described as 'widow' in her pass, in the constable's certificate, and in the order for reward, yet mysteriously the phrases referring to her husband's death in her examination were deleted at some point, leaving it doubtful whether she was or was not a widow – possibly since her husband was a soldier she herself had no idea.[29]

In other cases the route was mistaken. John Packman's pass to Scotland was made out via Ridge Hertfordshire, but he was sent back with his papers and a note overleaf dated five days later from James Smith in Bedfordshire, which reads, 'Convey the within named Vagrant to the Borough of St Albans, being sent the wrong road for Scotland'.[30] Ann Baker was wrongly sent from Warwick

25 DRO Midsummer 1745.

26 CA p&e 28 October 1783.

27 LMA WJ/SP/V/01/012/109.

28 LMA WJ/SP/V/01/007/108.

29 DRO QDV box 5 bundle 4.

30 LMA MJ/SP/1769/02/023.

to Southwark and ordered to be passed back to Warwick.[31] James Wills's pass from Middlesex to Plymouth omitted entirely to specify any route.[32]

Mistakes in names, dates and places are not infrequent, although not always significant. Place names in particular may refer simply to a hamlet or farm and do not appear on modern maps, so that conveying the vagrant to his settlement might depend heavily on local knowledge, even where the vagrant had honestly tried to say where it was. Elizabeth Smith, taken up in the City of London 10 January 1753, was ordered to be conveyed to Clifton Dorset, and the receipt dated 10 January 1752, although prewritten in the same hand except for the signature – presumably the clerk was not yet used to new-style dating. She was brought to Pentridge to be conveyed via Henstridge to her settlement at Clifton; Clifton Maybank is a tiny hamlet near Bradford Abbas, so small that modern maps may not show it, but using local knowledge Henstridge was deleted and she was ordered by the local justice to be passed to Milborne Port Somerset, 'that being the next precinct in the direct road to Clifton Dorset', where the tithingman accepted her, signed the receipt, and presumably conveyed her the 28 miles to Clifton Maybank.[33]

It is indeed surprising that such confusion does not occur more frequently, since there were no detailed gazetteers covering the entire country until the 1770s (for example, Paterson 1771), and a great deal of the actual passing must have depended on local knowledge. The use of printed forms, although a great timesaver, could also lead to error unless the inapplicable parts were carefully crossed out or altered; Elizabeth Strettenham was referred to throughout as 'he' and 'him'.[34]

Processing the vagrants: financial control

Much useful information, especially about the cost of vagrancy to the county, comes from the financial transactions involved. After the 1700 Vagrant Removal Costs Act transferred financial responsibility to the county, and especially after the 1714 Vagrant Act set up the chain of financial accountability, it becomes more feasible to assess the burden of vagrancy on the rate. Constables and vagrant contractors made lists of the vagrants they conveyed, sometimes noting the routes they used, and often details of any exceptional expenses such as extra subsistence for sick vagrants, burial and lying-in expenses, charges for guards,

[31] LMA MJ/SP/1795/12/051.

[32] LMA MJ/SP/V/01/040/74

[33] DRO QDV box 6 tithing of Pentridge bundle.

[34] LMA MJ/SP/V/01/035/51.

horse hire, and so forth. These lists were used to support their claims for expenses, and often survive, sometimes with the original bills, in Quarter Sessions rolls. For some counties high constables' accounts and treasurers' accounts yield important information about the cost to the county.

After reciting the provisions of the 1744 Vagrant Act, rules for making out certificates for conveying vagrants into the next county were laid down by Middlesex in 1749. The justice having made out the pass was directed to calculate the distance to the first parish in the next county and then note how the vagrant was to be conveyed and allow a sum of 6d per mile for conveyance and 6d for 24 hours' maintenance, this being the maximum the officer could demand from the high constable. A handy ready reckoner was supplied for the distances (probably from Clerkenwell Bridewell), viz. to West Ham Essex 4 miles 2s; to Egham Surrey 18 miles 9s; to Denham Bucks 18 miles 9s; to Northall Herts 15 miles 7s 6d; to Cheshunt Herts 11 miles 5s 6d; to Ridge Herts 17 miles 8s 6d. Justices were recommended to write out the amount of the allowance in words, clearly to guard against any fiddling of the figures to inflate the amount due.[35]

Only Dorset among the six counties in this study preserves many of these certificates, which are effectively orders for payment to constables taking the form of forwarding passes, and also constables' accounts noting the mode of transport, mileage and subsistence allowances claimed.[36] Constables' accounts are found sporadically among the sessions papers in other counties. These certificates or forwarding passes are mainly for vagrants passing through Shaftesbury: that is, for vagrants apprehended elsewhere and brought from another county to be conveyed to their settlements, a few to settlements in Dorset, but most through Dorset to yet another county. The certificates may well have been routine elsewhere but disposed of after the accounts were checked.[37]

These orders were made out by a local magistrate when the vagrant was brought into the county, included the mode of conveyance onwards and the mileage and subsistence allowance the constable could claim, and formed the authorization, duly receipted, for the constable to claim his expenses. The original pass and examination went with the vagrant; a duplicate was filed, if at all, only where the vagrant was apprehended and examined within the county. On arrival in the next county the receiving constable or his representative receipted the certificate to show that the vagrant had been duly handed over. Some of the receipts for the vagrants were made out at the same time and in the same hand as the certificate and simply signed by the receiving constable or

35 LMA MJ/SB/B/0106 47, 188–9.

36 DRO QDV six boxes.

37 There is a stray bundle in very poor condition among the high constables' papers in Westmorland, and a few scattered examples among Middlesex sessions papers.

his representative one or two days later without changing the date. One or two Dorset constables made their mark, or more likely the certificate was marked by someone else who received the vagrant in his absence; constables were expected to be literate – indeed it is hard to see how they could have followed written warrants from the justice or compiled their accounts if they had not been.

The passing system in practice

The objectives of vagrancy law were twofold, firstly to stop poor people wandering and begging and return them to their settlements, and secondly to punish a wide range of cadgers, frauds and socially irresponsible individuals. The passing system was designed to meet the first of these objectives, and for over a century followed the lines laid down in the 1714 Vagrant Act. Simple in principle, in practice all sorts of problems arose, chiefly from the assumption that everybody had a discoverable settlement, a basic misconception compounded by the increasing numbers of Scotch and Irish poor immigrants and of persons born 'in the army' or the colonies. Further problems arose from the complexity of the paperwork, from the lack of accurate geographical information, from the difficulties of travel and communication, and from the cost involved, especially as the system was widely used to plug gaps in the provision for particular groups.

In rural counties particularly, extra journeys and expense might be involved because a constable having apprehended a vagrant took him to be examined by a justice only to find the gentleman not at home. When Thomas Proctor, a dragoon from a regiment then lying at Manchester, died and was buried at Shap in 1770, the constable had to make five journeys to Orton, one of these at least to get Richard Burn's advice,[38] and five more to Kendal to get money, as well as sending letters to Manchester, Lowther, Penrith and Askham, and getting legal documents. Proctor was in custody to be taken before a justice when he died, quite probably at the constable's own house.[39] The constable's bill for Ann Wood in 1769 included, as well as the month lying in, a trip to Manchester of two days and a night to search for her marriage entry in the register, and four separate journeys to Read Hall Blackburn to see Mr Clayton the justice, on three of which he was not at home. These journeys cost £1 7s 4d, the lying in itself £1 2s 6d.[40]

---

38 Vicar of Orton and a doctor of laws, author of the standard justices' handbook *The justice of the peace and parish officer*, first published in 1755.

39 WRO WQSR 362/24.

40 LRO QSP 1948/9.

A constable might have to make extra journeys because the parish officers refused to accept the vagrant, usually because of a dispute about the vagrant's settlement. Wrongly refusing to accept a vagrant was however punishable by a fine of £20, which Daniel Lott incurred in Middlesex in 1787,[41] and the officers of Orwell in Cambridgeshire in 1791.[42]

Under the 1714 Vagrant Act, vagrants were to be passed to the next parish in the direct way to the place named in the pass, or if out of the county to the first place in the next county on the direct road. The 1740 Vagrant Act changed this to require vagrants to be passed house of correction to house of correction, perhaps to ensure they were punished there. In 1741 Susan Wellen widow and her two children Richard and Anne apprehended in Canford Magna as vagabonds were ordered to be conveyed to Lewisham Kent via Fisherton Anger house of correction and other houses of correction.[43]

But probably following protests from some counties that this often led to a long and expensive detour, the 1744 Vagrant Act reverted to passing vagrants constable to constable. As early as 1655 the inhabitants of Salford hundred gave as their reason for wanting their own house of correction that the distance to Preston house of correction made it of little benefit to them so that 'many tymes Idle Wandringe Vagrant and Loose persons passe with impunitie' (Tollit 1953, 80).

Quarter Sessions records rarely show what happened to vagrants on arrival, but some were put in the workhouse, like James Cakewick, apprehended in St James Westminster in 1765 wandering and laying in the open air, who was settled by apprenticeship in St Martin in the Fields, and delivered to the master of the workhouse there.[44]

Passing the vagrants: transport

The manner in which a constable, after apprehending a vagrant, conveyed him to the justice is obscure, and probably depended on the numbers involved and whether the constable had any help or transport available. He does not appear to have been reimbursed for this, but the mileages involved must usually have been insignificant. Probably the reward was intended to compensate, but the reward was not necessarily paid. The justices set the mileage rates, which were always less on foot than on horseback or by cart, but probably the vagrant, having been

41 LMA MJ/SP/1787/09/078 and /132.

42 CA information and complaint 6 May 1791.

43 DRO Midsummer 1742.

44 LMA WJ/SP/V/01/012/111.

examined and discharged, was often allowed to proceed unescorted, and given subsistence money, again at rates set by the justices, to cover the length of time his walk to the next parish would take. Most vagrants who were passed rather than committed were cooperative, and it is hard to believe the constable could actually spare the time to go to the next parish with each and every vagrant on foot.

Passes were also issued to travellers at their own request, probably to protect them from the vagrant laws, and seem to have been widely accepted, although legally invalid. They do not normally turn up in Quarter Sessions rolls, since they were not 'of record', but a stray example from Cambridge 8 December 1758 requests that Mary Langham singlewoman be permitted to go to Chatham 'without any of your Lett, Hindrance, or Molestation whatsoever, she demeaning herself orderly and not exceeding the space of ten days from the date hereof to accomplish her said Journey allowing her such relief as to you shall seem meet'.[45] There were many complaints about the issue of these foot passes, also known as 'walking passes', 'permit passes' or 'Scotch passes', which were officially only for soldiers and mariners.

Forged passes were not uncommon and a traveller with a pass might not be protected by it: William Cleveland was taken up in Sturminster Newton and sentenced to three months, although he was carrying a pass issued by a magistrate in Devon at the time, and there is no evidence the magistrates found this pass a forgery, though they probably suspected it. He claimed to be travelling from Plymouth Dock to Chatham and to have a pension from Chatham Chest, having been frequently wounded in his service aboard several of HM warships.[46]

How the vagrants were conveyed also varied from county to county, and there was evidently some confusion as to whether the mode of transport named in the original pass was obligatory for the entire journey. Cambridge justices rarely granted cart or even horse passes and protested to Essex in 1758 because all vagrants were sent out of Essex by cart (no doubt by vagrant contractor) requesting that they would in future convey by cart only vagrants unable to walk or ride; evidently the Cambridge justices assumed that they had to follow suit.[47] But most counties took the opposite view, and did what suited their particular circumstances. Westmorland, like Cambridgeshire, appears to have used horses or carts only for sick or heavily pregnant vagrants. Clearly if a vagrant turned lame or fell ill the original requirement to walk could not be adhered to, and common sense and economy generally prevailed.

45 CA Epiphany 1759.

46 DRO Easter 1791.

47 CA Q/SO/5 6 October 1758.

Cart passes were used in Middlesex only for sick vagrants until the appointment of their vagrant contractor in 1757, after which they were conveyed in batches in a covered cart. A great deal depended on the number of vagrants involved – it was often cheaper to pass a family by cart, especially if there were small children who could not walk or ride by themselves, for example Ursula Thorne and four children aged seven to twelve.[48] These inconsistencies were still presenting problems in 1785, when the Lancashire and Cheshire magistrates reported that some justices had specified the mode of conveyance in the pass itself, instead of in the certificate to the constable within each jurisdiction,[49] leaving the mode of conveyance through other districts on the route to the local magistrates. Magistrates had not always exercised their discretion in varying the mode specified in the original pass, resulting in very great additional expense.[50]

In the case of vagrants passed on foot, the law did not specify whether the constable was legally obliged to escort them but certainly many were simply given 'walking passes' and left to make their own way. Vagrants coming into Dorset with walking passes, partly because so many were military or naval personnel, seem to have been given simply a few pence subsistence and left to their own devices, and appear, if at all, in surviving constables' accounts. But all the other vagrants passing through Shaftesbury from other counties were conveyed forward either on horseback, or by cart. Certificates sometimes specified 'a double horse' – that is, either pillion behind the constable or two vagrants on one horse. The constable or his servant must have escorted vagrants going on horseback to bring the horses back, and probably the horses were linked together – obviously no risk would be taken of a vagrant just galloping off with the horse.

Dorset cart passes usually specified whether one, two or three horses were allowed, proportioned to the number of vagrants being carried, the distance, and probably the state of the roads. There seems no reason why Shaftesbury should have been different from the rest of Dorset, bearing in mind that the county picked up the bills. The distances and poor condition of the roads in Dorset may go some way to explain the preference for horse transport. On several occasions the transport of the king's baggage provoked adverse comments on the state of Dorset roads, even in summer. In July 1748 the officer commanding a detachment of General Frampton's regiment marching from Sturminster Newton to Evershot on their way to Exeter wrote to the constable of Sturminster Newton to explain that Henry Foster's wagon, which had been impressed to carry the troops' baggage, had been broken by the badness of the

48 DRO QDV box 3 bundle 5.

49 According to 1744 Vagrant Act s. 10.

50 LMA MJ/SP/1786/04/132, 5.

road, and that Foster ought to receive some compensation from the county, advising the constable to apply on his behalf 'as directed by Act of Parliament' (that is, the Mutiny Act).

In 1756 four pressed wagons carrying the baggage of a company of Scots Greys took three days to get from Shaftesbury to Bruton Somerset, a distance of 20 miles, 'as the roads has been so Excessive bad'. The four wagon owners petitioned Quarter Sessions, evidently with legal advice, explaining that, 'the weather then being very wet, and the River greatly risen on account of a prodigious heavy Rain', they could only reach Sturminster Newton the first day and Sherborne the second, so that including the return journey they were away three days, but by the express words of the current Mutiny Act they could not claim more than 1s per mile, which the officers had paid, giving them signed certificates to prove their claim, one of which they produced in court. They quoted the clause giving the justices power to pay extraordinary expenses: 'see the Stat. at large or Burns Justice number 401 title soldiers'. Duly impressed, the court ordered 20s paid to each petitioner out of county funds.[51]

Two female vagrants passed through Shaftesbury in 1753 had to be taken in a cart drawn by three horses, 'the Wether being bad'. As late as 1784 an owner claimed £1 10s 0d for extra time and trouble, his wagon being delayed ten days transporting army baggage between Dorchester and Sherborne, on account of the depth of snow that March. Dorset was not unique in this, however: even Cambridgeshire, a somewhat parsimonious county, permitted justices to allow a little extra mileage in cross-county passes if the roads were bad.[52] Hampshire in 1773 permitted an extra allowance not exceeding 6d per mile, at the discretion of the justices, for carrying army baggage from Petersfield to Godliman and Guildford 'on account of the badness of the Roads and the length of the Stages'.[53]

Dorset often allowed horse hire in bills, but in several bills late in the century charges for provender were struck out and not reimbursed. Transport could be a heavy item of expenditure: conveying Robert Thomas Dowland from Dorchester Gaol to Potterne in Wiltshire cost £7 14s 1d; the return journey took three days, and involved the hire of three horses, coach and chaise hire, and a guide from Devizes to Sarum.[54] In Lancashire sick prisoners were occasionally conveyed by sedan chair, and in Middlesex sick vagrants might be conveyed in a coach; in Dorset too a coach might occasionally be used, especially if the vagrant was furiously mad and needed a guard.

---

51 DRO Epiphany 1757.

52 CA Q/SO/5 18 January 1754.

53 HRO Q1/18 April 1773.

54 DRO Easter 1777.

Vagrants, if not furiously mad, were generally tractable compared with felons – conveying William Cleaton, a vagrant committed by the mayor of Shaftesbury in 1785, to Sherborne Bridewell cost 16s 0d including hire of two horses, but when the mayor committed William Church to Dorchester Gaol in the same year on a charge of feloniously stealing two cows it cost £2 16s 0d to convey him there, including drivers, turnpikes, expenses on the road for two constables and the prisoner, and hire of a chaise, 'the Constable being unable to convey the Prisoner with Safety without taking that Method'.[55] Sick casual poor taken up and processed as vagrants were obviously only too glad to gain access to shelter, treatment and transport. Vagrants under conveyance do not seem to have been fettered, and some certainly escaped on the way (Eccles 2006, 89). A North Riding clergyman suggested that constables should be equipped with collars marked with the name of the town to lock on vagrants while in custody to prevent them escaping (Cockburn 1963–66, 511). The receipts for vagrants were intended to ensure that constables could not simply let them go and claim the money, so that if a vagrant did escape the constable got no expenses, but he does not otherwise seem to have been held accountable, nor was the Middlesex contractor.

Some of the vagrants arriving in Shaftesbury had been conveyed considerable distances, many coming from London, others going to the London area from Devon and Cornwall. Since the pass itself was not normally receipted, the intervening stages are usually unidentifiable, but a rare survival exists in Dorset: Elizabeth Gray, a soldier's wife with her two children, was passed to Shaftesbury from Liverpool in April 1755 en route to West Stour, a few miles west of Shaftesbury. Receipts from constables endorsed on her examination record her journey from her apprehension on 9 April. She reached Latchford near Warrington 12 April, Falk o'the Mill Staffordshire 14 April, Sutton Coldfield Warwickshire 16 April, Northfield Worcestershire 18 April. On the eighteenth she passed through St Nicholas and St Peter Without Worcester to Twining Gloucestershire, finally arriving in Shaftesbury 26 April. Even in this case there may well be one or two stages unrecorded, especially during the last few days of her journey.[56] Probably most if not all constables owned horses, and some also carts, but where vagrants were sent by cart or by more than one horse it may be the extra mileage allowance was intended to cover the cost of hire and help. Dorset constables' bills rarely include hire of vehicles as a separate item, and neither gaol nor bridewell possessed vehicles – after 1774, when the prisoners no longer walked in chains to the sessions, the keepers hired carts.

---

55 DRO QDV box 4 bundle 14.

56 DRO Midsummer 1755.

Although in the early 1740s after the 1740 Vagrant Act came into force Dorset vagrants were passed by the bridewell keeper to the bridewells in neighbouring counties as the law directed, to Taunton or Shepton Mallett in Somerset and Fisherton Anger in Wiltshire, when this stipulation was reversed in 1744 the county promptly reverted to the older system of passing vagrants constable to constable. It would clearly have been out of the direct route and far more expensive to have passed a vagrant from Poole to Plymouth via Sherborne. There was no financially foolproof method, constables were suspected of overcharging, but if the bridewell was inconveniently situated they might still be the cheaper alternative.

By 1750 vagrants in Dorset were conveyed by the constable in the parish of apprehension the whole way to the constable in the nearest out-county parish, along the most direct route; Dorset also had vagrant contractors from time to time, often long-serving constables. Vagrants apprehended in Shaftesbury or conveyed through the town were taken by different routes according to their ultimate destination. Those going to Devon and Cornwall went via Henstridge Somerset, a distance of 10 miles. The hire of a cart and three horses to Henstridge came to 8s 4d, a cart with two horses 6s 8d, the allowance on horseback was 2s 6d, with two horses 4s 2d. Most of those going to the London area went via Martin or Donhead St Mary Wiltshire, which was only 4 miles from Shaftesbury. Later Semley Wiltshire was preferred to Martin, perhaps because of a change of constable or a request from Wiltshire. Other transit parishes included Pentridge and Charmouth.

Conveying vagrants within the county was often considerably more expensive than passing them into the next county – four vagrants summarily convicted in Shaftesbury were sent 16 miles to Sherborne Bridewell in a cart with three horses at £1 1s 4d;[57] this cost factor may have deterred some justices from committing vagrants. Thomas Boyle had been passed from Lambeth Surrey and brought to Shaftesbury to be conveyed to Clifton, near Bradford Abbas, a journey of 24 miles. He was conveyed by two horses, probably because one horse could not carry two men so far, at a cost of 10s, plus 2s for two days' subsistence, 'no justice being in town'.[58] Rachel Highcraft and her two small children had been conveyed to Shaftesbury from Southwark; conveying them from Shaftesbury to their settlement at Dallwood cost £1 3s 6d, involving two days' subsistence for Rachel and the older child (sucking children did not count) and a 42-mile

57 DRO QDV box 3 bundle 6. Order 12 November 1751.

58 DRO QDV box 3 bundle 5.

journey with two horses and a man.[59] Dorset at least seems to have paid for the return journey.

Constables were not expected to travel on Sundays; an extra day's subsistence was paid, but it is not clear where the vagrants stayed overnight. Many villages and towns had small lock-ups variously known as the cage, round-house, watch-house or simply prison; in some cases workhouse accommodation was used, especially for sick vagrants, in other cases quite likely the constable put them in a stable loft or outbuilding on his own property. The Middlesex vagrant contractor put them in a semi-basement and a stable loft until 1792 when the justices insisted on better accommodation. Gilbert proposed in 1782 that the justices should provide a cage or lock-up house in every market town to be paid for by the county and managed by the constable, and pay for the maintenance of vagrants for 24 hours until the constable took them before a justice (Gilbert 1782, 15–16), but this clause did not appear when the new Vagrant Act was finally passed in 1792. It may already have been the arrangement in most counties: in 1771 Hampshire ordered a round-house to be erected in the East Soke near Winchester to secure delinquents until they could conveniently be taken before a justice.[60]

Hampshire was very keen for villages to keep their stocks properly maintained, although who sat in them does not appear from the records of Quarter Sessions – possibly vagrants, although nothing in any vagrancy act in force in the eighteenth century authorized such a measure. Middlesex on the other hand abandoned stocks in the seventeenth century (Shoemaker 1991, 162). One justices' handbook said the constable might put a person who deserted a child in the stocks until he took it up, but this cited no legal authority.[61] Unrecorded informal justice may have been fairly common, however: in 1828 a Yorkshire justice attributed much of the alarming apparent rise in juvenile crime to the decline of such measures – 'I remember in former days, persons were taken and pumped upon, or something of that sort; but now they are handed over to the Police, and tried on it'.[62]

The stocks remained in use for village summary justice in some places in northern counties well into the nineteenth century (Morgan and Rushton 1998, 127–8) and the stocks at Odiham still survive,[63] now moved from their original position outside the bridewell to stand near the church. Maintaining the stocks

---

59 DRO QDV box 3 bundle 11. These mileages are those given in the documents; modern distances might be different because of changes in the road network.

60 HRO Q/3/9 Midsummer 1771.

61 Giles 1744, 18–19. The same author makes a number of errors however and cannot be considered a reliable authority.

62 1828 Report on criminal convictions PP vol. 4, 4.

63 See Plate 6.

might be tricky though – in 1767 Mary Dennis was committed for stealing the iron off the stocks at Upwey.[64]

Dorset vagrants got a generous 1s per day subsistence, enough for a night's lodging and supper in a local alehouse. Probably they were given the subsistence money rather than the constable providing a meal. On two occasions in 1770 vagrants, evidently with walking passes and unescorted, complained to the tithingman of Martin that they had not been given their subsistence money by the previous officer and were paid it without question.[65]

Passing the vagrants: Irish vagrants

As early as 1572 masters of ships could be fined 20s for bringing Irish and Manx vagrants, and such vagrants were ordered to be sent back. We have noted that the 1662 Settlement Act applied only to persons with settlements in England or Wales and to no others, and that by the 1714 Vagrant Act fines were imposed on masters of vessels bringing persons 'likely to live by begging'. There was no poor relief system in Ireland or Scotland, and by 1744 increasing immigration meant that more detailed arrangements had to be made for dealing with vagrants from overseas, more particularly from Ireland. Measures to compel masters of vessels to take vagrants at rates set by the justices were put in place, although a master could only be compelled to take one vagrant per 20 tons burthen of his ship.

Often passes and examinations of Irish vagrants say they are 'settled' in some parish in Ireland by birth or apprenticeship, and require them to be passed there. In practice the pass was valid only to get them on board and after that nobody cared much what happened to them. Peter Flynn, a blind boy of fifteen whose mother died in Cambridge Bridewell in 1768, was sent to Ireland as his late mother's settlement since she was married in Co. Cavan, although she had since been in England 23 years and he was born in St Giles in the Fields.[66] Ironically, had he been a bastard, he would have been deemed settled in St Giles. Derk Credelo, a Dutchman apprehended begging in Fulbourn in 1776, was ordered to be passed to the nearest seaport to return to Holland following his sentence, unless he agreed to join the navy.[67] William Cleveland was born in Plymouth New England, and passed from Sherborne Bridewell to Exeter to be sent back to America,[68] and Rosannah Johnson and her three children, apprehended begging

[64] DRO Easter 1767 gaol calendar.

[65] DRO QDV box 2 bundle 10.

[66] [66] CA Q/SO/7 January 1768.

[67] [67] CA Q/SO/7 February 1776.

[68] DRO Easter 1791 calendar.

in Moor Crichel Dorset and discharged at midsummer sessions 1799, were put on board the Guernsey packet at Weymouth by the verbal order of the chairman.[69] It is highly unlikely that Credelo and Cleveland were finally repatriated, but if they were Essex and Devon must have paid their passages, following the rules for Irish vagrants. The repatriation of Americans and foreigners was not envisaged in the law.

Irish vagrants obviously had to be sent by sea, yet Middlesex did not send them from one of the Thames ports but passed them county to county across the country. Nor did they send vagrants to Northumberland for Scotland by one of the many coastal vessels. In the first place county to county was the method laid down by law, in the second this method spread the cost among the intervening counties. Until relatively late in the century all Irish vagrants passed home by Middlesex were sent to West Chester (Parkgate in Cheshire); later in the century other routes were sometimes followed probably in response to complaints by Lancashire and Cheshire: those going to Cork, for example, were sent via Bristol, yet as late as 1797 Patrick Mahan was sent to Cork via Liverpool.[70] Hampshire did however send Peter and Mary Taylor to Southampton to be carried by the first ship to Scotland, although this was by no means the usual practice.[71]

In the case of Irish vagrants a lengthy delay at the port of embarkation might occur due to adverse winds. This bore hard on those counties that had to maintain these vagrants and also pay for their passage (Place 1985). Although it had been a common practice long before, the cost of repatriating the Irish became particularly contentious after s. 33 of the 1819 act legitimated their passage home even where no act of vagrancy had been committed, and was still a matter of grave financial concern to Middlesex in 1833.[72]

---

69 DRO NG/PRI: D1/1.

70 LMA MJ/SP/V/01/040/50.

71 HRO Q1/17 10 July 1759.

72 1833 Report on Irish vagrants PP vol. 16; 1834 Report on vagrancy PP vol. 38 Appendix E 21–5.

Chapter 3
Vagrancy Law in Practice

Vagrancy law in action

Turning from statute law against vagrancy to the law in action, we may note that vagrancy was to a large extent 'victimless crime', or rather, the parish or county was the victim. In this it resembles riot, nuisance and public order offences – it was often used as an alternative to these charges – rather than petty larceny or assault. Its prosecution consequently depended on official law enforcement agency rather than personal initiative to a much greater extent than property crime. We may also perceive it as a particular example of the modification of statute law from below through the use made of it by the justices. Much good work by historians has demonstrated the wide gap between the 'bloody code' as it lay on the statute book and its application in practice, not entirely down to the judiciary but to refusal of juries to convict, or their returning partial verdicts such as finding thieves guilty 'to the value' of a sum that turned capital larceny into petty larceny, often out of sympathy with the accused and in defiance of the facts (Beattie 1986, 284–6, Beattie 2001, 26–8). Courts, juries and justices might render statutes nugatory by simply not enforcing them: Peter King cites the refusal of local courts to enforce a 1788 decision that gleaning was illegal as an example where they defeated the aims of farmers by siding with the poor (P. King 2006, 7).

By the eighteenth century the power of the Privy Council to supervise the activities of the county justices had declined. The circuit judges in their charge to the grand jury passed on government policy statements and had a supervisory role, and the court of King's Bench could, but rarely did, deal with complaints about the behaviour of individual justices (Hay 2002, 19–22; Landau 2002, 46–70); in extreme cases the Lord Chancellor could remove a justice from the commission of the peace. Otherwise counties were largely independent of parliament, and applied, ignored and adapted legislation as they saw fit; within counties individual justices were similarly free of county interference to a considerable extent.

Non-conformity to statute law was only seen as a problem when it raised complaints in parliament or in King's Bench, and counties, justices and parish officers all assumed they could adapt or ignore it when they thought proper. Extra-legal initiatives can be found at all levels: the government itself, to give only one example, clandestinely paid salaries to Bow Street justices at the time when the Fieldings were experimenting with the horse patrol, the Bow Street runners and public offices, and eventually the whole system became official, despite some misgivings on the part of individuals who thought it gave too much scope for government patronage and interference. Some of the expense caused by the military fell on the counties without any statutory authority, simply by failure to make other provision.

Counties handed over the conveying of vagrants to vagrant contractors, although this solution to their problems in implementing the conveying of vagrants enjoined by vagrancy law never had statutory authorization. To avoid the greater cost of passing them with the correct vagrant passes Berkshire came to an extra-legal arrangement with the two Maidenhead parishes for splitting between the parishes and the county the cost of subsisting vagrants with walking passes going westwards along the Bath road, although the county was well aware it was an evasion of the statute, and when the parishes asked for more money refused on the grounds that 'the present Allowance ... is not strictly legal' (Neuman 1982, 113–16). The Speenhamland system was an extra-legal measure, though widely practised in the southern agricultural parishes. In the industrializing north, rather than apprehend them as vagrants or allow them to beg from the public many townships developed vagrant offices where poor travellers could get a bed and supper, also without statutory authority.

In a Dorset case Ann Tanswell, a female beggar, was held in bridewell for over four years, double the maximum sentence anyone could receive under vagrancy law, apparently because she had no known settlement or place of birth to which she could be sent; perhaps a rare example of oppressive behaviour by the court itself, but it is not clear what could legally be done in such a case other than maintain the person at county expense in bridewell, and perhaps the fault lay rather with the law itself.[1] Courts and justices alike would sentence likely men to whipping and imprisonment but offer enlisting in the army or navy instead.

Justices often failed to follow correct procedure, but much of this was due to the increasingly onerous paperwork to be dealt with by magistrates, few of whom had any reward other than status and local influence. In Middlesex some justices persistently declined to obey directives from the county, due partly to the pursuit of gain by trading justices and partly to individual justices disagreeing with county policy when it appeared to put cost before humanity.

Justices cut corners: for example, where a vagrant was committed the pass for conveying him to his settlement was not supposed to be made out until after the sentence was carried out or the court discharge obtained, and then by the

---

1 DRO Easter 1789, Midsummer 1793.

committing justice. In Cambridge Edward Bartlam was ordered to be brought before the justices sitting at the Rose tavern at the end of his sentence to have his pass made out.[2] But many justices, at least in Middlesex after the 1792 act made a minimum period of seven days in bridewell mandatory, made the pass out at the same time as the *mittimus*, partly to save time and trouble – otherwise the bridewell keeper would have to take the vagrant back to the committing justice to get the pass – and partly to ensure that no other justice received the fee for the pass at the end of the sentence.

George Story examined and committed several vagrants apprehended in Shadwell in 1792, but after the seven days the vagrants were passed by John Staples, who sat at the Whitechapel office. John Staples also sat on the accounts committee and presumably this shortcut was acceptable unless the committing justice complained. Often too in Middlesex the turnkey's receipt for the vagrant endorsed on the pass and examination is the only evidence that the vagrant ever was committed.

Justices were in the strong position of being indispensable to county administration and to law and order, but Middlesex referred the cases of fifteen justices to King's Bench, successfully in twelve cases, alleging irregularities, self-interest and dereliction of duty against this small minority, mostly 'trading justices' (Hay 2002, 21, 45; Landau 2002, 47, 50–52).

Parishes felt free, in managing the poor, to adopt such measures as refusing relief to those they disapproved of – tipplers, for example – or those who kept a dog and were therefore deemed not to be in actual want. The select vestry of Uffington Berkshire threatened to fine £5 any parishioner who employed a non-parishioner except at peak agricultural seasons, without any statutory authority to levy such fines, and many Berkshire parishes employed salaried assistant overseers long before legally empowered to do so (Neuman 1982, 154, 181). London parishes adopted their own system of issuing 'friendly passes' to avoid the expense and hassle of a pauper removal or the illegal issue of vagrant passes for the same purpose: pre-printed forms were available and took the form of a polite request addressed to the parish officers, 'Gentlemen, the bearer, Ann Brown, upon examination appears to belong to your parish. Your taking her without an Order of Removal will much oblige, and the like favour shall at any time be returned by, Gentlemen ...', signed by the overseer with the date and parish (Hitchcock 2004, 147).

Peter King has convincingly demonstrated how the justices of the peace quietly changed the law from the margins by the manner in which they applied or ignored it (P. King 2006), and vagrancy was a particular case in point. The

2 CA Q/SO/8 16 July 1784.

contribution of juries to modification of the letter of the law did not of course apply to vagrants since even those who appeared in court were not entitled to jury trial, the case being decided by a majority of justices present at the sessions. Counties and overseers alike, concerned about finance, thought justices too lenient to vagrants and too sympathetic to the poor. In addition, much of the difficulty in enforcing vagrancy law even when counties and justices sought to do so was caused by members of the public exercising their own autonomy, and persistently giving to beggars in defiance of all attempts to stop them. Despite suggestions that giving to beggars should itself become a criminal offence this was evidently considered a step too far, and never happened.

Vagrancy law as applied by the justices was very different from vagrancy law on the statute book otherwise the streets would have been running with blood round the whipping posts. The routine whipping of all vagrants seems never to have happened in the eighteenth century, and was less and less common as the century progressed. The most likely explanation is embodied in resolutions of the Middlesex bench in 1757 and again in 1775, urging magistrates to distinguish bogus crippled and sick vagrants from the genuine and whip the bogus,[3] namely that individual justices had been doing that very thing for some time at their own discretion, and found most vagrants brought before them to be genuinely crippled, sick, deserted or destitute. The justices in practice limited the penal provisions of the law to those they judged to be voluntarily idle and dishonest, and either discharged or passed the unfortunate; passes noting that the vagrant had been punished are conspicuous exceptions, and virtually confined to the earlier years after the passing of the 1744 Vagrant Act, at least until 1792 when in Middlesex for some time it was regularly noted that the vagrant had been committed for seven days.

Summary justice is of course singularly difficult to pin down, leaving no official record of orders to whip vagrants, and there may have been particular justices, particular times or particular places where vagrants met with harsh treatment. Moreover the minority committed may have been routinely whipped on admission to bridewell, but by the last quarter of the century, when the justices took a more active role in the supervision of bridewells, keepers were generally forbidden to whip prisoners without an order from the visiting magistrates. There were exceptions, however: at the London bridewell the keeper was allowed to give up to thirty lashes with the cat o' nine tails at his own discretion as late as 1818 (Henderson 1999, 139). Even the 1792 Vagrant Act, although widely observed to begin with, failed to reinstate whipping for simple begging, and the seven days' imprisonment was mostly the preferred option, even for men.

---

3 LMA MJ/O/C/006 14 July 1757, MJ/SP/1775/12/063.

Richard Burn identified many areas of confusion in statute law: he devoted over fifty pages of his *History of the poor laws* to a list of defects in the laws needing clarification or amendment and drew attention to the fact that case law often produced divergent judgments and made things worse, not least because the handbooks often failed to keep up to date, 'for where precedents once get into any edition of a book, they seldom get out again, let the law alter as it may' (Burn 1764, 242–95, 126). As early as 1742 a commentator wrote, 'The statute laws are now becoming so voluminous and intricate, and by making and mending new quibbles and blunders which daily arise like Hydra's heads, are in such a way of increasing, that ... I fear they will become the grievance of the subject, and the shame of the nation' (P. King 2006, 23). The passage of time did nothing to improve matters. Statute law was often ambiguous, leaving many cases open to question or to differing interpretations; obsolete statutes lay on the books unrepealed, leaving the way open for their use in particular cases long after.

For example, the penalties for bastard bearers incorporated in the 1609 Vagrant Act (7 James I c. 4 1609 s. 7) were not included in the piecemeal repeal of other clauses, and though a dead letter in some counties, remained in use in others, such as Gloucestershire, well into the nineteenth century. Again, the statutes against inmates were virtually unused in the eighteenth century; on the contrary, overseers commonly encouraged or even obliged paupers to take in other poor as lodgers as a method of easing the poor rate. Steve Hindle points out that in the seventeenth century the law against inmates and the consequent demolition of cottages was at odds with the requirement to house the poor (Hindle 2006, 61), and in 1601 the then Secretary of State Robert Cecil's speech against enclosures eloquently described the potential dangers of such contradictory legislation:

> yf the poore being thruste out of their howses go to dwell with others, streight we ketche them with the statute of inmates; yf they wander abroad and be stubborne, they are within the danger of roagues; yf they be more humble and vagrant baggars, then they are within this statute of the poore to be whipte and tormented. (Hindle 2004, 303)

But the law against inmates could still be used: in 1761 Robert Beaumont was fined 13s 4d for lodging William Turth and his wife in his cottage as inmates,[4] and in 1771 a warrant was issued for the apprehension of William Thompson for lodging inmates in St Sepulchre Cambridge.[5]

4 CA Q/SO/6 3 April 1761.

5 CA Q/SO/7 18 January 1771.

Yet the Middlesex bench in 1744 sought a law against harbouring inmates, especially loose idle disorderly persons or reputed thieves or vagabonds living by pilfering or cheating, 'there being at present no Law for the speedy and effectual punishment of them'.[6] They do not appear to have noticed that the statute against inmates was still in force, or that s. 23 of the 1744 Vagrant Act, passed six months before, made harbouring vagrants punishable by a fine or a month in prison. Probably what they had in mind was more like the Disorderly Houses Act passed subsequently in 1752 (25 Geo. II c. 36). However, as late as 1775 William Nicholson was prosecuted in the same county for a misdemeanour in lodging inmates:[7] the prosecution took the form of a Crown action, and bail was posted in £80 for the defendant and in £40 each for the sureties.

Laws were poorly drafted and therefore inconsistently applied. Much legislation was introduced for very limited areas, such as the numerous local watch and paving acts and the acts permitting the development of a particular stretch of road or canal, or for short periods of time, notably the constant changes in taxation; even the crucial Mutiny Act governing recruitment and arrangements for the army was passed annually, to give the illusion that there was no standing army. By the end of the eighteenth century the volume of legislation must have made it impossible for lay justices to have much in-depth knowledge of the law, hence the need for justices' handbooks. Justices, not having a clear-cut brief for their powers, simply did what they thought best, although when acting as a group they might often have put the interests of the county before those of a parish or individual, and of course they then had the clerk of the peace to advise them, or they might ask learned counsel for an opinion. Parishes often complained that individual justices were too ready to grant maintenance orders in defiance of the overseers, who kept a close eye on the parish budget, and who might be using their power to give or withhold relief as a disciplinary tool.

The overlap between statute law and common law left a good deal of room for manoeuvre, and the virtual absence of supervision gave the justices the opportunity to make their own law to some extent, sometimes with good results later incorporated in statute law. The 1819 act allowing the passing of Irish and Scotch poor (59 Geo. III c.12 1819 s. 33) was a case in point: moving for leave to present the bill, Sturges Bourne stated, 'at present these persons were committed as vagrants' – his bill would propose magistrates should have power to pass them to the nearest seaport without committing them. Despite decades of complaints by counties about the expense there seems to have been no objection to this clause, although in the act as passed the route was not specified (Parliamentary

6 LMA MJ/O/C/005 18 October 1744.

7 LMA MJ/SP/1775/05/034.

Debates XXXVII col. 1057). The widely practised discharging of vagrants without punishment and with a pass, the prevention of which had been one of the chief objectives of the 1792 Vagrant Act, was also ultimately permitted by s. 6 of the 1824 Vagrant Act, 'a most humane provision, not to be found in any preceding law' (Anon [a barrister] 1824, 44). Probably the exemption of female vagrants from whipping in the 1792 Vagrant Act, at a time when the main aim of the law was to tighten up enforcement, followed its widespread abandonment by justices persuaded that the great majority of them were victims of circumstances.

The summary justice of vagrancy law, widely applied to other offences and extended throughout the eighteenth century and into the nineteenth, both by statute law and the practice of the justices, may have acted as a stalking horse for that general expansion of summary justice that began to excite alarm in the nineteenth century, principally because it threatened to affect the middle classes (Sweeney 1985). Certainly the storm of protest against the inclusion of indecent exposure in the 1822 Vagrant Act was principally down to panic at the idea that middle-class gentlemen might be accused of it. In a critique of the 1824 Vagrant Act an anonymous barrister, broadly supportive of the new act but anxious to ensure it maintained the correct class bias, objected that the clause dealing with persons refusing to maintain their families was too general as including all classes of society as well as the labouring class 'to which, of course, it is intended to apply' (Anon (a barrister) 1824, 26). Yet in the eighteenth century vagrancy law seems rarely to have been used oppressively, and even more rarely to have rocked the class boat.

Vagrant appeals and Rex v. Ringwould

A further layer of legal confusion was added by appeal judgments in superior courts, which might fail to filter down to the lower levels or be ignored by the justices since there was no mechanism for disseminating and enforcing these rulings, and although precedent was generally accepted as binding in English law, it was perhaps not seen to have equal force with statute law – itself widely ignored at the level of the individual justice of the peace. The much-used handbooks for justices might fail to keep up with these judgments although justices must have relied on them extensively, since sets of the statutes were too voluminous, expensive and inadequately indexed to be a practical reference tool, even after they became available, and even distributed free by the government in some cases (Devereaux 2005, 94–7). But counties acquired them as well as copies of handbooks such as Burn's, so that the decisions of the bench in court were probably more firmly grounded.

Higher court judgements might also, however impeccable from the point of view of jurisprudence, fly in the face of common sense and cause further problems in practice. One such judgment that seems to have taken immediate and general effect particularly concerned vagrancy law, namely the decision in Rex v. Ringwould in 1777 that no appeal by a parish against a vagrant pass could lie, based on the argument that a vagrant pass by a single justice was a warrant in execution, intended only to stop the wandering and begging, and was not the equivalent of a pauper removal by two justices that determined the settlement or enabled the settlement to be decided on appeal (Nolan 1825 vol. 2, 238–40). Some historians and many early nineteenth-century writers seem unaware that vagrant appeals had previously been perfectly normal, and simply state that a parish could not appeal against a vagrant pass (Taylor 1989, 134; P. King 2006, 31; 1815 Mendicity report, 69). In the 1805 edition of Burn's *Justice* John Burn, the then author, noted that the Rex v. Ringwould and Rex v. St Lawrence Jewry verdicts were contrary to the 1744 Vagrant Act, which directed that an appeal did lie to Quarter Sessions (Burn 1805 vol. 4, 647; 17 Geo. II c. 5 s. 26). The law was so confusing that it is small wonder the justices simply did what seemed best in a given situation.

This peculiar judgment ignored the fact that vagrant passes had been appealed by parishes for decades in exactly the same way as pauper removals, giving due notice of intention to appeal to the parish where the vagrant was apprehended, and Quarter Sessions making the adjudication to quash or confirm the pass, and that therefore the court decided the settlement, not the single justice. They were certainly less common than pauper removals however, and when in 1758 Joan Dominey was sent on a vagrant pass from Hawkchurch to Cerne Abbas Dorset and Cerne appealed, giving due notice, John Tucker Esq. wrote to the clerk of the peace, puzzled as to where the respondents must appear or submit to the court. He explained that there was a similar case tried at last Bridport sessions, the only such case he remembered since he began attending sessions, but he was at the Bull swearing in militiamen at the time and did not know what had happened on that occasion.[8]

A full set of vagrant appeal papers is rare as hens' teeth, but in the case of Thomas Woodward, St George Hanover Square removants v. St James Westminster appellants, the original pass and examination, the case for the respondents, the petition of the appellants, the order appointing the hearing

---

[8] DRO Easter 1758.

before Quarter Sessions, and the court judgment all survive.[9] The vagrant himself appeared in court as a witness and the court allowed the appeal and ordered him to be returned to St James. Only the pass and the word 'vagrant' distinguish this case from a routine pauper removal appeal. Whether this was an example of a parish trying to use the vagrant laws to avoid a pauper removal or a genuine confusion about Woodward's settlement cannot be determined, since the grounds of his settlement in St James, which must have emerged in court, were not included in the judgEment, but the case does demonstrate that the same redress was open to the receiving parish in a vagrancy case as in a pauper removal, until King's Bench in its legal wisdom decided it was no longer available.

To take a few examples out of many vagrant appeals, Jane Yarr, a soldier's wife, was taken up in Kendal with her two young children and passed to Skelsmergh in 1769, which she declared was her husband's settlement. Skelsmergh gave notice of appeal against the vagrant pass, which was noted 'Ordered to be quashed by consent of the Attorneys on both sides'.[10] Also in Westmorland William Atkinson and his wife were apprehended begging in Nether Staveley in 1775 and passed to Over Staveley. On appeal against the pass it appeared that, although he was born in Over Staveley, he was settled in Nether Staveley by the latest of a series of hirings and the vagrant pass was quashed. His examination unfortunately does not survive, but possibly the justice who passed him did not make a sufficiently detailed enquiry into his settlement.[11] Settlement examinations could be extremely lengthy and complicated to take and write down, but vital in any future appeal.

Vagrant appeals, like pauper removal appeals, could cross county boundaries: in Hampshire Thomasin Cook was apprehended in 1741 begging in Preston Candover with her bastard child and passed to Chilton Somerset; Chilton appealed, counsel argued the case on both sides in court, and the pass was quashed.[12] Likewise in 1751 a vagrant pass for conveying John Holmes and his two children from Warrington to Loweswater Cumberland was quashed by Lancashire magistrates on Loweswater's appeal.[13] In Hampshire there were six vagrant appeals between 1741 and 1746. In the first case in 1741 Illfield, the appellants, did not appeal against the vagrant pass conveying a woman and three children to Chichester until they had already maintained them six months. The

9 LMA MJ/SP/1768/07/049a–c.

10 WRO WQSR 346/19–21.

11 WRO WQSR 387/25.

12 HRO Q1/13 1741.

13 LRO QSO 2/120.

court was evidently in doubt whether there was some time limit for vagrant appeals, and the case was eventually removed by *certiorari*.

Vagrant passes were quashed or confirmed, sometimes with the agreement of both parties, sometimes by decision of the court, with counsel representing removants and appellants exactly like pauper removal appeals. In Hampshire as early as 1741 the vagrant pass conveying Ann Elms from Alverstoke to Cheshunt was quashed,[14] and in the same county vagrant appeals were heard as late as 1781, when Droxford appealed against an order of 16 October 1780 for conveying Dinah Wells and her son William, vagrants apprehended in Alton, to their parish.[15] This appeal had been received and respited at the previous sessions on the motion of Mr Missing, counsel for Droxford, and was withdrawn in April also on the motion of Mr Missing. The grounds were not cited, but possibly Mr Missing had become aware that vagrant appeals were now illegal.

This new ruling obliged the receiving parish to resort to a pauper removal by two justices if it disputed the settlement, with a possible pauper removal appeal by the removing parish to follow; the upshot may have been perversely to encourage the passing of paupers by vagrant pass. By 1815 the disadvantages of this ruling were obvious: a Westminster vestryman giving evidence to the mendicity enquiry complained of the abuse by City parishes of passing paupers as vagrants 'knowing that there is no appeal against a vagrant pass'.[16] In 1825 Nolan roundly declared that removing paupers by vagrant passes was illegal *because* no appeal lay (Nolan 1825 vol. 2, 237–40), yet it is hard to see what action could have been taken to stop it. It could be hard on the vagrant too: in 1795 Ann Baker was 'missent' from Warwick to Southwark, and simply ordered to be passed back again.[17] A vagrant might be shuttled backwards and forwards in this way if neither parish was prepared to relieve the vagrant as casual poor or to use the pauper removal process, particularly where the settlement was difficult or impossible to determine.

Naturally appeals by vagrants themselves are extremely unusual, although Hay refers to a few cases (Hay 2002, 32–3): in most instances the vagrant was summarily passed, committed or whipped, and there was neither time nor opportunity for an appeal. There were a small number however, all in Middlesex. One Israel Walker was committed to Clerkenwell Bridewell in 1751 as a common cheat and gambler having no settled abode but wandering from place to place, accused before Henry Fielding Esq. of playing an illegal game called 'Hussell Cap' and cheating Colin Campbell gentleman by pocketing the 15s stake money as it

14 HRO Q3/6 Easter 1741.

15 HRO Q1/19 24 April 1781.

16 1815 Mendicity report, 69.

17 LMA MJ/SP/1795/12/051.

lay on the table. Walker appealed through his attorney, protesting he could not possibly be within any statute against rogues and vagabonds, he was a wholesale dealer in brandy, had lived in St Margaret's Westminster more than two years, did not know hussell cap was illegal, and that far from cheating Campbell he had lost to him and 'parted in friendship'. There were other witnesses however and his appeal was dismissed: he was sentenced to six months in bridewell under the 1744 Vagrant Act.[18]

Francis Rhodes first escaped a charge as a rogue and vagabond for fortune telling in 1770 when he appealed successfully on a technicality against the warrant of committal, on the grounds the warrant said he was charged but did not say he was convicted (Paley 1814, 187–8). In 1792 he was summarily convicted, under the 1744 Vagrant Act, before John Spiller Esq. and sent to Clerkenwell Bridewell for unlawfully telling the fortunes of James Bolton and his child. He was then forty-seven and lived at Curtain Road Shoreditch where he made a living by making and selling medicines and 'teaching the use of the Globes'. He owned books and astrological tables and witnesses referred to him as 'the doctor'. He appealed against this conviction too, but this time the court upheld the conviction and sentenced him to six months' hard labour.[19]

James Vandercom and James Shields each appealed unsuccessfully against convictions under the 1792 Middlesex Justices Act as reputed thieves and vagrants.[20] The appeal of Arthur Connolly, apprehended under the same act on the same charge, was more successful. He was examined at Queen Square Public Office Westminster and committed, but he put in bail in order to lodge an appeal against the conviction, and requested an appeal hearing. The committing magistrate was given notice to attend the hearing. At the hearing in October 1795 Connolly, represented by counsel, had his appeal upheld and his conviction quashed, possibly on a procedural technicality although the grounds are not given.[21]

Several of the lottery vagrants brought within the vagrancy laws by the 1787 Lottery Act (27 Geo. III c. 1 1787) appealed; crucially, although those convicted under this act were dealt with as rogues and vagabonds, they could not be summarily convicted, but their cases had to be referred to the sessions, thus giving much greater opportunity to appeal. Robert Taylor appealed successfully against his conviction as a lottery vagrant in 1791. The conviction was quashed, not necessarily because he was innocent, but because he had been summarily tried and convicted before a single magistrate, William Addington

18 LMA MJ/SP/1751/02/38–42, 81.

19 LMA MJ/SP/1792/03/008–9, MJ/SP/1792/07/002–3.

20 LMA MJ/SP/1793/04/014–015.

21 LMA MJ/SP/1795/10/102 i–ii.

Esq., contrary to the act. If he had been triable summarily, as vagrants generally were, he would no doubt have spent six months in Clerkenwell Bridewell, the usual sentence for lottery vagrants.[22] We may note that, although the act had been passed several years before, the magistrate was either ignorant of this clause, or ignored it. Richard Gee successfully appealed against the length of his sentence as a lottery vagrant, offering to go to sea – the offer was accepted and his sentence halved from six months to three.[23] In these cases we seem to be a long way from the summary conviction and instant punishment envisaged in the vagrancy laws of earlier in the century, even as these 'vagrants' themselves were a far cry from the rough sleepers and street beggars who formed the majority of Middlesex vagrants (Eccles 2008, 213–20).

More exceptionally, in linked cases, two seamen's wives appealed against vagrant passes in 1784, appeals that seem to have arisen from St George Middlesex, the removing parish, failing to follow the pauper removal procedure and using vagrant passes as a short cut; Shadwell then appealed against the vagrant passes. Mary Robson's petition and appeal stated she was the wife of William Robson who had been away at sea about four months and was expected home in two months. She had lodged in St George Middlesex in good credit upwards of two years, but 'being deceived in not having received Monthly money left by her Husband and being very big with Child and near her time of lying in was unable to support herself and Child'. She applied to St George for relief, was examined as to her settlement, and signed the examination annexed to the vagrant pass but

> was not informed that the Preamble to the said Pass contained a reference wherein your Petitioner and her Child aged upwards of one year was described as Vagabonds and had been apprehended as such. That your Petitioner was conducted to the House of the Revd Dr Mayo ... where your Petitioner has been since informed that she and her Child was charged before the said Justice with being Vagabonds (viz.) wandering abroad and laying in the open Air in the said parish of St George.

They were then taken by the officers of St George to St Paul Shadwell and delivered to one of the overseers of the poor. She had never wandered abroad and laid in the open air as stated in the pass or committed any act of vagrancy whatsoever either in St George or anywhere else 'but on the contrary hath constantly demean'd herself in a decent and reputable manner and never was in a situation to be deem'd under the odious description of a vagabond'. The petitioner

22 LMA MJ/SP/1791/04/113.

23 LMA MJ/SP/1791/04/107.

conceived herself aggrieved by the act of Rev. Dr Mayo in having signed the said pass and been conveyed to Shadwell. She appealed against the pass and sought a hearing. The court ordered the officers of St George to have notice of the appeal and summoned them to attend court the following Thursday.

The brief for St George, after reciting her petition *verbatim*, stated she had applied several times to the parish officers for relief at Shadwell, but they refused to receive her without a pass (i.e. without a pauper removal order). Mr Wright, who appears to have been another justice of the peace in St George, not being at home at the time of her removal and the beadles who usually remove paupers being sick was the reason of her going in that manner (by a vagrant pass). Mr Wright on hearing of the matter informed the vestry clerk of St George that he should receive back the pauper and send her with a legal order (a pauper removal order), but the overseers of Shadwell insisted on appealing against the pass. The ground of her removal was that she was born in Shadwell, never gained another settlement and did not know her husband's settlement. Mr Wright trusted that, having offered to receive back the pauper and send her with a legal order, the order would be quashed without costs.[24]

Mary Ann Magsby's petition was virtually identical, except that she had two children and was not pregnant, and that she was alleged to be settled in Shadwell by her husband renting a house in Love Lane at £8pa and paying land tax on it. She too had been taken before Rev. Dr Mayo and signed the settlement examination without being informed that the pass stated she and her children had been apprehended wandering and begging and lying in the open air in St George, which she also denied.[25] The court set the appeal hearing for 9am the following Thursday, when both parishes were summoned to appear, and quashed the passes. The most likely explanation of this odd affair is that St George had passed the women as vagrants to avoid the problem of only one magistrate being available, and Shadwell did not know at the time it insisted on the appeal that no appeal was now legal, so the women were then induced to make their own appeals to get round the problem. The Rex v. Ringwould ruling, although decisive about parish appeals, had declined to say whether the same judgement would be good if an individual vagrant appealed. Certainly the bench had no trouble accepting that they had a power to hear the appeals and to quash the passes, although they were probably well aware that they were hearing a parish appeal disguised as a personal appeal by the women.[26]

---

24 LMA MJ/SP/1784/10/140.

25 LMA MJ/SP/1784/139.

26 LMA MJ/SB/B/0316.

No action appears to have been taken against the egregious Rev. Dr Mayo, and one wonders whether other alleged vagrants signed examinations unaware that they were in fact being charged with vagrancy, since very few of them were literate, even if they had been given time to read their own pass and examination. But then again, probably those who were looking for a lift home found being labelled a vagrant a small price to pay.

Abuses or solutions? Bending vagrancy law

Throughout the eighteenth century there were complaints, louder at some times than others, that the vagrant laws were 'abused', almost all demanding stricter enforcement or tougher penalties. This generally meant the laws were considered insufficiently severe to deter beggars, or that vagrants were costing the ratepayers too much money. Parishes were accused of getting casual poor passed as vagrants to avoid the expense of removal orders or to shift the cost to the county, and some justices were suspected of conniving at the practice. Rogers notes that the suspiciously low expenditures of some urban parishes for removals and litigation suggest some parishes did manipulate the law to their advantage: the Holborn area, for example, with the rookery of St Giles in the Fields, where itinerant poor clustered in cheap lodging houses, and where low rents and geographical mobility provided a precarious poor rate base (Rogers 1991, 138).

Justices and pamphleteers alike complained that constables were negligent and failed to apprehend vagrants, or even colluded with them and did very well out of it. Peace officers on the other hand complained that there was no point apprehending vagrants because the justices never punished them, and constables certainly could not always count on the support of the general public in their attempts to clear the streets. The Middlesex vagrant contractor, under orders to identify repeat offenders and take them before a justice to be punished as incorrigible rogues, commonly noted that the magistrate 'desired he (more often she) might be conveyed on' because of sickness, advanced pregnancy, or lunacy. Towards the end of the century and early in the next it was claimed that the poor, especially the Irish, were exploiting the vagrant laws to their own advantage, jaunting about the country at public expense. The old stereotype of the jolly beggarman raised its head again. To enquire whether there was a grain of truth in these complaints, and if so why, will be the main purpose of this section. It is not claimed that these abuses were universal, but that they happened often enough to give grounds for these complaints, and also that some of them were sensible attempts to deal with situations that statute provisions failed to remedy.

Such complaints led to the 1792 Vagrant Act, with its insistence on preventing vagrancy being a soft option and ensuring that all vagrants were punished, but the problem, and the complaints, did not go away. In fact the vagrancy problem worsened in the nineteenth century, particularly in the lean times following the Peninsular War, and the whole vagrancy issue contributed to the pressure for abolishing the Old Poor Law and adopting again the repressive and punitive attitudes that had from time to time surfaced over the centuries, and had been a constant theme in statute vagrancy law.

In 1796 the Society for Bettering the Conditions of the Poor set up the first real social research into the vagrancy problem, as opposed to the 1777 enquiry into numbers in bridewells that was not concerned with the causes of vagrancy. Led by Matthew Martin Esq. this enquiry continued until 1803 when a report was presented to Lord Pelham; continued with government support and finance and based after further enquiry on some 4,500 cases, the results were later reported to the 1815 Parliamentary Committee on Mendicity. The enquiry was conducted by selling tickets for the charitable to give to beggars in the West End of London instead of cash. These tickets entitled the recipients to relief at the Mendicity Society's office, where they were asked twenty-six questions about the reasons for their begging, and their sex, settlements, age and so forth noted.[27] This ticket system was also widely adopted in the north where townships, in an attempt to curb the indiscriminate charity commonly believed to encourage vagrancy, set up vagrant offices and encouraged householders to send beggars there with a ticket instead of giving them money (Hastings 1981, 155–6). Martin concluded tentatively that about half the beggars were genuine cases of distress, although he admitted it was hard to assess the true proportion because the impostors refused the tickets and avoided official contacts.

Although the initiatives of the Society for Bettering the Conditions of the Poor and the Mendicity Society in addition to the reports of parliamentary committees on mendicity in the early nineteenth century made a serious attempt to understand the causes of the problem in individual cases, they could not propose any practical solution to vagrancy as a whole. Other charitable societies tried to help particular groups: there were societies to help the Irish and the Scotch, for example. There were legal changes too: in 1819 the passing of Irish and Scotch poor as vagrants without exacting the punishments for vagrancy belatedly legalized a practice that had been going on for decades but had been particularly condemned as an abuse of vagrancy law. We noted that the passing system was quietly dropped in 1824 yet many counties still had pass-masters in

[27] 1815 Mendicity report, 5–8.

1833, suggesting that parliament and the counties were not always singing from the same hymn-sheet. These pass-masters *may* have passed only Irish and Scotch under the 1819 act, but the imprecision of the terminology makes it impossible to be sure: the 1828 and 1833 parliamentary reports on Irish and Scotch vagrants use 'vagrant' throughout, although legally those under discussion were paupers removed under the 1819 act, as witnesses occasionally remembered to point out.

The northern 'vagrant' offices were coping with many mobile poor who had almost certainly not been convicted for vagrancy offences, nor were they all Irish and Scotch. The vagrancy laws had perhaps never been fit for purpose if the aim was to stop wandering and begging. Colquhoun thought vagrancy law had over sixty-two years ceased to fit the case, many forms of vagrancy had ceased to exist or to be dangerous, and it was only enforced by means of 'occasional punishments of an individual who happens to be particularly obnoxious' (Colquhoun 1806 (1) 76), an assessment borne out by the court records. By the early nineteenth century the sheer scale of the problem, especially of dealing with the huge numbers of Irish beggars, made the vagrancy laws almost unenforceable. The Liverpool stipendiary magistrate said the Vagrant Act was 'a dead letter in the whole place; we are choked out', giving an example of a woman brought up by the overseer for begging: when he decided to send her to gaol the overseer protested, 'She has six children; if you send her to gaol I must take the children, and it will be a great loss to me.' He accordingly did not commit her and they were all sent to the workhouse, but the magistrate observed, 'If this is to be the process, there is an end of the Vagrant Act in Liverpool' (Rose 1988, 15 note 31).

There were indeed a few writers throughout the period who grasped that the causes of vagrancy were not the innate criminality and idleness of the 'inferior sort', but outside their control; even these humane authors however could not suggest a viable solution, and in the prevailing economic and political climate it is hard to see what could feasibly have been done. Neither could magistrates propose a workable alternative, but throughout the period they had a better understanding of the problem than members of parliament and adapted vagrancy law to cope with particular problems.

Since magistrates enjoyed a large measure of autonomy, they could often successfully defy even their own colleagues on the county bench: in practice, only bribery and financial malfeasance were likely to result in action. An act of 1751 extended judicial immunity, and also protected constables executing their warrants (24 Geo. II c. 44 1751). Placed at one remove from the pressure of ratepayers demanding minimal relief, especially to strangers, they were often notably more sympathetic towards the poor, a fact often complained of by overseers, although vestries might simply decline to implement their rulings

(Neuman 1982, 73–4, 100, 165), and the justices had no more power to control vestries than the bench to control its own members or the government to control the justices.

I would argue that many 'abuses' of vagrancy law were a creative and sensible attempt by magistrates, parishes and conceivably the poor themselves to plug gaps in the legal provision for poor travellers, especially military personnel and their families, those who fell sick or lay in on perfectly reasonable journeys, and those with no legal settlement. Magistrates saw these people face to face and were well aware of the gaps: they were generally quite able to sort out the unfortunate from the cadgers and criminals, and to suit their actions to the individual case, and they could by questioning the alleged vagrant discover and block any moves on the part of a parish to pass people as vagrants if they did not consider the aims of the parish reasonable. These 'abuses' often imply a degree of wisdom and humanity on the part of the justices somewhat lacking in the legislation itself.

No doubt parliament, locked into a strictly parish-based system of provision for the poor and obsessed with putting a stop to wandering and begging, took a different view or the 1792 Vagrant Act could not have specified the punishment of all 'vagrants', despite there still being no legislation to address the problems of legitimately travelling poor (Zouch 1766, 34). The settlement certificate system seems never to have functioned for those whose migration was not intended to be long term, and an optimistic expectation that parishes would relieve them as casual poor was often circumvented by parishes. The poor law and settlement law between them had grown horns on which successive governments were impaled, and no amount of tinkering with vagrancy law would get them off.

In addition to the widespread refusal of magistrates to exact the statute law penalties, the areas where vagrancy law was most frequently abused – or from another point of view, adapted to plug gaps in legal provisions – were for coping with pregnant female travellers and women giving birth on the road (Chapter 4), coping with poor sick travellers (Chapter 5), facilitating the travel of service personnel, and coping with Irish and Scotch poor becoming chargeable.

'Abuses' worked both for and against the poor: in favour of the poor where they plugged gaps in the provisions for them, or were used to mitigate the rigours of other laws, and against them in enabling the justices to punish those unable to pay fines or enter into acceptable recognizances in such cases as assault, and those whose behaviour the justices found reprehensible although no statute actually made the behaviour illegal, most notably prostitutes.

The adaptation of vagrancy law by the justices

Counties themselves passed people as vagrants who were not objects of vagrancy law. Lancashire magistrates passed John O'Brian, Henry O'Brian and Richard O'Brian 'as vagrants' to Ingleton although they were originally indicted for assaulting James Standen, traversed the indictment, and then refused or neglected to find sufficient sureties for their appearance at the following sessions to try the traverse and were remanded back by order of court. Probably they were acquitted of the assault or the prosecution was dropped and they were passed to Ingleton partly in consideration of their time awaiting a decision.[28]

Justices were sometimes party to the manipulation of vagrancy law by individuals and parishes, to the irritation of the counties, who often had great difficulty in controlling their own justices. Cockburn claims the justices did little to remedy the inherent weaknesses of the poor law, largely because of preoccupation with the fiscal aspect (1963–66, 513), but although this is true of county benches, individual justices often acted in defiance of the county and of the parishes on the side of the poor. Middlesex in particular waged sporadic battles with errant justices whose lax approach to punishing and passing vagrants, following the proper documentary procedures, and issuing rewards undermined attempts to control costs and to ensure that statute law was enforced. Such justices no doubt agreed with the Fieldings that many of those accused of vagrancy and petty crime were guilty only of poverty.

Justices cut corners by issuing passes at the same time as committal warrants, although the correct procedure was to do so after the vagrant had been punished; they signed blank passes and left them for their clerks to complete; they signed passes but did not seal them; and they came to quiet arrangements with fellow justices or parishes behind the scenes. Individuals from the lower ranks of society, particularly vagrants, although legally entitled to complain, were seldom in a position to do so, so that any oppressive use by justices of their powers was unlikely to come to light. Even the Robson and Magsby cases do not seem to have resulted in action against the justice's abuse of vagrancy law,[29] which seems to have arisen from a desire to oblige the parish rather than to stigmatize the women, although their indignation may well have been quite genuine. The abuses of vagrancy law by justices were mostly for administrative convenience or to plug gaps in the poor law provisions, sometimes for the fees, but it is rare to find evidence that they used it as an instrument of class oppression. They did however stretch it to deal with petty crime and immorality not specifically illegal under statute law.

---

28 LRO QSP 1921/2.

29 See pp. 60–2 above.

The abuse of vagrancy law by parishes: using vagrancy law to avoid removal orders

The Middlesex bench certainly attributed some of the rising cost of vagrancy to the use by parishes of vagrant passes as a substitute for removal orders to avoid the maintenance of casual poor.[30] In the North Riding the practice was said to be rife in the 1780s (Hastings 1981, 153–4). The justices at the St Albans Tavern meeting convened by the Proclamation Society in 1790 and attended by representative magistrates from most counties, heard that in London, Westminster and parts of Middlesex and Surrey justices removed paupers by pass from one parish to another, though they had not committed any act of vagrancy. The delegates were reminded that the expense of a vagrant pass fell upon each county, and the parish to which the vagrant was sent had no appeal from such a pass (after 1777), but before it could challenge the settlement it must remove the pauper back by a removal order, and then prove the settlement of the pauper, a responsibility that would otherwise lie upon the parish originally removing. Such passes were therefore not only illegal but a fraud upon the kingdom in general and extremely unjust (Proclamation Society 1790, 3). There are many examples among the cases of travelling sick poor, suggesting that they did so in other counties too, yet it is difficult to find proof, mainly because of the close similarity between the pauper and vagrancy procedures and the loose use of terms. Furthermore neither parish nor magistrate wished the collusion to be obvious since the county bench, for financial reasons, was much less likely to take the same point of view.

Vagrancy law was very clearly used, or abused, to avoid removal orders in the case of very young children, undoubtedly with the knowledge of the magistrate who issued the pass. Legally no lone child under seven could be a vagrant but must be passed by a pauper removal order (Burn 1805 ed. vol. 4, 628), yet several cases of their being passed as vagrants occur. Anne and Mary Pitman, aged six and nine months respectively, who were passed through Sherborne in 1753, had been apprehended as rogues and vagabonds in Sts Philip and Jacob, near Bristol, and were on their way to Gillingham Dorset. They may have been orphaned or deserted, but they clearly were not rogues and vagabonds. They were duly passed on horseback and the constable was paid 6s for conveying them.[31] One can only speculate who looked after the baby, and how she was fed.

---

30 LMA MJ/O/C/006 21 April 1757.

31 DRO QDV box 6 Sherborne 1753–54.

Often it is apparent that these 'vagrant' children had been living in the parish for some time, the evidence about their settlement being supplied by a parish officer or a neighbour. In August 1782 seven-year-old Susannah Merchant was apprehended in St Botolph without Aldgate Middlesex 'wandering abroad and destitute of support and habitation' and passed to St Mary Whitechapel. One Mary Whitnell said she knew the child well, having been present at her birth, and that she was born on Salt Peter Bank in St Mary Whitechapel. Susannah *could* have been wandering and begging, but more likely had become suddenly dependent after living in St Botolph for some time.[32] In another case John Skutt of St Mary Whitechapel, probably the beadle, reported that Matthew Hoare's mother had said during her lifetime that he was a bastard born in Musbury Dorset. She had died two months previously, leaving Matthew to the tender mercies of St Mary. St Mary could only legally send him by pass to Dorset if he had committed an act of vagrancy, otherwise they would be obliged to go through the whole process of giving due notice of removal to Musbury, getting a warrant of removal from two justices, and financing his journey there. Whether or not he was really lying in the open air, by charging him with the offence they could pass him immediately and at county expense.[33]

Parishes might even pass young children with the collusion of relatives: in 1756 Ellen Clayton deposed that her grandchild Mary Cholmley aged six was the lawful daughter of William and Hannah Cholmley both deceased. Hannah Cholmley came with the child to Manchester 'as a stranger' and died leaving Mary 'destitute and forced to wander and beg of its Grandmother this Examinant for Relief and Support'. She further stated that William Cholmley was settled at Spitalfields by renting at more than £10pa 'where this Vagabonds last legall Settlement is likewise it not being of Age to have gained any future Settlement'.[34] And not being of an age to be a rogue and vagabond either. We cannot know whether Ellen Clayton could not afford the child, although she had a husband and was able to sign her name, or did not want her. In either case, by making her statement, whether or not under pressure from the parish, she enabled the overseers to pass Mary from Manchester to London at the expense of the intervening counties.

Catherine Crofts, a child not yet nine years old, was apprehended in St Botolph without Aldgate Middlesex as a 'vagabond wandering and begging destitute of habitation'. The examination of her mother was taken, who said Catherine was born in Brown's Buildings Rosemary Lane in St Botolph without

---

32 LMA MJ/SP/V/01/021/20.

33 LMA MJ/SP/V/01/021/085.

34 LRO QSP 1734/12.

Aldgate City of London (that is, the other half of St Botolph, part of which was in Middlesex and part in the City). Clearly she was a bastard and hence settled by birth, but whether the mother or the parish was keen to get rid of her or both, she was passed to the City side of St Botolph for them to support her.[35]

In October 1790 Hannah Puttenham and Thomas Humphrey, her son by a previous marriage, were apprehended in Uxbridge. The boy, aged ten, was stated in his pass to have been wandering abroad, lying in barns and outhouses, and not giving a good account of himself, but if his examination was taken it was not filed. In practice the examinations of young children were only taken if no adult was in a position to make a statement. His mother, although examined as a rogue and vagabond, did not admit to any of these acts of vagrancy, she was not asked about her own settlement, nor was she passed, but she said Thomas was the son of her former husband Richard Humphrey, settled at Sevenoaks Kent. Her present husband Daniel Puttenham had deserted her and she had no means of maintaining the child. Thomas Humphrey was passed to Sevenoaks as a vagrant.[36]

Whether he had any current connections in Sevenoaks or would end up in the workhouse was irrelevant – Uxbridge would be rid of him. Very possibly Hannah was settled in Uxbridge by her second marriage, and becoming unable to maintain the boy on her own had applied for relief, which the overseers were unwilling to grant, envisioning being obliged to support the pair for years to come. They could not avoid maintaining the mother if she was a settled pauper, but they were not legally obliged to maintain the boy, since he was over seven and no longer a 'nurse-child'. Neither were they keen to remove him as a pauper in view of the inevitable delay and the cost of keeping him until the removal order was confirmed, especially if Sevenoaks appealed. They therefore claimed he had committed acts of vagrancy (which may or may not have been true) and passed him promptly to Sevenoaks. Neither we nor the county bench could be sure whether the whole business was a put-up job, to avoid the delay and expense of removing the lad to his settlement, or whether he had really been committing acts of vagrancy, and either way his mother was in no position to protest. These and other cases involving young children are particularly tragic examples of the impact of settlement law, and of the use of vagrancy law to divest parishes of responsibility for them.

No record exists that suggests the counties involved in the child cases just cited objected to this flagrant manipulation of vagrancy law, but in 1746 Dennis and Susannah McGruddy were apprehended wandering and begging in Stoke Newington and committed by Henry Spurling Esq. to Clerkenwell

---

35 LMA MJ/SP/V/01/026/23.

36 LMA MJ/SP/1790/10/011.

Bridewell. It is not clear how the case came to the attention of the Middlesex bench – perhaps the bridewell keeper Henry Wallbanck raised the matter – but the justices decided that as they were 'children of very tender years' they ought not to have been sent to the house of correction, and ordered Stoke Newington to relieve them as casual poor and to reimburse the keeper for maintaining them in the bridewell.[37] Quite likely the parish could not find out where the children were settled, and was trying to avoid maintaining them long term as casual poor, with the connivance of Henry Spurling.

The abuse of vagrancy law by parishes: using vagrancy law to remove the irremovable

Settlement law was largely responsible for the passing of Irish and Scotch paupers home as vagrants, since they were otherwise irremovable. It is even possible that the Irish were deliberately excluded from settlement law because of increasing numbers coming to England due to the harvest failure of the 1640s, and that once the 1700 act made the removal of vagrants a county charge the exclusion turned out to be a Pyrrhic victory. The problem was particularly pressing in Middlesex: by the later eighteenth century whole parishes such as St Giles were largely settled by Irish poor, most of whom were in need of relief although there were few residents paying poor rate. A parish-based relief system was completely unsuited to such a situation and unsurprisingly such parishes either ignored the begging (which the poor mostly did in more affluent adjacent parishes) or used vagrancy law to get rid of them if they applied for relief.

The St Albans Tavern justices' meeting was told that Irishmen and others coming to harvest work were passed home without any examination, merely on application and the payment of a small fee, and without the punishment ordered by the 1744 Vagrant Act. The Proclamation Society considered this a great grievance and heavy expense to many parts of the kingdom. The Society stressed that vagrancy law was for prevention and punishment of offences, not to relieve parishes of the burdens of poor relief, or of removing paupers as prescribed by the poor laws (Proclamation Society 1790, 4).

But obviously all a parish had to do to pass Irish and Scotch poor as vagrants before 1819 was to refuse relief; the paupers' only recourse then was to beg, when they could legally be apprehended and passed as vagrants. Although most of them were genuinely within vagrancy law in the sense that they were destitute and begging on the streets or door to door, as their

---

[37] LMA MJ/SB/B/1030, 29.

examinations state, some do appear to have been passed as vagrants without doing any such thing. For example, in 1760 Alexander Call, his wife and five sons were 'apprehended' in Levens Westmorland and passed to Scotland. The parents and three sons were born in Scotland, another son near Cockermouth, and the youngest in Levens. However, since the youngest was a year old, it seems more than likely that they had been living in Levens for some time and had recently become chargeable, and being irremovable under settlement law, the parish passed them as vagrants.[38] No doubt the justice who took the examination and made out the pass warrant was well aware of the situation and obliged the parish; whether the Call family was happy about it we shall never know.

In 1815 Montague Burgoyne Esq., honorary secretary of a society for the relief of Irish poor, took the view that because of the expense very few were removed under poor law procedure, and hence were allowed to live in intolerable squalor, becoming a health hazard to the metropolis at large.[39] Matters were no better after the 1819 act allowing Irish and Scotch paupers to be passed legally by the vagrant conveyance system: in fact, for a few years numbers and costs increased as even more parishes seized the opportunity to clear out their non-settled paupers.

The clerk to the sitting alderman at Guildhall told the 1828 committee that parishes would give a tiny amount in relief and promptly complain to the justices about the applicant to get him removed, citing the case of a poor Irishman who had lived twenty-two years in St Giles without Cripplegate and had no wish to go to Ireland. He asked for 2s 6d to buy some hay-bands to sell because an injury to his leg prevented him working; the parish gave him 6d, refused more, and, to get him passed as a vagrant, complained to the sitting alderman who instead gave the man the half-crown, and he went away 'thankful and satisfied'.[40]

Complaints that Scotch and Irish vagrants, especially the Irish, were exploiting the vagrancy laws to get free travel and subsistence back to Ireland became a howl of protest by the early nineteenth century. The 1819 act allowing them to be passed home as vagrants without punishment merely acknowledged a situation that had been developing for decades. One might see a certain poetic justice in the Irish vagrant problem, largely caused by centuries of neglect and exploitation. The Chief Baron of the Exchequer in Ireland commented on the London riots of 1768 involving militant Irish

38 WRO WQSR 285/11–12.

39 1815 Mendicity report, 10.

40 1828 Report on Irish vagrants PP vol. 4, 17.

coalheavers, 'England has sown her laws like dragon's teeth, and they have sprung up, armed men' (Linebaugh and Rediker 1991, 30). By the end of the century the Irish, not armed but very expensive, had turned England's settlement and vagrancy laws, intended to exclude and punish them, into a system of subsidized travel.

The abuse of vagrancy law by the poor: using vagrancy law as a subsidized travel system

The Irish were not alone in exploiting vagrancy law in this way. The St Albans Tavern meeting was told that in London, Middlesex and parts of Surrey

> passes are granted generally and indiscriminately to all persons whatever; and that many persons, even voluntarily, apply for them; and that the punishment, as ordered by the 17th Geo. II, commonly called the Vagrant Act, is seldom inflicted; by which means many persons who are not objects of the vagrant laws, by their own desire are conveyed to the distant parts of the kingdom at the public expense (Proclamation Society 1790, 2–3).

It is entirely possible that some vagrants were perfectly willing or even eager to be passed home at no expense to themselves; remarkably few escaped from the Middlesex contractor's carts, despite there being nothing to restrain them (Eccles 2006, 89). Deserted wives, recent widows, and others suddenly finding themselves bereft of support might themselves want to go home to their settlements, and officers and pauper collude in the operation, with or without the justice's knowledge. Indeed if a genuinely needy pauper was destitute and refused relief as casual poor by the parish, he or she would immediately become a vagrant by being forced to beg or starve, exemplifying the thinness of the line between poor and vagrant, and bearing in mind that a vagrant in the legal sense was not necessarily wandering.

To take only one example among many, Mary Goldsborough was passed as a vagrant from Soham Cambridgeshire to Spilsby Lincolnshire in 1774. According to her examination her husband was settled at Spilsby and she had herself lived there, but he had now run away and left her and her infant son, and being in very great distress she did beg and was relieved by the overseer of Soham.[41] It is impossible to reach behind such an examination to ascertain the real situation. Had the Goldsboroughs been on a journey or had they lived

[41] CA Easter 1774.

in Soham for some time? Had she really been deserted or had they parted temporarily to allow her and the baby to be carried home? Had she begged in the street or did she apply to the overseer, who took the vagrancy route rather than maintain them as casual poor or get a removal order? Did applying for relief count as 'begging'? It certainly did in London by 1828 as we have seen, and it seems unlikely the stratagem was exactly novel. It is hardly surprising that county benches bemoaned such 'abuse' of vagrancy law and yet were powerless to stop it.

The agency of the poor has been fruitfully explored recently (Hitchcock, King and Sharpe 1997) and can also be detected in the operation of vagrancy law. In some cases a degree of accommodation, even collusion, between the authorities and the 'vagrant' seems probable. Elizabeth La Grove was the widow of a Frenchman, who when she first knew him was a soldier in General Bragg's regiment. She married him in Ireland and they had three children. Her husband had recently died a pensioner of Chelsea College, but he had never gained a settlement. Soon after his death she 'went away' and left her children a charge to Chelsea, where she was apprehended as a vagrant. She was passed to Ireland, presumably with the children. A suspicion arises that she 'ran away' from the children in order to engineer a pass home to Ireland, possibly with the knowledge or even at the suggestion of the parish officers.[42]

A similar suspicion arises in the case of Leonard Kirby, apprehended in St Leonard Shoreditch in 1768 and accused of 'running away and leaving two children whereby one of them is likely to be chargeable to St Leonard Shoreditch'. He was actually apprehended together with the six-year-old daughter he was supposed to have run away from, and said his wife had left him, and his other child was at Wimpole Cambridgeshire where he was settled in right of his father who had rented a farm at over £100pa some years before. There is no indication he was punished; rather, he was passed 'by a proper carriage' to Wimpole.[43] Meanwhile in Cambridgeshire Elizabeth Kirby was in the house of correction accused of deserting her son aged four at Wimpole. She appeared in court on 15 April 1768 and was discharged the same day and told to 'endeavour to maintain her said son', but the court made an order at the same time for the overseers of Wimpole to apply her husband's goods, now in their hands, to the maintenance of his wife and child.[44] Here we seem to have a marital rift resulting in both parties taking advantage of vagrancy law, Elizabeth by 'deserting' her son to force the overseers to use her husband's estate for her benefit, the runaway husband to

[42] LMA MJ/SP/V/01/009/01.

[43] LMA MJ/SP/V/01/013/01–02.

[44] CA Easter 1768 calendar, Q/SO/7 Easter 1768.

get a lift back home. This case is unusual chiefly in that both sides of the story survive in the records of two different counties.

William Anderson, apprehended in Ratcliffe Stepney in 1772 having 'run away and left his daughter Elizabeth Anderson aged about four whereby she became chargeable to Ratcliffe' had lately been left a widower and very possibly wanted to go back to his settlement at Newcastle-upon-Tyne to get help from relatives to look after the child, but he could not afford the journey. He too was passed with her as a vagrant.[45] Similarly Alexander Bowie, a discharged soldier, was passed to Edinburgh in 1766 as a rogue and vagabond apprehended in Plymouth threatening to run away and leave his two children on the parish. Such a threat did indeed bring him within vagrancy law, but one suspects the parish officers and the justice knew very well that he could hardly travel to Edinburgh with the children under his own steam, and their only other course of action would have been to maintain the family long term as casual poor.[46]

In other cases too it is possible that the vagrant was displaying a degree of agency in getting a vagrant pass, with the cooperation of the magistrate, a possibility that is however hardly susceptible of proof. In Cambridgeshire Michael Rickwood was passed to Mildenhall Suffolk in 1767, having been apprehended in Trumpington as a rogue and vagabond wandering about and frequenting houses of ill fame. In his examination he said he was settled at Mildenhall by birth and his father was also settled there; he had been looking for work as a bricklayer in the Cambridge and Trumpington area and had lodged in houses of ill fame 'and is now desirous of being sent home' to Mildenhall.[47] There is no record of his being punished, and he apparently got what he wanted. Very probably the justice who dealt with the case accepted his story and was well aware that his only alternative if he genuinely could not find work was to beg, since it was unlikely that Trumpington would relieve a fit man as casual poor. It is also possible that he had applied for relief and been 'apprehended' and that the initiative came from the parish. In Middlesex Mary Cotton 'apprehended' in St Botolph said in her examination she had been informed by letter that her late husband had died possessed of an estate at Malpas Cheshire worth £7 10s 0d per year. She gave no other information but was passed to Malpas; most likely she had been chargeable and the parish was happy to accommodate her.[48]

The documents unfortunately conceal as much as they reveal of what went on in the justice's parlour leading up to the issue of a pass and there is no way of knowing for sure whether these vagrants, with the collusion of the authorities,

45 LMA MJ/SP/V/017/01–02.

46 DRO QDV box 2 bundle 5.

47 CA Easter 1767.

48 LMA MJ/SP/V/019/08.

were manipulating the law to supply their needs, but such a suspicion was commonly voiced as an 'abuse' by pamphleteers who wanted the severer elements of the law enforced, and these examples, together with cases of sick travelling poor treated as vagrants, supply some corroborative evidence. By the second half of the century it seems that most of the vagrants who were merely poor and unfortunate had little to fear from the operation of vagrancy law in practice, and that it might be a godsend to them. There is even occasional evidence that, as pamphleteers alleged, they were becoming all too aware of the uses of vagrancy law, like Ann Penniston and Sarah Davies, two stroppy soldiers' wives passed to Great Yarmouth from South Brent Devon where they were apprehended begging relief, probably from the parish officers, and declaring they would not leave the parish until they got it.[49]

Stretching vagrancy law: passing military personnel and their families as vagrants

We have already noted that the government never made proper financial provision for discharged servicemen beyond the certificates that functioned as a licence to beg, but many of the discharged soldiers were sick or disabled and many had their families with them; these army families including sick and discharged men fell on the parishes as casual poor, or more often on the county as vagrants.

Seamen were slightly different in that their families did not usually accompany them from port to port, knowing that they would lose contact as soon as the man's next ship sailed, but some certainly did so and were then obliged to beg their way home or be passed as vagrants; discharged men might be landed at ports a considerable distance from their settlements and were given no travel allowance to go home, nor were serving men paid off promptly on disembarkation and therefore had no stock of money to pay their own way. A group of serving marines taken up in Dorset as vagrants, probably on applying for relief, were marching in a regular manner in full regimentals at the time, but said they had been given no subsistence money for twelve months and were 'destitute of necessaries to go aboard' their next ship.[50] Navy pay, due to the admiralty's method of paying off ships alphabetically and turning men over from one ship to another, was notoriously often months and even years in arrears.

---

[49] DRO QDV box 2 bundle 6.

[50] DRO Easter 1743.

The eighteenth century experienced a succession of wars, and soldiers, sailors and militiamen were on the move a good deal. Army numbers fluctuated wildly: for reasons of economy the government would recruit large numbers of men on the outbreak of war, and discharge them equally abruptly on the cessation of hostilities. The eighteenth-century army lived a nomadic life: since a standing army was politically sensitive few barracks existed in England and no permanent military hospitals except those for the chronically sick and disabled such as Greenwich and Haslar for the navy and Chelsea for the army.

Baggage transport costs were shared between the county and the government: the county provided wagons impressed by the constables, and the officers paid a mileage allowance to their owners. If, however, as commonly happened, the journey took longer than one day, or the wagon was damaged, the extra cost fell on the county because there was no provision for it in the Mutiny Act. Similarly, as long as men were marching with the regiment they were billeted at a standard rate paid for by their officers, but if they fell behind the county found itself picking up the bill for the same reason. The Mutiny Acts throughout the eighteenth century forbade any wives or children to be carried on the baggage wagons, and soldiers had to share their own rations with their families unless the women were 'on the strength' and worked as laundresses or nurses. Most however were not, and like the men fell on the counties if for any reason they could no longer march with the regiment; large numbers might be left behind at ports of embarkation, and again fell on the counties, with or without the notorious walking passes.

The arrangements for service personnel and their dependents were unsatisfactory because no government was prepared to fund the cost of returning discharged men to their settlements, still less that of their wives and children. Soldiers were never paid enough to finance their own travel arrangements – only Irish agricultural labourers were worse off financially (Trustram 1984, 19). Seamen were left to make their own way from one vessel to another – only pressed men enjoyed the unwanted privilege of an escort. Parliament's answer was to set up a certificate system that allowed men to beg, but it was never clear whether these certificates *entitled* them to help from individuals, parishes or counties, or merely protected them against penal vagrancy charges. These military passes were 'walking passes' authorizing the man to beg for relief, and to pass 'without let or hindrance' provided he kept to a stated route, but not to any help with transport. In course of time 'walking passes' became an abuse, or a way of plugging a gap in statutory provision, depending on one's point of view (P. King 2006, 18–20).

The system of issuing certificates to soldiers was poorly organized and men sometimes got their passes from any accessible 'credible person'; the whole system depended too much on commanding officers of regiments, magistrates and peace officers in or near seaports (Zouch 1786, 11). Discharged seamen in theory could go to any justice at the place of their disembarkation and obtain a pass; soldiers were supposed to be given a certificate at the time of their discharge, either by the officer of their unit or if they had been in one of the very few military hospitals by one of the staff there, and some such were issued, although they were often suspected of being forged, and did not necessarily protect a man. Chelsea out-pensioners do not seem to have been issued official certificates to prove their credentials but might nevertheless be passed as vagrants, although they do not seem to have been punished.

In Cambridgeshire Hugh McDonald and Dugald MacPherson were picked up as vagrants in Royston on 26 May 1759, despite both having certificates issued by Vice-Admiral Holburne on 2 February to the effect that they had been discharged from Haslar naval hospital unfit for service. According to their examinations they were both pressed men, had served in different ships, and were sent to the hospital on different dates but discharged together. Suspicion may have been aroused by McDonald's age – he admitted to being sixty years old and said he had been on board the *Unicorn* two years – or they may have been genuinely disabled and engineered their own apprehension in order to be passed back to Scotland. Either way, they were not committed but given vagrant passes.[51]

Military passes were often suspected of being forged and were particularly likely to be so, since they did not necessarily limit the bearer to travel to his settlement, and allowed him to make his own way without being apprehended. The passing of soldiers' wives by military pass either to their settlements or to follow the regiment was not legally possible, but they were often given the much-criticized walking passes. They were also often given horse passes or cart passes as vagrants in case of need, especially those who were visibly pregnant, lame, or burdened by several small children.

As many as sixty soldiers' wives and a hundred children were passed from Dorchester in 1757 on a single occasion at a cost of £76 13s 0d, of which the county reimbursed £39 0s 0d. They were passed as vagrants to their respective settlements, settlement examinations taken and vagrant passes issued, but no duplicates filed. It took between three and four days to complete the paperwork and pass them through Wiltshire, Somerset and Devon, during which time they were subsisted in Dorchester. The whole situation was occasioned by the sudden march of the men from the camp at Dorchester to the Isle of Wight.[52] Dorset

---

51 CA Midsummer 1759.

52 DRO Michaelmas 1757 Dorchester constables' account.

also subsisted large numbers of persons with walking passes in the last quarter of the century, many if not most of them seamen, soldiers, and their families, and the bench accepted constables' unsubstantiated claims; probably they took the view that it was more cost effective to pay a few pence subsistence than to refuse and involve themselves in vagrancy cases, and possibly a revolt on the part of the constables. As the numerous petitions to the bench to be relieved of the office show, Dorset had enough trouble finding suitable men prepared to serve as constables without harassing those they had.

Most of the persons passed through Dorset were apprehended elsewhere and heading to destinations mainly in the south of England and London; it is explicitly noted on a few constables' lists of persons relieved that many of the men were mariners, and some women were mariners' widows and wives. The mariners' destinations were mainly seaport towns, and taken in conjunction with periodic demands for more men, it seems clear that vagrancy law was being used to facilitate and pay for the travel of poor mariners to and from ships, not to and from settlements. Although orders were received periodically from the admiralty by the Lords Lieutenant, requiring magistrates to take up as many 'straggling seamen' as possible and get them on board naval vessels, no particular way of doing this was specified; the men were to be sent 'by proper persons' to the ports and handed over to naval personnel. The county had no proper persons to call on except the constables so the established mechanism for apprehending and passing vagrants was used. Nor were government funds available for the purpose.[53] Dorset more than once conveyed a man to a port, only to have the receiving officer refuse him as unfit.

There was by the later eighteenth century very little enthusiasm for the routine punishment of vagrants, and a system of simply passing them at public expense if they appeared to be genuine poor, travelling for reasonable purposes, seems to have been tacitly but widely practised. Doubtless the repeated wars of the eighteenth century, with their inevitable large displacement of soldiers and sailors, their wives and families, both on mobilization, and the abrupt demobilization of men that normally took place at the end of hostilities, had helped to promote this tolerance. This reflects the role played by parliament's own expedient of permitting licences to beg to service personnel under vagrancy law in legitimating the very mendicancy the vagrancy laws were so keen to suppress. Both in this case and in the case of the sick poor, parliament had never provided a workable alternative, and it was left to magistrates at the coalface to find a method of coping.

---

[53] That is, in the eighteenth century. In 1801, when the war against revolutionary France ended, funds were provided for repatriating Irish service families from Bristol (1834 Report on vagrancy, Appendix E, 61).

Those counties that lay on marching corridors were particularly burdened with discharged and sick men and their families. Since one of the principal marching corridors lay through Westmorland (see Chapter 4 for further details), and the army was not particularly efficient at looking after sick or lame men, several soldiers had to be looked after by the parish overseers there. Soldiers' wives needing such support were even more numerous: a large number on this corridor either gave birth on the road or were given vagrant passes because of advanced pregnancy. Although vagrancy was far less common in Westmorland than Middlesex, the impact of the army was much greater, and in Dorset of the navy.

In 1803 previous regulations were relaxed so far as to allow the baggage train to carry soldiers, their wives, children or servants, forbidden by earlier mutiny acts. Soldiers were also permitted to swear an affidavit declaring their settlement (43 Geo. III c. 20 1803 ss 50–51), a practice that had been permitted by the Mutiny Acts as long ago as 1746 (19 Geo. II c.11 s. 25). This document, sworn before two justices, was intended to be preserved for use on future occasions to prevent repeated examinations. Where this had not been done vagrancy law might be used, which of course required only one justice – particularly useful in emergencies when only one justice was available.

In 1756 William Smith, a soldier in Lord George Beauclerk's regiment of foot, swore before Hugh Robinson Esq. that his legal settlement was Warton Lancashire, and he had a wife Jane whom he had married twelve years ago, and three children. Jane Smith and two of the children were then passed to Warton (presumably the third child was elsewhere). The wife, although passed as a vagrant, and alleged to have been apprehended 'wandering and begging' in Appleby ('rogue and vagabond' was deleted from the printed form), was not herself examined, and the family was clearly travelling as a unit, probably with the regiment.[54]

The three children aged between two and nine years old of Francis Bushbey, a soldier in the 13th regiment of foot settled at Bridgmount Bedfordshire, were passed there from Stoke Damerell (now Devonport) with a vagrant pass; they were alleged to have been wandering and begging unable to give a good account of themselves, but were clearly with their father, who was examined and made a settlement declaration. Probably he was about to embark and this was a way to have them escorted home.[55]

Isabel Morrison on the other hand was travelling by a 'Scotch pass', evidently a walking pass, when she turned lame and was unable to travel further. She was the

54 WRO WQSR 266/30–31.

55 DRO QDV box 2 bundle 5, pass 29 September 1766.

widow of a soldier in Lord George Beauclerk's regiment settled at Trowbridge Wiltshire, who had lately died at Perth.[56] Lord George had paid the passage of her two children in the London wagon, and no doubt issued her pass. The pass had taken her on foot as far as Barton Westmorland when she turned lame and applied for relief. No duplicate pass survives, but most likely she was passed the rest of the way to her settlement as a vagrant by a horse pass.

The withdrawal of military permission to beg in 1792 was a dismal failure and had to be reinstated in 1803, perhaps because it adversely affected recruitment of men for the French war. Edward Quin Esq. of the Irish Charitable Society estimated that seven out of twelve of the Irish who applied to the society were servicemen returning from the Peninsula, many with families, and with no means of going home except by pass – 'we have known a man with a wife and six children, coming from the Peninsula'; sometimes these men had 9d, 1s or 2s per day, hopelessly inadequate for eight travellers' food and lodging.[57]

Stretching vagrancy law

Statutory provisions could in practice be stretched by courts and justices to cover situations not specifically included: for example, the introduction of payments to cover prosecutors' costs in 1752, intended to encourage the prosecution of felons, was extended by county courts to cover other categories of prosecutor (P. King 2006, 10). The extension of walking passes to travellers other than the military was illegal and widely condemned as an abuse of vagrancy law, but many of these passes were nevertheless issued by justices aware of the limitations of poor law provision. The use of vagrant passes to convey home sick travellers, soldiers' families and those with no settlement was often the only sensible way to avoid their being a long-term liability as casual poor, or being denied casual relief and forced to become vagrants or worse to survive.

Expensive though it may have been to the counties, no doubt many individual justices were perfectly prepared to see the practicality of this solution, and either issued walking passes or vagrant passes. There was after all little the county could do to prevent the issue of vagrant passes to non-settled poor who had 'asked relief', and thus instantly turned into vagrants by 'begging'. But in 1760 Middlesex threatened to lay an information in King's Bench about the issue of passes signed by a Yorkshire magistrate, Mr Bell Esq., irregular because no act of vagrancy was stated to have been committed, and because although they had

56 WRO WQSR 290/13.

57 1815 Mendicity report, 19.

complained some time previously of 'this great evil' he still continued.[58] The threat may have worked, or they may have realized King's Bench was unlikely to take action in such a case.

Extensions of vagrancy law may also be seen operating to plug gaps in the criminal law, or as an alternative to other available legislation, for reasons of cost, or to moderate the impact of harsh statutes. It was a general practice in English law to enact a statute in broad terms and leave the specific applications to be worked out in detail by the courts, an approach very generally employed by courts and individual justices in developing vagrancy law in practice. Parliament itself, partly in an effort to find alternatives to the severity of the 'bloody code', made some offences statutorily punishable under the 1744 Vagrant Act, such as lottery offences (Eccles 2008) and loitering with intent to commit a felony (32 Geo. III c. 53 1792 s. 17). This latter clause in the Middlesex Justices' Act raised a storm of protest in the parliamentary debates preceding its enactment, opponents pointing out that in effect it made a person punishable for an offence he had not actually committed, and that 'intent' was impossible to prove.[59]

It passed into law nonetheless, but although clearly open to abuse it is hard to determine from the existing evidence how unjust it was in practice; in 1821, although the clause was still in use, and had indeed been extended, its teeth may have been somewhat blunted by the sparing use made of it. A defender of the clause complained about the restrictive interpretation of it by the chairman of the Westminster bench (Allen 1821, 11–13). But in the last quarter of the eighteenth century, even before the Middlesex Justices' Act introduced 'evil fame' as a legal term, the Middlesex bridewell calendars listed a very high percentage of persons committed under 'evil fame', which in the case of men usually meant they were reputed thieves and in the case of women prostitutes, although even the Middlesex Justices' Act gave no authority for using the term 'evil fame' to punish prostitutes. This act applied only to the metropolitan area, and provincial county courts used this 'guilty until proved innocent' approach less often, although it was implicit in vagrancy law all along, on the assumption that anyone 'not giving a good account of himself' was up to no good and punishable as a vagrant.

Lenient as they often were to the sick and destitute, the justices did not hesitate to stretch the law where no specific law existed to deal with those whose behaviour they found objectionable, often by adapting vagrancy law. The Middlesex bench considered a complaint of extortion against two justices for making threats of

58 LMA MJ/O/C/007 10 July 1760.

59 Parliamentary History vol. 29 1464–76.

prosecution for disobedience to 'Statutes that never were enacted',[60] but felt perfectly free themselves to deal with offenders against statutes that never were enacted in what they conceived to be the public interest. These were chiefly 'moral' offences such as prostitution and gambling but also offences such as body-snatching,[61] which was not illegal because a corpse under English law was not property and therefore could not be stolen (Richardson 1988, 59, 68, 70, 86).

Other counties too contrived to prosecute offences not statutorily illegal, sometimes using vagrancy law, sometimes simply mentioning no relevant legislation. In 1753 Dorset prosecuted Elizabeth Soper for maliciously attempting to infect her parish with smallpox. This case arose from a dispute with the parish of Rhyme Intrinseca, and her behaviour probably reflects the impotent rage that often led the poor to threaten arson. On 6 August the overseers took action against her for refusing to affiliate her bastard child, born in May; on the same day two justices issued a *mittimus* committing her

> for carrying her bastard child into the house of one Joseph Michel in Yeovil and putting it to bed to the said Michel who then lay sick in the smallpox and returning again with it to Rhyme Intrinseca with a malicious intent to infect the inhabitants of the same with the said distemper.

The informant in the case pointed out that there were believed to be above a hundred people in Rhyme Intrinseca who had never had smallpox. She was continued for two sessions on the same two charges, but by Easter 1754 she had given in and sworn the child to Silas Murley of Montague Somerset, and she was discharged.[62] The parish had got what they wanted, and whether the smallpox charge was merely a little extra pressure or based on genuine fears the bench evidently decided six months in bridewell would do to make their point. This holding of persons from sessions to sessions, thus ensuring punishment without the case actually being decided, could be contested using *habeas corpus* by persons with means, but not by the poor.

Mary Tabor of Tollesbury, 'an Idle and disorderly person, and of bad behaviour', was tried at Essex Quarter Sessions in 1768 charged with threatening to inoculate her children against smallpox 'in order to spread the Distemper', and Daniel Sutton, who pioneered a less invasive method of inoculation, was indicted for a nuisance at Essex Assizes in 1766 in an attempt to stop his practice, although there was no statute in existence against inoculation, and

60 LMA MJ/O/C/010A March 1778.

61 LMA MJ/SP/1767/05/026, MJ/SP/1798/02/024.

62 DRO Michaelmas 1753, Easter 1754.

indeed other inoculators were active in Chelmsford at the time (Smith 1987, 45). Thus different legislative provisions were used in similar cases.

Justices stretched the existing laws against gambling, which were themselves special cases of a general clause in the 1744 Vagrant Act making any person 'playing or betting at any unlawful games or plays' a rogue and vagabond. Certain games were illegal by statute, others were not, partly because gamesters constantly invented new games or changed the names of old ones to evade these laws. In the case of Israel Walker mentioned above (pp. 58–9), Walker had a fair point in arguing that he did not know hussell cap was illegal: no statute made it so, unlike certain other games such as passage, prohibited in 1740 (13 Geo. II c.19 1740 s. 9), and roly poly or roulette in 1745 (18 Geo. II c. 34 1745), but the justices assumed they could use the clause against any game they themselves deemed unlawful, whether declared illegal by statute or not.

In 1782 Middlesex appointed a committee to consider the laws against gaming and whether an amendment should be sought in parliament to stop 'the pernicious practice of gaming with EO tables and other Games and Devices', but evidently they decided the existing laws could be stretched to include the new scourge.[63] In Dorset Steven Styley, a pedlar from Andover, was arrested as a rogue and vagabond for using an EO table in the streets of Dorchester and thereby defrauding several people of their money, summarily committed under the 1744 Vagrant Act, and imprisoned for a month.[64] This interpretation had become accepted as a legitimate extension of vagrancy law by 1806, when Colquhoun listed as persons who could be taken up under the 1744 act 'low gamblers with EO tables' along with ballad singers, hurdy-gurdy players, vagabonds with dancing bears and monkeys, and a number of other offenders not actually mentioned in the original act (Colquhoun 1806 (1), 38–41).

The justices in all counties were using vagrancy law to deal with suspicious persons long before the notorious 'sus' clause in the 1792 Middlesex Justices Act became law. In Westmorland in 1747 a family of tinkers was apprehended as vagrants 'suspected of felonious practices'. No felonious practices were proved, but the men in the group were all whipped as vagrants.[65] In Dorset Jane Moores was committed in August 1749 charged by the officers of Puddlehinton as a very disorderly person and on suspicion of setting a house on fire in the parish.[66] Middlesex used a vagrancy charge to hold suspect persons for further examination, for example Thomas Shaw, committed to Clerkenwell Bridewell in July 1778 charged with being able-bodied idle and disorderly, unable to prove

63 LMA MJ/O/C/010A April 1782.

64 DRO Easter 1794, NG/PRI: D1/1 1794.

65 WRO WQSR 196/21–2.

66 DRO Epiphany 1750 gaol calendar.

on examination that he exercised any lawful trade, 'for further examination'.[67] This holding of suspects indefinitely for further examination eventually became a scandal, although a 1752 law did allow justices to commit suspicious persons for six days in order to advertise them in the newspapers in search of evidence (25 Geo. II c. 36). Dorset used vagrancy law to hold a suspected Jacobite, described as 'a gentleman of figure', while enquiries were made (Eccles 2010 (2)). A similar procedure could be used as a quasi-punishment for the poor, very common in assault cases, namely to demand sureties and hold the individual indefinitely from one sessions to another 'for want of sureties', whereas more affluent offenders simply obtained the sureties and walked free.

When justices were at a loss for how to proceed in certain cases they could often fall back on vagrancy law. In Dorset G. Goddard gave his opinion citing various precedents in riot cases; this particular riot was about a bull baiting at Marnhull. Goddard wrote that he doubted a bill of indictment would lie, 'There is such a Bull-baiting Grand Jury this sessions', but went on to suggest using vagrancy law, 'the Bull-keeper seems to be punishable with less doubt; for he seems to be in the nature of a vagrant under some of the statutes as the 39 Eliz c4 21 Jas ch 28, 12 Ann etc.' He referred to Dalton's opinion[68] that bear baitings and bearwards were prohibited by those statutes 'and consequently Bull keepers should share the same Fate being within the meaning of same Law'. Bull baiting was however thought to improve the meat, and continued into the nineteenth century, often with gentry support (Cockayne 2007, 97; Malcolmson 1973, 45–6, 66–8). In the end five rioters, presumably including the bull keeper, were taken away by the bridewell keeper and his guard on a warrant for contempt in refusing to give evidence about the riot 'so great is the confederacy of these rascals, that like ye FreeMasons all are Secret, and no evidence is to be got, who were the chief Transactors'. The grand jury certainly did find 'no bill' to a charge of riot at the sessions, but there is no record whether these five were ever punished or the whole case dropped.[69]

The concept of new situations being triable 'within the meaning' of an existing law seems to have operated usefully in adaptations of vagrancy law. It is probable that vagrancy charges, needing a very low burden of proof and involving no jury, were used in preference to other legislation as a handy means of ensuring some sort of punishment where a case was weak, no alternative legislation existed, or nobody could be found to prosecute, especially where the accused was either a stranger or poor. Forgery of some documents, chiefly financial instruments, was statutorily punishable by a fine, imprisonment or the pillory (McGowen 2002,

67 LMA MJ/SP/1778/07/097.

68 Michael Dalton, author of *The countrey justice*, one of the most popular handbooks before Burn.

69 DRO Midsummer 1740.

121), but forgery of passes, not expressly illegal under vagrancy law, was often summarily punished using it.

Alternative legislation often did exist, and might be used on occasion where the aim was compensation rather than punishment – in assault or fraud, for example. In the Israel Walker case above he could equally well have been prosecuted for a misdemeanour, as was Michael Kennedy, indicted for a misdemeanour in winning a certain sum of money at cards of James Scarlet in Rex v. Michael Kennedy, a case between two seamen.[70]

In other cases vagrancy law might be used in addition to other legal provisions: in Cambridgeshire William White was committed for behaving in a disorderly manner and trading as a pedlar without licence in Newmarket. He confessed, said he could not pay the fine, apologized, and promised to leave town immediately, whereupon he was discharged 'having been committed near three months'.[71] It was not unheard of for the court to discharge vagrants in consideration of a period in bridewell awaiting trial. He had obviously been charged both as a disorderly vagrant and as an unlicensed pedlar, which carried a fine of £5. The act relating to the licensing of hawkers itself laid down that a hawker convicted of trading without a licence who could not pay the fine should be punished as a common vagrant (9 & 10 William III c. 17 1698 s. 3). Similarly a twofold charge was preferred against a Lancashire labourer, Charles Butterworth, who was charged with being idle and disorderly, not able to give any good account of himself, and with stealing 'two pieces of Bays the property of Richard Scholes out of his warehouse in Rochdale'; thus if Scholes did not prosecute, or the grand jury found no bill, Butterworth could still be punished as a vagrant.[72]

Obscurity surrounds both the choice of charge and the conduct of such cases in court, since the different charges required different trial procedures, but this belt-and-braces approach was by no means uncommon. Middlesex prosecuted a man 'seen to pick pockets at Upton' as a vagrant, possibly because none of the individuals allegedly robbed would prosecute, thus avoiding both a possible failure of the grand jury to find a bill and an acquittal by the petty jury. He was sentenced to six weeks' imprisonment.[73] In Cambridge in 1787 John Fletcher was committed as a rogue and vagabond for playing with cups and balls at Linton fair, but the complaints laid against him by two different informants

70 LMA MJ/SP/1757/12/12, probably a *qui tam* action – that is, a personal suit with Crown support (on these choices see Lieberman 2002, 140–41, 155). It was possible under 9 Anne c. 14 1710 for a gamester losing more that £10 at a sitting to sue for it within three months.

71 CA Q/SO/7 1771.

72 LRO QSO 2/127.

73 LMA MJ/SP/1793/04/008. For examples in the City see Beattie 2001, 26–9.

included assault and theft. Perhaps neither informant wished to prosecute, which cost time and money, or the committing justice doubted the other charges could be proved if the case went before a jury. The prosecution finally came to court however as the King v. Fletcher, on an indictment preferred by one of the original complainants, and was found a bill; the indictment did not mention the theft, but was for assault and trespass. Fletcher, who had already been in prison from midsummer to Michaelmas, pleaded guilty and was imprisoned until the next sessions unless he enlisted in the navy.[74] Probably more theft cases involved vagrants than appears, since indictments routinely describe the accused as 'late of' the place where the offence took place, not of the settlement or residence of the accused: John Fletcher was described as 'of Linton', but he was settled at Tharp Northamptonshire and travelled in muslins with his uncle.

On the other hand, 'idle and disorderly' servants might be punished under vagrancy law, when their real offence was theft, and its use could thus mitigate the rigours of the law (Ignatieff 1978, 20, 25; Beattie 1986, 18; P. King 2002, 108). It may be noted that on the evidence Israel Walker could have been charged with capital theft since the stake money he filched amounted to 15s. The Walker case neatly illustrates the flexibility of vagrancy law both in making it possible to prosecute offences not specifically illegal, and in mitigating the most severe provisions of the law, themes that will be explored further below.[75]

74 CA QS/O9 5 October 1787.

75 Chapters 6 and 8.

Chapter 4
Lying in Upon the Road

Section 25 of the 1744 Vagrant Act in practice

> And whereas Women wandering and begging, are often delivered of Children in Parishes and Places to which they do not belong, whereby they become chargeable to the same; Be it therefore enacted by the Authority aforesaid, That where any such Woman shall be so delivered, and become chargeable, it shall and may be lawful for the Churchwardens or Overseers of the Poor of such Parish or Place, to detain such Woman in their Custody, until they can safely convey her to some Justice of the Peace, who shall examine her, and commit her to the House of Correction, until the next General or Quarter-Sessions, who may (if they see convenient) order her to be publickly whipt, and detained in the House of Correction for any further Time, not exceeding six months; and upon Application by the Churchwardens or Overseers of the Place where she was so delivered, the Justices at such Sessions shall order the Treasurer of the County or District to pay them such a Sum of Money as shall be adjudged a reasonable Satisfaction for the Charges such Place has been put to on such Woman's Account; and if such Woman shall be detained and conveyed to the Justice as aforesaid, the Child of which she is delivered, if a Bastard, shall not be settled in the Place where so born, but the Settlement of such Woman shall be deemed the Settlement of such Child; any Law to the contrary notwithstanding. (1744 Vagrant Act s. 25)

In exploring the practical workings of this clause, potentially vindictive, it will be argued that the 1744 Vagrant Act provided welcome relief to parishes by shifting the cost of maintaining women lying in upon the road from the parish to the county, without in practice oppressing the great majority of these women, and in the next chapter that parishes later illegally extended this provision to minimize the expense of poor sick travellers, sometimes with the tacit approval of justices.

The Yorkshire magistrate Henry Zouch pointed out in 1766 that begging had not been suppressed precisely because so many legitimately travelling poor needed help, and 'must of course be passed away as vagrants', assuming that parishes would not support them as casual poor (Zouch 1766, 33). Thus the provisions of vagrancy law were stretched to plug a gap in the poor laws. It is not suggested that this was a universal practice, but it was sufficiently common to cause tensions between parishes, individual justices, and counties.

It had always been possible for the parish to petition Quarter Sessions for relief when travelling poor had cost money, but the justices were not obliged to grant the petition, and were no more anxious to pay than the parishes. Section 25 of the 1744 Vagrant Act however opened up an alternative: the overseers might detain a woman lying in and becoming chargeable until they could safely carry her before a justice, who was required to examine her and commit her to the house of correction until next Quarter Sessions; the court could then order her to be publicly whipped and detained for any further time not exceeding six months. But crucially the costs incurred by the parish were to be paid by the county, and the child if a bastard was no longer to be settled in the parish of birth, or sent there by pass for want of other settlement, but take the mother's settlement. Legally, therefore, if a woman gave birth to a child in any parish other than her parish of settlement and could not pay her own way she came within the act; as we shall see in the case of sick vagrants, 'wandering and begging' was widely interpreted as signifying 'travelling and asking for help' even from parish officers.

Until the enactment of s. 25 pregnant travelling women, especially single women, represented a potentially heavy expense to a parish if they should happen to fall in labour on the road. Although a normal delivery itself cost very little since midwives' fees were low, it was usual at this period to allow a full month for the lying in, and any other children with the woman would also have to be maintained for that period. Moreover, bastards were legally settled wherever they were born, even if affiliated to a known father with a settlement, so that a parish might be saddled for generations to come with a stranger's bastard and his progeny (or hers if she should also have bastards or marry a man with no settlement). The 1609 Vagrant Act (7 James I c. 4 1609 s. 7) in making provision for the punishment of bastard bearers did nothing to change this legal situation, but the 1744 Vagrant Act did so in the case of travelling women.

Although there was no statutory right to relief for casual poor (in the sense of non-settled poor), any expense for travelling poor lay on whichever parish they happened to be in when they fell ill or labour came on; parishes on busy roads might find this a particular problem, and numerous cases arose where women in labour and the sick were treated inhumanely. The 1744 Vagrant Act however lifted this financial burden in respect of women lying in: under s. 25 such women, married or single, if 'wandering and begging' and chargeable to the parish were *ipso facto* vagrants and liable to be committed by a justice to the house of correction. The parish however could then reclaim the expense of their care from the county, and had no future responsibility for the child if a bastard.

Depending on how vigorously the courts chose to make use of the provision for punishing the women, this might be seen as a step forward for both woman and parish. In the sixteenth and seventeenth centuries heavily pregnant women might be hustled out of the parish, as were several women at Pattingham Staffordshire in the seventeenth century, including one 'soe greete with child that I was feereful shee would have cryed out before I should have bee shutt of hir' (J.R. Kent 1981, 38).

Even in the eighteenth century where parishes did not use the loophole provided by s. 25 the same thing might happen (Marshall 1926, 239). In Ealing it was quite common for pregnant women to be given a shilling and told to go on, although some were delivered in the cage or in the workhouse (Lightning 1966, 9) and in April 1760 the accounts for Canterbury cathedral include one shilling 'for putting out a poor Vagrant woman out of our precincts because she was thought to be in Labour' (Rickard 1995, 18). Snell quoted a comment of Sir William Meredith that among other examples of parish inhumanity met with every day were 'removals of women with child and in labour, to the danger of both their lives, lest the child should be born in the parish' (Snell 1984, 43 note 30). Clearly where the provisions of s. 25 were used to shift the cost, but the penal provisions were not applied, the act could be beneficial to the woman as well as the parish.

It might have been expected that the 1744 Vagrant Act would have made the harrying of women out of the parish for fear of the expense less common, and perhaps in the case of single women it did so up to a point, as the child was no longer settled by birth; but the vagrancy acts only allowed a parish to claim for the lying in of those women apprehended, examined and committed as vagrants, not for every stranger in that situation. Middlesex at least once refused to pay for a woman lying in at Stanmore on legally erroneous grounds, probably because they suspected some fraud on the part of the parish.[1]

It was by no means unusual for women travelling under a vagrant pass to be delivered at some point on the journey, particularly as pregnant women might be passed the length and breadth of the country, which could take days or even weeks, and often travelled on very rough stretches of road. In 1750 Elizabeth Browne was under a pass from the North Riding to Shadwell and had reached Enfield where, while under the care of the passing constable, she fell from the horse. This caused her to go into labour and he sent for a midwife, nurse, and other assistance. Mary Bitter swore an affidavit in support of his petition that

1 LMA MJ/SP/1768/09/068.

the vagrant was so ill that she, Mary, had to sit up with her almost three weeks, and expected 18s for her attendance and the woman's maintenance. She thought the bill amounting to £2 12s 6d in all was very reasonable. Middlesex must have thought so too, and paid it in full.[2]

There was of course no question of women under pass being whipped or committed under s. 25, as they were supposed to have been punished before being passed. Likewise the county was indisputably responsible for any costs incurred. References to these cases are virtually confined to notes of the expense: for example, the Dorset treasurer's accounts noted a payment of £3 4s 0d to Mrs Jane Weston of Dorchester for her trouble and expenses for the lying in of a woman at her house on a vagrant pass,[3] and in Lancashire in 1765 the constable of Dalton with Hutton was ordered £2 2s 6d for Elizabeth Brown 'being brought to bed as the said Constable was passing her by virtue of a Vagrant Pass'.[4] Female vagrants once committed might be delivered in the house of correction while awaiting their appearance at sessions or serving a term of imprisonment for a vagrancy offence, but in that case they were delivered and lay in like any other female prisoner; they did not become chargeable to the parish where they were apprehended, which was the nub of the offence. Sarah Lackington was committed to Sherborne Bridewell as a rogue and vagabond 27 February 1789, and gave birth while awaiting the Easter sessions, when she was discharged for want of prosecution; her commitment ensured she gave birth in the bridewell and not in Minterne.[5]

But most women lying in on the road were not under pass but travelling poor. The grey area between travelling poor and vagrants is particularly wide and murky when assessing the use of vagrancy law to parishes in offering a way to lessen the financial impact of emergency situations such as women falling in labour or people falling sick, meeting with accidents or dying as they travelled through. There are many cases where women were apprehended only after, and because, they fell in labour; it is not unusual for a woman to be described as a vagrant or a beggar in the petition to Quarter Sessions for the costs, but as 'a poor travelling woman' in the bill of expenses or the baptism register. It seems likely that women falling in labour in parishes not their own and sick travellers were especially prominent among those complained of as 'oppressing' the counties by being passed and paid for as vagrants by this legal sleight of hand.

Westmorland is a special case in that it seems clear that there the justices came to accept the logic of shifting the cost to the county, and by the end of the

2 LMA MJ/SP/1750/04/14.

3 DRO QFA/1 1759–60.

4 LRO QSO 2/134, QSP 1871/25.

5 DRO Easter 1789.

century routinely paid for medical and midwifery expenses for travelling poor as vagrants. Westmorland did not have a great vagrancy problem in general: fewer than 300 vagrants came to the attention of sessions in the period 1740–1800, and there was clearly nothing like the pressure on the county that was experienced on the other side of the Pennines. It did however have an unusual number of women lying in upon the road, who formed 14 per cent of Westmorland vagrants; the great majority were soldiers' wives, almost all delivered in parishes in the north of the county.

A small cluster of cases around mid century may have been the catalyst for Westmorland to develop an unusually relaxed attitude to the funding of women lying in on the road as vagrants, even when they had not been apprehended. In 1749 Cornelius Knot, a soldier, complained to Quarter Sessions that when his wife fell in labour in Bongate the constable

> violently and without compassionating her Circumstances forced her out of Bongate and into Appleby [Appleby St Lawrence, the other Appleby parish]. That the said Wife was immediately after brought to Bed by reason of the Violence used by the said Constable [and] was in great Danger of losing her Life.[6]

The court ordered that the money spent by Knot in medicines should be reimbursed, probably by Bongate. It is possible this case alerted the bench to the undesirability of laying the financial burden for such cases on the individual parish.

Soon afterwards the only example of a case when Westmorland refused to pay the bill occurred in Shap: late in 1751 Agnes Carr and Eleanor Thompson both fell in labour in the street. Neither of the women was described as a vagrant; Agnes Carr was 'a poor travelling woman', and although Eleanor Thompson was a sailor's wife travelling by pass she was apparently unescorted, and the pass was probably issued by a naval officer. Shap petitioned the court for the £1 15s 7d the two of them had cost, pointing out that it had a numerous poor of its own and 'by reason of the great Road laying through it is greatly oppressed by poor Travellers disbanded men and soildjers Wifes and their Children and hath often suffered by accidents of this same Nature'.[7] The petition was rejected, but it may not be fanciful to suggest that these cases and the Cornelius Knot case coming before the court within a short time drew the magistrates' attention to the difficult situation faced by those parishes that lay on one of the only two main roads through the county. One of these roads ran east–west over Stainmore,

6 WRO WQSR 207/9.

7 WRO WQSR 226/26–7.

and the other north–south roughly along the line of the present M6. This road, although nowhere near as busy as the great north road, was a marching corridor to and from the barracks in Carlisle (Houlding 1981, 37) and passed through Burton, Kendal and Appleby. Shap and several other poor and thinly populated parishes all lay on or near this road in mountainous and challenging country and undoubtedly had more than their fair share of soldiers and their families needing help. No fewer than fifteen of the thirty-nine women lying in did so in Shap, a place so small it did not even have its own midwife, who had to be fetched from Bampton.

Two years later Shap petitioned again. James Gordon, a Chelsea out-pensioner, and his wife Sarah were on their way to Scotland, arrived in Shap, and put up at the Queen's Head on 30 March 1753. Sarah 'fell sick' and died the following day about noon. The bill submitted by the overseers shows that Hannah Sanderson the Bampton midwife had been fetched but makes no mention of the child, so that presumably Sarah Gordon died undelivered or the child was stillborn and buried with her.[8] Deaths in childbirth undelivered, although rare, were not unheard of in the eighteenth century (Eccles 1982, 125–8). The petition went on,

> the said James Gordon having nothing to defray the Expences of his Wifes Funerall, and the Parish Officers not having Notice of the Affair and no reasonable Time to apply to any of his Majesties Justices of the peace to advise how to proceed in such an Affair before it was necessary that the Corps should be buried; and as misfortunes of this nature has often happened to us, of which the Parish itself has born the whole Expence we the said Parish Officers humbly begg that the Honourable Bench will take the Affair into their Consideration, and order that the said Expences may be defray'd out of the Vagrant, or other County Sess as they shall judge meet.

The honourable bench did exactly that and paid the £1 5s 6d bill, plus 5s towards the court fees of 10s 2d. The Gordons were travelling poor, not vagrants, and Sarah for obvious reasons had not been apprehended and punished as such.

Two vagrant women also fell in labour in 1753 and were both committed as vagrancy law required, and the bills paid in full. In 1754 two more cases came up in Shap; both these women were soldiers' wives, neither of them vagrants. Ann Worral was taken to Kendal, presumably under a vagrant pass, but not committed.[9] Ann Bracon was with her husband, an Irish soldier in General

[8] WRO WQSR 235/21–2.

[9] WRO WQSR 245/31–3.

Steward's regiment of foot quartered in Carlisle. Hugh Bracon swore an affidavit that his wife, hindering their march, was left behind at Shap where she was delivered of a female child, baptized at Shap 12 September 1754.[10] He sought help to convey her and the child to Carlisle. The overseers of Shap were allowed £1 9s 0d 'for relieving maintaining and removing of Ann Bracon a Soldier's Wife from Shap to Penrith', presumably en route to Carlisle, although her settlement was Ireland.

Evidently the Westmorland bench had now decided the law was an ass, and were passing and paying for these women as if they were vagrants, but without complying with the requirement to commit them. Although the Mutiny Act made provision for a soldier to make a settlement declaration in respect of his wife, it did not allow the wife or family to travel at government expense. Even vagrancy law did not allow a soldier's wife to be passed anywhere but to her settlement, yet here the justices stretched the law far enough to pass her to her husband in Carlisle, possibly bearing in mind that he was Irish and had no settlement there or anywhere else. If they had acted strictly legally they would have been obliged to pass her to Ireland, and both economy and humanity informed their decision to let her follow the regiment. The whole thing was however entirely extra-legal.

In 1758, when the overseers of Great Asby petitioned for the lying-in expenses of Mary Gordon, they emphasized that they had acted properly under vagrancy law: they 'in pursuance of the statute in that case made did after the birth of the said child detain and convey the said Mary Gordon before Ri. Burn clerk one of his majesty's justices of the peace'. Richard Burn added a postscript in his own hand: 'I know the facts in this petition to be true. I think there is a settled allowance in the Bottom in such cases of 15sh over and above the court charges' (the most northern wards in Westmorland were often referred to locally as 'the bottom' of the county). The £1 19s 6d claimed by Great Asby was allowed, plus legal fees.[11] This document is the only evidence in her case, and it is quite possible she too was one of the 'grey area' cases, a traveller dealt with as a vagrant for financial and practical reasons.

None of the thirty-four surviving bills for a lying in was for as little as 15s, however: they ranged from 19s to £3 3s 0d, with an average of £1 12s 9d. Sometimes the justices allowed less than the whole claim, but mostly, especially where the bill was sufficiently detailed, they allowed the whole amount; they even added the court fees to the total claimed. Court fees might amount to a significant sum: in the case of Hannah Matthews they accounted for 22s out

10 WRO WQSR 252/10.

11 WRO WQSR 270/20.

of a total of £2 12s 0d, compared with 15s spent on looking after her, 1s to the midwife, and 14s to the nurse for the month's lying in.[12]

By 1758 then, Westmorland parishes were aware that the Westmorland bench was disposed to grant petitions for lying-in expenses; often they went through the form of getting the woman examined before a justice, but decreasingly often as the century wore on, and in four cases of heavily pregnant women the county used the same mechanism as well. The woman's application for help, it could be argued, was 'begging'. Ann Hedges, born in America and married there by the regimental chaplain to a soldier in the 22nd regiment of foot who had died at West Florida about four months previously, was 'apprehended' in Brough in 1765 on her way to her late husband's settlement in Oxford, presumably under an army pass.[13] She had been landed at Leith seven weeks before with her two children, both of whom had since died on the road. She was seven months pregnant and lame in the leg from a wound received at the battle of Martinico, penniless, and not able to travel either on foot or on horseback. She was passed to Oxford, presumably by cart. Clearly she had herself asked for help and the 'apprehension' was a legal fiction so that she could be passed at county expense. At least three other soldiers' wives were marching with the regiment at the time they fell in labour, and were coped with as vagrants.

Magistrates might have been expected to make an exception for soldiers' wives, as it had been common for many years in other counties to pass soldiers' wives and children as vagrants.[14] The fact that so many of the pregnant and lying-in women in Westmorland were soldiers' wives, four of them lately widowed, was no doubt an additional factor encouraging the magistrates to stretch the provisions of the Vagrant Act to deal with the perceived hardship to parishes caused by the lack of proper provision for them. It is significant that only two of the soldiers' wives were committed (13 per cent), compared with ten of the other women (71 per cent).

Middlesex also passed pregnant soldiers' wives in need of relief, but Middlesex magistrates were usually careful to mention they were begging. Mary Morse and her child were apprehended in August 1757 'on the great Western Road in the Hamlet of Hammersmith laying down and begging'. She was married to a soldier in Lord Home's regiment 'late ship of from the camp at Chatham to the Isle of Wight' and on her way to her husband's settlement at Gloucester, but 'being big with child not having 10 days to reckon' and having nothing to support herself was unable to travel further.[15] Later the same month Mary Frazier was on the

---

12 WRO WQSR 238/14–16.

13 WRO WQSR 319/14–15.

14 See pp. 75–80.

15 LMA MJ/SP/V/01/009/01.

same road very big with child and with three other children. Her husband had been shipped off from Bristol and had given her a guinea to take her to their settlement at Norwich, but she had now run out of money and had been obliged to ask relief. She was put in Clerkenwell Bridewell 'to be rested', and then passed by the vagrant contractor.

In Westmorland there were fifteen women as well as the soldiers' wives who were 'vagrants' only in the sense that they gave birth where they had no settlement and their lying in was funded by the county, but all of these occurred in 1786 or later. In 1799 John Burn, son of Richard Burn, who continued to edit his father's handbook after the latter's death in 1785, sent a note to inform the overseers of Shap that John Jones a soldier in the Welsh militia had reported that his wife lay in at Shap the previous day and he had nothing to support her with, and that the overseers must support her until she could safely follow the regiment and would presumably be reimbursed by the county. The overseers' bill was 19s 0d – for bed, fire, washing, attendance and food 6s 6d; cash paid to John Jones 5s; coach hire 7s 6d.[16] The county did indeed pay, though there was no pretence that she was a vagrant.

By then it was normal in Westmorland for the county to reimburse the overseers for women lying in on the road, whether the woman was a vagrant or not, and the legal fiction that they were vagrants was no longer necessary. Westmorland certainly continued this practice even after it became legal in 1795 for parishes to claim the expenses of sick non-settled poor from the parish of settlement (35 Geo. III c. 101), but how well this provision worked is obscure, and in any case many of the Westmorland travelling poor were Scotch or Irish and had no settlement to claim from. Strictly speaking however, this creative use of the vagrant law was an 'abuse'; the Middlesex justices certainly took a dim view of it, but were powerless to prevent it.

Cambridgeshire also tried to limit the payment of costs to those cases where the parish officers had acted in accordance with vagrancy law. In 1751 the justices allowed a guinea to Oakington for nursing and maintaining a poor travelling woman brought to bed in the parish, but ordered that in future no allowance must be made to a parish unless they got the vagrant examined and sent away properly. Fifteen years later at the midsummer sessions they ordered that no part of Oakington's bill of £4 14s 8½d for nursing Margaret Tinker, a vagrant delivered of twins there, and for burying one of them, should be paid by the county. Although no duplicates were filed for her, possibly Oakington was

16 WRO WQSR 560/12.

able to prove they had acted correctly because at the Michaelmas sessions the justices relented, not indeed so far as to pay the entire bill, but they allowed £2.[17]

Looking after the women – or not

In Westmorland the women seem to have been looked after reasonably sympathetically, although cases of harsh treatment did occasionally occur, such as the case of Cornelius Knot's wife. Esther Egerton, wife of a private in the Caithness Fencibles travelling with three other children, gave birth to a fourth child in Shap 24 October 1799. Shap did not claim for her lying in and she probably went on to Kendal of her own accord, arriving by 12 November. She then, possibly for the first time, approached the parish officers, but the overseer sent her on to Burton 'in a severe storm of wind and rain, and [she] was then very weak and not able to travel'. She and all her children had to be lodged at the Wheatsheaf and a midwife sent for; very probably she was losing blood. Next day a constable took her to be examined by a magistrate, who passed her as a vagrant to Ireland. Since both she and her husband were Irish there was no legal alternative, although she may originally have been planning to rejoin her husband in Liverpool, where the regiment was then lying. She may even have been able to do so since Irish vagrants were passed from Liverpool and Lancashire was unlikely to insist on paying her passage. Burton claimed £1 7s 3d for the family's two days in the parish, which the county no doubt paid.[18]

Parishes were still notoriously anxious to spend as little as possible on the relief of non-settled poor, so much so that cases of very callous treatment occurred. Flora Mackneil, a 'strolling Scotswoman' about sixteen years old and pregnant by a Scotsman she believed had since died, arrived in Barton Lancashire in 1752 and was harboured in John Cletherall's house for about a week, no doubt an alehouse. But when she fell in labour Cletherall's wife forced her out of the house to Mary Hudson's in Myerscough, where she was immediately delivered without any assistance. Flora Mackneil was taken before a magistrate and examined, but only after she became chargeable to Myerscough, when she said (or the clerk wrote) she had 'wandered and begged' in Myerscough since her delivery – in other words, she had been lying in at their expense. The overseers of Myerscough's expenses amounted to £1 16s 10½d for three weeks and four days

17 CA Q/SO/6 18 July 1766, 10 October 1766.

18 WRO WQSR 563/16, 23.

lying in, baptizing and burying the child; legal and travel expenses brought the total up to £3 2s 2½d, which the county duly paid.[19]

In 1750 Susan Stuart and her daughter Susan had been some days in Ormskirk, but when she fell in labour she and her child were conveyed to Aughton about one o'clock in the night, put in a hen house and left there,

> and nothing upon her only they pulled a little old thatch to lye upon – it being a very cold night about six in the morning she was found in that destitute condition in labour – a midwife was immediately got but she poor woman was grown very weak and being almost starved had a hard labour and she languished till she dyed – and after her death the child she was delivered of dyed about a week or ten days after.

Significantly, in Aughton's petition 'a Travelling Woman' was crossed out and 'vagrant' substituted; evidently the same reasoning was operating as in Westmorland, since she had certainly not been apprehended before this tragic event. The case had cost the parish the large sum of £3 8s 10½d, but the county paid.

What happened to Susan, now an orphan, is not recorded, and nobody seems to have faced prosecution for this heartless affair.[20] In Hertfordshire in 1693 however the churchwarden and constable of Broxbourne were presented for 'by colour of their offices, removing an unknown woman, who was with child, from Broxbourne to Ware, thereby causing her death', but the case was probably dropped, at least no outcome was recorded (Hardy 1905 vol. 1, 409).

The grey area between casual poor and vagrants proved unfortunate for Sarah Kelly in Dorset. She was taken before John Tucker Esq. in February 1747 for 'committing acts of vagrancy' in Whitchurch; in other words, for seeking help. Her husband, a pressed Irishman, had written to her three months previously asking her to come to Plymouth where he was on board the *Princess Amelia*, but when she got there she found his ship had sailed for Portsmouth. She then set off for Portsmouth and admitted she had asked several people for small beer, who also gave her food. She had reached Axminster when she fell in labour and gave birth to triplets, two stillborn girls and a boy who died soon after. The overseers there relieved her and buried her children, and about a fortnight later got a horse to convey her to a public house in Charmouth but did not take her before a justice. Next morning she was taken to John Crabb, tithingman of Whitchurch, who conveyed her to Chideock and from there to Longbredy. The officers at Longbredy however, sticklers for the proper forms, refused to

---

19 LRO QSO 2/121, QSP 1668/5, 7.

20 LRO QSO 2/120, QSP 1653/15, 26.

receive her without a vagrant pass, and the poor woman was taken back to John Crabb, who had taken care of her since. John Tucker Esq. then committed her to bridewell. John Crabb claimed 19s 8d for 'taking care of Sarah Kelly in her weak and sickly state', and for his journeys, including horse hire and a guide for three days taking her to Sherborne Bridewell, and several journeys with his own horse. It may have been unfortunate for him too as he was not paid the 19s 8d for his journeys, but he did receive 10s reward for 'apprehending' her.

This case is unusual in that she was clearly supported initially as casual poor, but conveyed as a vagrant, until Longbredy refused to relieve her, when she was dealt with officially under vagrancy law.[21] Parishes had a choice: some would relieve such a woman as casual poor out of the poor rate, others would not; quite likely the attitude of both the ratepayers and the county to such borderline cases greatly influenced overseers' course of action. Unfortunately without much more research into the relief of travelling poor by parishes it is impossible to say how widespread the use of vagrancy law to avoid the expense was, but it was certainly *believed* to be widespread.

Parish officers were the obvious people to whom the woman, or her husband if with her, applied for help, and it was one of the burdens of office that they might have to look after her themselves. Anne Campbell was delivered at the constable of Orton's house in 1750, and Mary Peal at the overseer of Bampton's house the following year.

Probably in most cases where the petition came from the individual who had taken in the woman, he would have been the overseer or constable, but the sources do not always make it clear, since parish officers were often simply indicated by their names and trades, not by their office. George Huck of High Borrowbridge said in his petition that Elizabeth Dixon came to his house in a cart at 5 o'clock in the morning on 20 February 1793 and bore a child an hour after. She stayed there until 3 March and was then taken to Shap, where the child, a bastard, was baptized – Mary daughter of Elizabeth Dixon base begotten 'born at Hucks being on her journey to her Settlement at Bampton'.[22] Elizabeth Dixon was probably under a cart pass and delivered to Huck in his capacity as constable, but she might simply have been dropped off at Huck's as a nearby house or inn when she fell in labour.

Some were certainly looked after by innkeepers: Sarah Gordon fell in labour and died at the Queen's Head in Shap; Margaret Cleasby came to George Drummond's inn at Thrimby on 30 April 1785, fell in labour the same night, and

21 DRO Easter 1747.

22 WRO WQSR 517/7.

stayed until 1 June.[23] Other individuals in whose houses women were delivered may have been simply members of the public; the Mary Medcalf in whose house at Ravenstonedale Rebecca Doubleday was delivered in 1765 may or may not have kept some sort of victualling house. The three women who fell in labour in the street were no doubt taken to the nearest available place. The wife of William Barnett, a private in the 43rd regiment of foot, 'being upon their March from Scotland to Lincoln' was delivered in the house of Mrs Ann Parker in Appleby.[24] Apparently it was a difficult case and Mr Jackson a man-midwife was summoned; he charged 10s 6d, about four times as much as the Bampton midwife who laid four of the fifteen women delivered in Shap. The only other items on the bill were four days' lodging to Mrs Parker, and 10s cash given the soldier's wife by order of the mayor of Appleby when she left. Mrs Parker may equally well have kept an alehouse or simply lived near where William Barnett's wife fell in labour.

None of the Westmorland women was taken to a workhouse, but in other counties, better provided with such institutions, workhouses were sometimes used. Women passed by the Middlesex vagrant contractor who fell in labour at the Islington pass-house were generally taken to a workhouse for the delivery and lying in; the workhouse then charged the county. A typical case was Elizabeth Somerby, who was brought to the pass-house in the afternoon of 22 January 1784 with her husband and three children, went into labour at 8pm, and was immediately taken by coach to Islington workhouse, where she gave birth to a girl at 2am, who died about three hours later. Her husband and children were passed immediately via Ridge to Bedfordshire, but she stayed in the workhouse for a while. The case cost Middlesex £1 2s 6d.[25] Despite the thousands of vagrants passed through the contractor's hands between 1777 and 1794 only fourteen women fell in labour in his house, and one who had been brought from the City 'sick' miscarried; another gave birth in the Colnbrook pass-house, where she stayed for twenty-nine days.[26]

In Hampshire at the Michaelmas sessions in 1789 William Burgess's wife, then in custody for a misdemeanour, was suddenly taken in labour in court and the bridewell keeper was ordered to 'immediately convey her to a proper Place of Reception, where she can have proper Care taken of her, and that the Expence thereof be repaid out of the County Rate'.[27] This place might have been the bridewell sick ward, which by now all prisons had to have, or a nearby workhouse. Mary Rayner was apprehended in Newmarket as a rogue and

---

23 WRO WQSR 470/21.

24 WRO WQSR 382/8.

25 LMA MJ/SP/1784/02/006, MJ/SP/1784/02/033.

26 LMA MJ/SP/1780/06/24.

27 HRO Q1/21 October 1789.

vagabond 14 January 1790, and the constable finding 'by examination of her body' that she had the smallpox put her in the pest house with the consent of the overseers, to avoid spreading the infection, where she bore a bastard 18 February 1790, before she was over the smallpox. She was committed to the bridewell 2 March and discharged and passed at the April sessions.[28]

Some of the women were delivered before coming to the notice of the authorities: Ann Sherwood was delivered in an outhouse at Stoke Charity Hampshire, probably by herself,[29] and Ann Derrick otherwise Bromley was delivered in the open street near Ealing workhouse and taken there afterwards; the workhouse matron said the usual charge for a woman lying in at the workhouse was 40s, and maintenance was about 2s per week.[30] It was popularly believed that vagrants and soldiers' wives were such a hardy breed that they generally had easy labours and hardly needed to lie in at all (Eccles 1982, 86; 1990, 36–7), and indeed several, like William Barnett's wife, seem to have moved on after a very short time. In Westmorland Margaret Wakefield was delivered of a bastard in Henry Bland's barn at Orton and promptly made off, but she was pursued, examined and committed to the house of correction.[31] Others too had given birth in barns or outhouses and were discovered only later.

Although the Vagrant Act specified the woman must be detained until she was fit to be taken before a justice to be examined this period varied a good deal, and in at least a quarter of the Westmorland cases the full month was allowed. In a few cases the time was much shorter, mainly for soldiers' wives, who were not always passed to their settlements, as they should have been under the act, but might be allowed to follow the regiment, especially if the husband himself had asked for help. In that case naturally the woman was anxious to go on as soon as possible in order to catch up before the regiment moved on.

Two of the thirty-nine women delivered in Westmorland died, a maternal mortality rate of 5.1 per cent at a time when the general maternal mortality rate was about 2.3 per cent (Eccles 1977, 8–11). It is of course only possible to know the outcome in cases where a bill including funeral expenses for the woman survives, or a petition mentioning her death, and the Westmorland rate may not have been typical. In Middlesex, because the contractor moved women in labour promptly to a workhouse, none of the outcomes is known, and in many cases although a payment is recorded for the event no detail survives; the amount charged varied a great deal depending on how long the woman lay in, how much

28 CA Easter 1790.

29 HRO Q10/6/2 Easter 1774.

30 LMA MJ/1741/02/36.

31 WRO WQSR 224/11, 14–16.

care she needed, whether she had other children with her, what journeys and so forth were involved, and whether the baby died.

Bills often included much that was not directly spent on the care of the woman. There might be legal fees, numerous journeys fetching and carrying the woman to be examined or committed, or to find out the woman's settlement or get advice, fetching and carrying the midwife, funerals, clothing for the child if only a yard of flannel, and occasionally for the woman a shift or a pair of old stays. The bills generally included a fee to the midwife, normally 2s 6d to 5s, and sometimes a small amount to a nurse or 'neighbour women' called in to help. Occasionally the bills included payments to apothecaries for medicines: for example, 2s 2d to Dr Loadman for physic and a plaster. The cost of lodging, food and drink naturally depended partly on the length of time the woman lay in and whether she was alone. A poor woman travelling from Liverpool to Whitehaven with her husband and two children in August 1786 fell in labour before her time near Sandygap. She was carried to Burton and delivered. The overseers' bill included 6s to the midwife 'Giving more Attendance than Common', sugar, tea, barley, wine, ale, butter, soap, meal, bread, beer, neck of mutton for broth, potatoes, lodging and attendance, and totalled £1 8s 9d. The court allowed £1 14s 9d, adding in the court fees; but there was no pretence that she was a vagrant.[32]

Enforcing s. 25 – a clause more honoured in the breach than the observance

In Westmorland two women died before they could be examined, and three fell in labour in the street; in such cases it was scarcely possible to comply immediately with the instructions of the Vagrant Act to take the woman before a justice. But most were examined a few days later, and about one in four committed to the house of correction; there is no indication that any of the women, including those committed, was whipped. One of the bastard bearers and a self-confessed beggar were the only two detained beyond the next Quarter Sessions.

Although the Vagrant Act did not distinguish between bastard bearers and lawfully married women, four of the five women who had borne bastards were sent to the house of correction, three others were widows, and the marital status of the rest is not clear, but none of the women recorded as married was committed. The married women were most likely simply to be relieved and the expenses claimed from the county, but most of them were soldiers'

---

32 WRO WQSR 437/7.

wives, especially in the last quarter of the century. In other counties however it would appear that the part of the Vagrant Act requiring such women to be committed, and authorizing the magistrates in sessions to order them whipped and imprisoned up to six months, was somewhat more likely to be enforced, although nevertheless remarkably few women were whipped.

Some magistrates, although they conformed to the law, were obviously sympathetic to the women. William Jones Esq. committed Mary Burgen, who was delivered of a bastard in Little Sheir Lane in St Clement Danes, and taken before him at the month's end 'pursuant to 17 Geo. 2 c5'. Having checked that the parish had no objection, he wrote to the court, 'I shall be glad if you will discharge her tomorrow and not let her be confined till the day of Gaol Delivery'.[33] Counties varied a good deal: in Lancashire thirteen of the twenty-one women who lay in were committed, in Cambridgeshire only one out of six, in Dorset six out of eight; those who lay in under a vagrant pass need not be committed. The clause in the 1714 Vagrant Act dispensing the sick, pregnant and old from the punishments mandatory for other vagrants had been dropped in law, but it seems this exemption was largely continued in practice.

In Hampshire however Mary Gatehill gave birth to a bastard in Hurstbourne Tarrant and was committed as a vagabond; in court at the Michaelmas sessions 1745 she was ordered 'in pursuance of the Act of Parliament in that case made to be publicly whipped in Winchester' and detained a further period of three months in the house of correction,[34] and in the same county in 1768 Sarah Prior lay in of a bastard and was whipped together with other vagrants listed in the Easter calendar.[35] In Lancashire Margaret Blexenden was begging in Pendleton and lay in there. She was committed to the house of correction and at the midsummer sessions ordered to be whipped there and discharged forthwith.[36] These three were the only ones who were definitely whipped under s. 25 out of nearly a hundred women in these six counties.

On the other hand pregnancy might lead to a woman's release from bridewell. Tam Doland had been in Clerkenwell Bridewell since April 1764 under sentence as an incorrigible rogue, and made oath in January 1765 that she expected to be confined within a month. This combined with her having become infirm through her imprisonment persuaded the bench that 'her continuing longer in Prison in that Situation may be of ill Consequence to her in her Health' and to order her release, provided she had been imprisoned only for vagrancy.[37]

---

33 LMA MJ/SP/1749/04/19.

34 HRO Q1/14 Michaelmas 1745.

35 HRO Q10/6/2.

36 LRO QSO 2/128.

37 LMA MJ/SB/B/0157.

Possibly it would be cynical to suggest her sickness and delivery in bridewell might also have had ill consequences to the county's finances, but then again, possibly not.

1 William Hogarth, *Four times of day: Night* (City of London, Metropolitan Archives). Note vagrants sleeping under a bulk (bottom left)

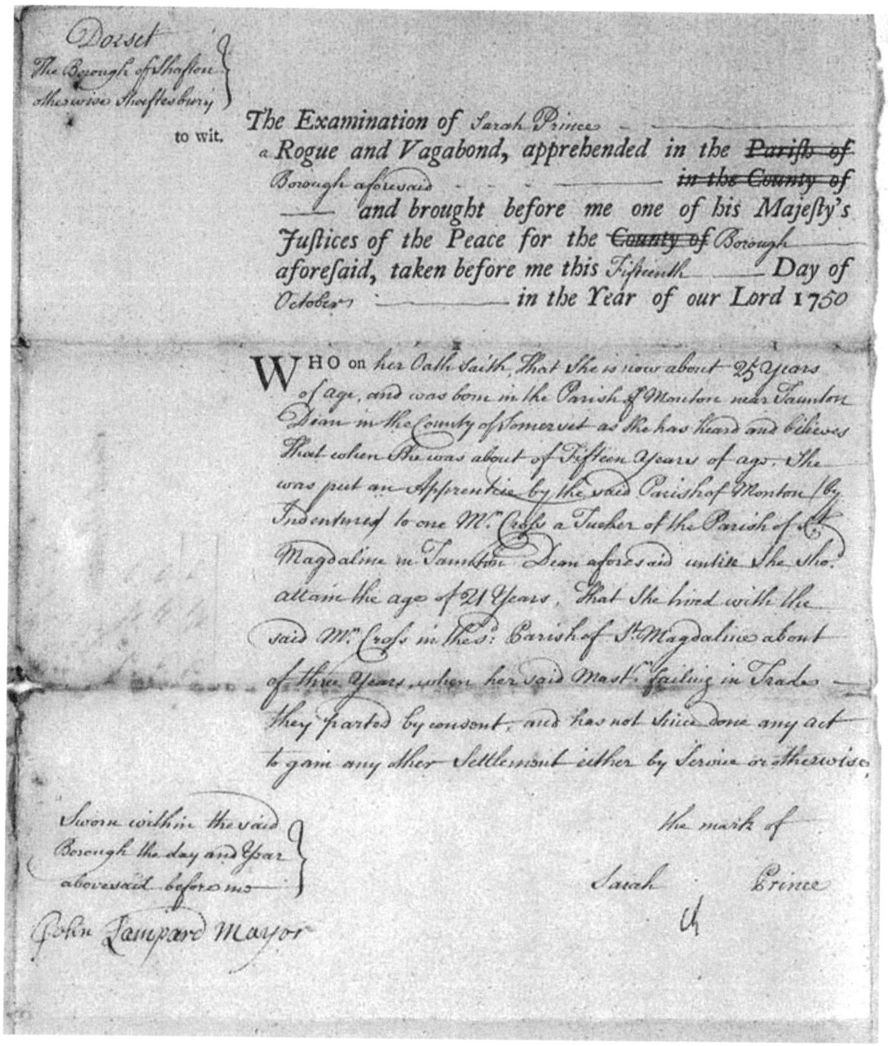

Dorset
The Borough of Shaston otherwise Shaftesbury } to wit.

The Examination of Sarah Prince a Rogue and Vagabond, apprehended in the ~~Parish of~~ Borough aforesaid ~~in the County of~~ and brought before me one of his Majesty's Justices of the Peace for the ~~County of~~ Borough aforesaid, taken before me this Fifteenth Day of October in the Year of our Lord 1750

WHO on her Oath saith, That she is now about 25 years of age, and was born in the Parish of Monton near Taunton Dean in the County of Somerset as she has heard and believes That when she was about of Fifteen Years of age, She was put an Apprentice by the said Parish of Monton (by Indentures) to one Mr. Cross a Tucker of the Parish of St. Magdaline in Taunton Dean aforesaid untill She sho. attain the age of 21 Years, That She lived with the said Mr. Cross in the sd. Parish of St. Magdaline about of three Years, when her said Mast. failing in Trade they parted by consent, and has not since done any act to gain any other Settlement either by Service or otherwise.

Sworn within the said Borough the day and Year abovesaid before me } John Lampard Mayor

the mark of Sarah Prince

2 Vagrant examination of Sarah Prince (by permission of Dorset History Centre)

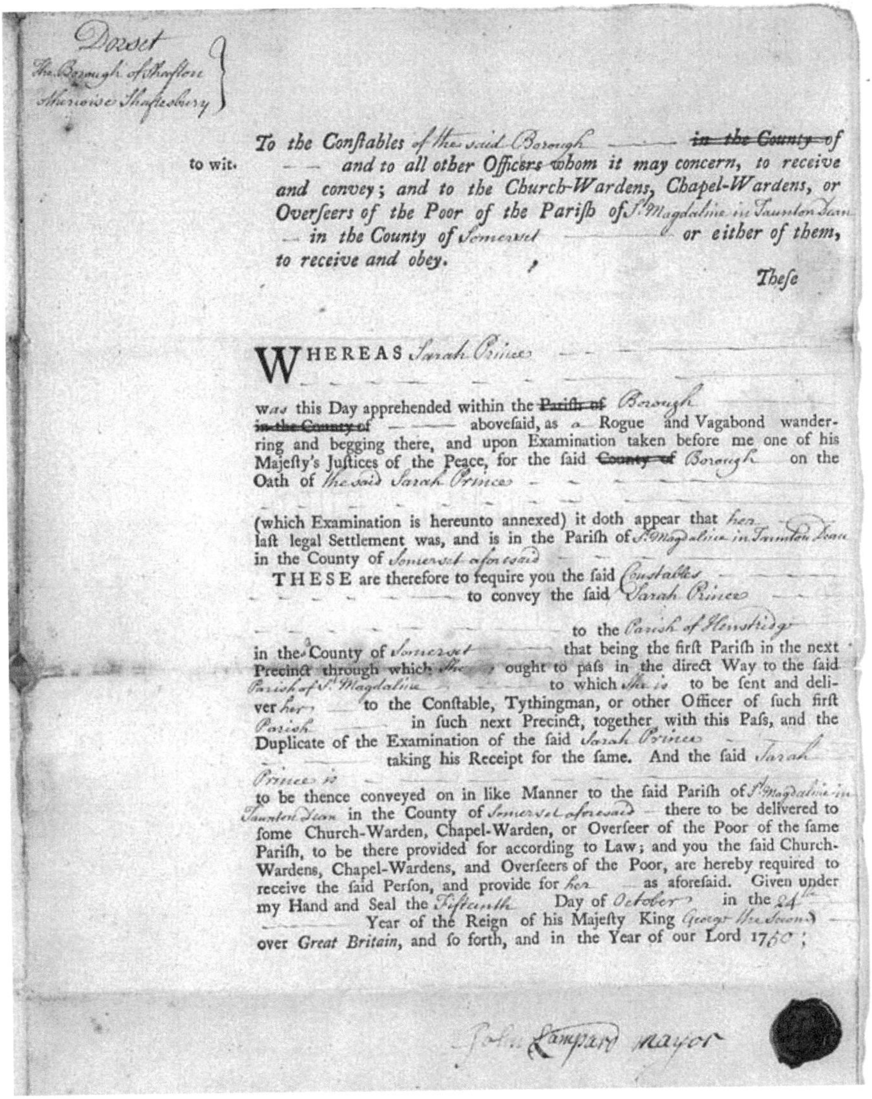

Dorset
The Borough of Shaston
otherwise Shaftesbury } to wit.

To the Constables of the said Borough ——— ~~*in the County*~~ *of*
—— *and to all other Officers whom it may concern, to receive and convey; and to the Church-Wardens, Chapel-Wardens, or Overseers of the Poor of the Parish of* St Magdaline in Taunton Dean
— *in the County of* Somerset ——— *or either of them, to receive and obey.*

These

WHEREAS Sarah Prince ———

was this Day apprehended within the ~~Parish of~~ Borough ~~in the County of~~ ——— abovesaid, as a Rogue and Vagabond wandering and begging there, and upon Examination taken before me one of his Majesty's Justices of the Peace, for the said ~~County of~~ Borough on the Oath of the said Sarah Prince ———

(which Examination is hereunto annexed) it doth appear that her last legal Settlement was, and is in the Parish of St Magdaline in Taunton Dean in the County of Somerset aforesaid

THESE are therefore to require you the said Constables ——— to convey the said Sarah Prince ———

——— to the Parish of Henstridge in the County of Somerset ——— that being the first Parish in the next Precinct through which she ought to pass in the direct Way to the said Parish of St Magdaline ——— to which she is to be sent and deliver her to the Constable, Tythingman, or other Officer of such first Parish in such next Precinct, together with this Pass, and the Duplicate of the Examination of the said Sarah Prince ——— taking his Receipt for the same. And the said Sarah Prince is ——— to be thence conveyed on in like Manner to the said Parish of St Magdaline in Taunton Dean in the County of Somerset aforesaid — there to be delivered to some Church-Warden, Chapel-Warden, or Overseer of the Poor of the same Parish, to be there provided for according to Law; and you the said Church-Wardens, Chapel-Wardens, and Overseers of the Poor, are hereby required to receive the said Person, and provide for her as aforesaid. Given under my Hand and Seal the Fifteenth Day of October in the 24th ——— Year of the Reign of his Majesty King George the Second ——— over *Great Britain*, and so forth, and in the Year of our Lord 1750;

John Lampard Mayor

3 Vagrant pass for Sarah Prince (by permission of Dorset History Centre)

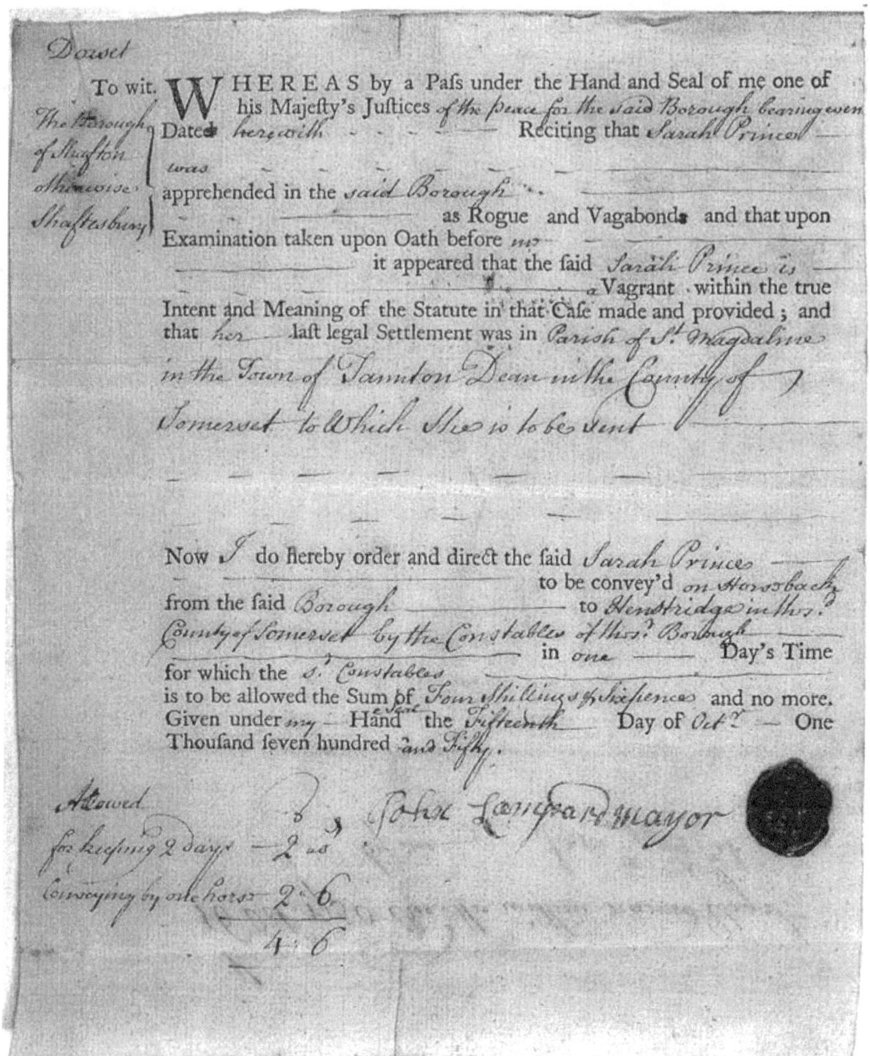

Dorset

To wit. The Borough of Shafton otherwise Shaftesbury

WHEREAS by a Paſs under the Hand and Seal of me one of his Majeſty's Juſtices of the peace for the said Borough bearing even Dated herewith — Reciting that Sarah Prince — was — apprehended in the said Borough — as Rogue and Vagabond and that upon Examination taken upon Oath before me — it appeared that the ſaid Sarah Prince is a Vagrant within the true Intent and Meaning of the Statute in that Caſe made and provided; and that her laſt legal Settlement was in Parish of St. Magdaline in the Town of Taunton Dean in the County of Somerset to Which She is to be Sent

Now I do hereby order and direct the ſaid Sarah Prince to be convey'd on Horseback from the ſaid Borough to Hendridge in the s.d County of Somerset by the Constables of the s.d Borough in one Day's Time for which the s.d Constables is to be allowed the Sum of Four Shillings & Sixpence and no more. Given under my Hand and Seal the Fifteenth Day of Oct.r One Thouſand ſeven hundred and Fifty.

John Lampard Mayor

Allowed

for keeping 2 days — 2 0

Conveying by one horse 2 6

4 6

4 Certificate for constable's expenses for conveying Sarah Prince (by permission of Dorset History Centre)

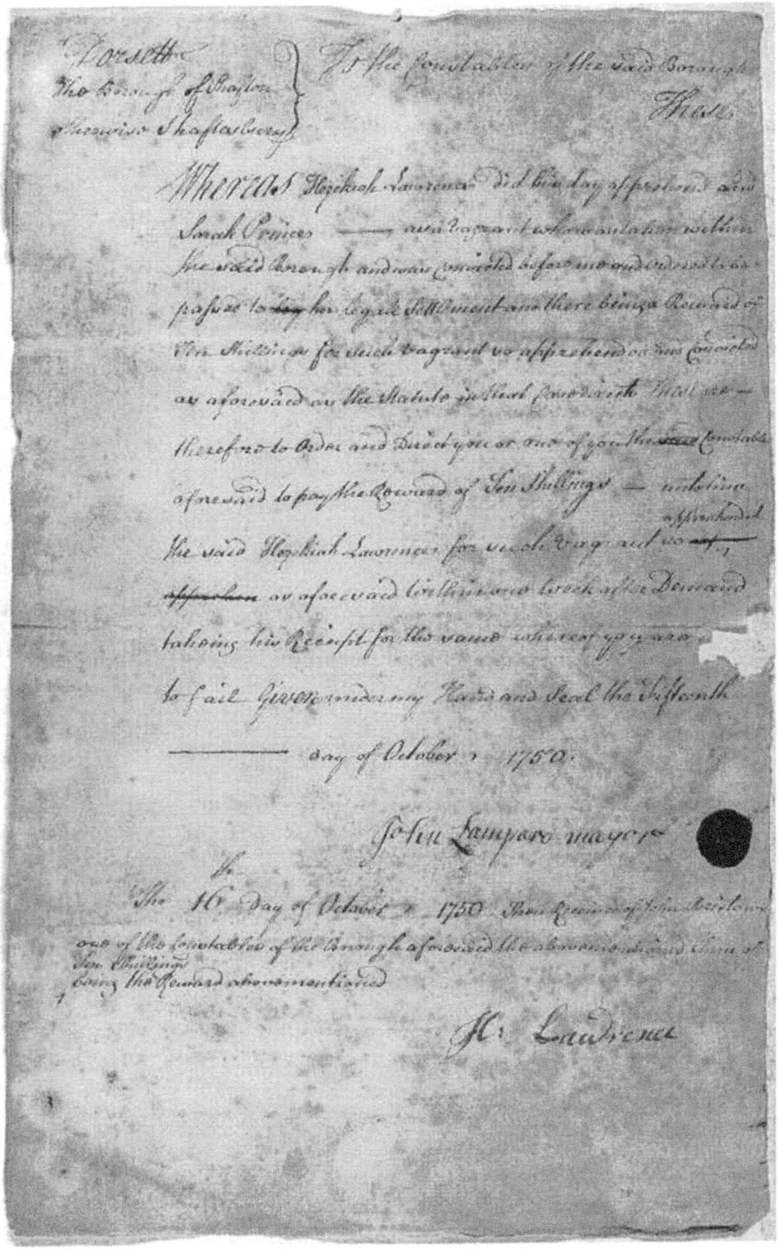

5 Certificate for payment of reward for apprehending Sarah Prince (by permission of Dorset History Centre)

6 The stocks and whipping post at Odiham (courtesy of Hampshire Constabulary History Society)

7 William Hogarth, *Industry and idleness* Plate III (City of London, London Metropolitan Archives)

8 William Hogarth, *The Harlot's Progress* Plate IV (detail) (City of London, London Metropolitan Archives). Note the inscription over the stocks 'Better to work than stand thus'

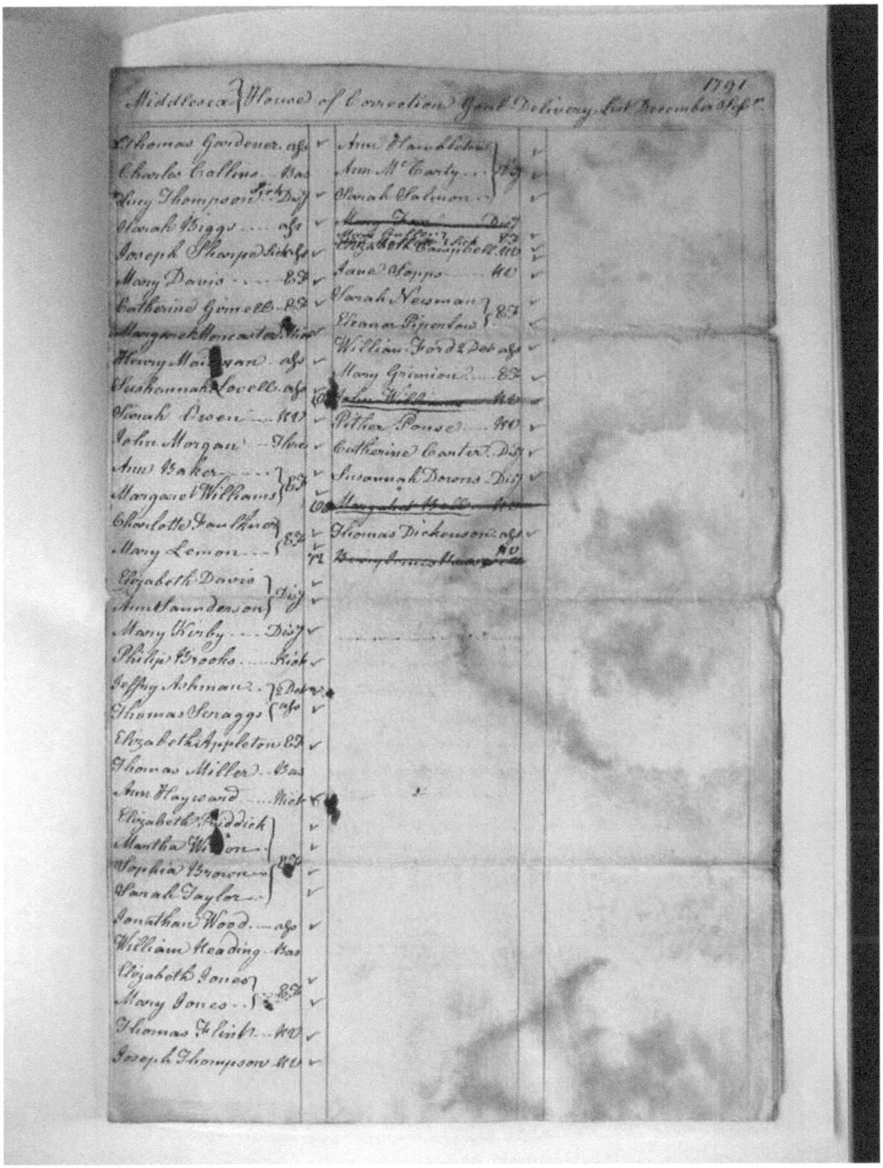

9 Clerkenwell Bridewell calendar (London Metropolitan Archives), LMA MJ/SP/1791/07/009

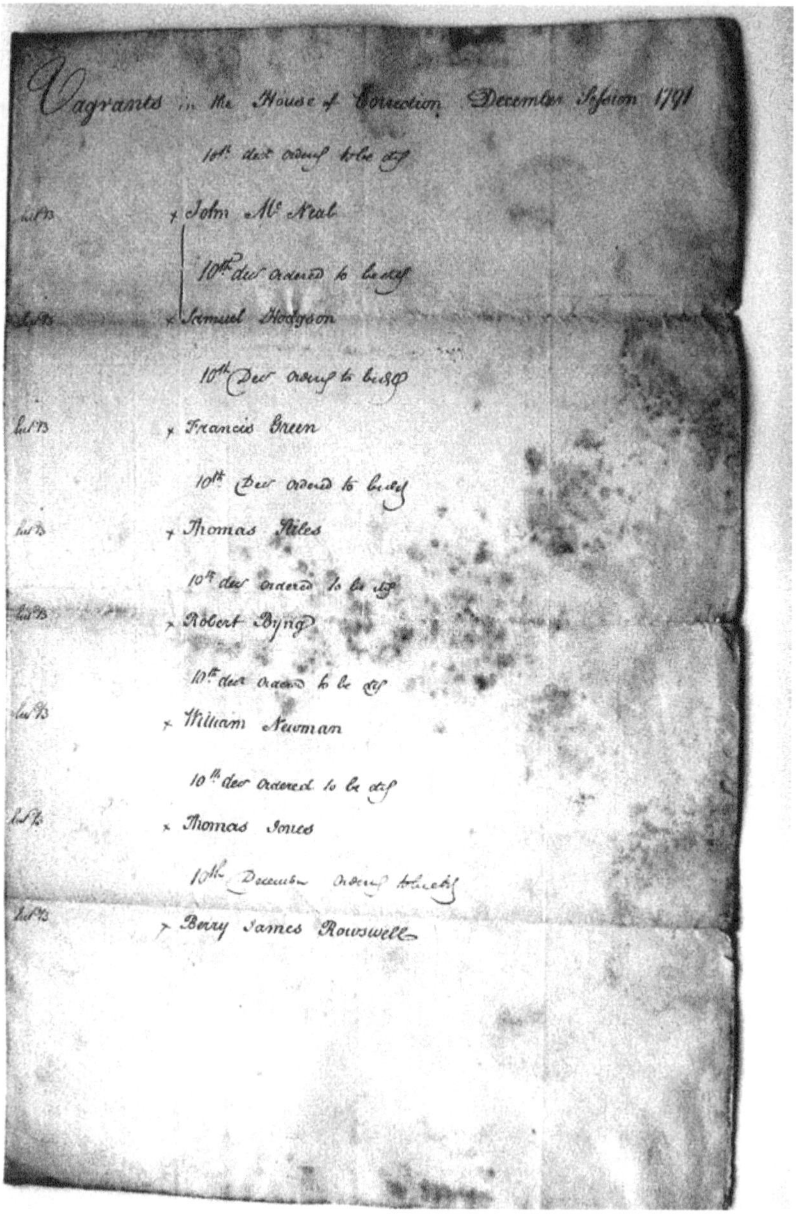

Vagrants in the House of Correction December Session 1791

10th dec ordered to be

John Mc Neal

10th dec ordered to be

Samuel Hodgson

10th Dec ordered to be

Francis Green

10th Dec ordered to be

Thomas Stiles

10th dec ordered to be

Robert Byng

10th dec ordered to be

William Newman

10th dec ordered to be

Thomas Jones

10th December ordered to be

Berry James Rowswell

10 Clerkenwell Bridewell calendar (London Metropolitan Archives), LMA MJ/SP/1791/12/012.

Chapter 5
Vagrancy Law and Coping with Poor Sick Travellers

An act of 1691 (3 William & Mary c.11 s. 29) forbade relief to persons not in the parish books other than by order of one justice or of Quarter Sessions 'except in cases of pestilential diseases, plague or small pox, for such families only as are infected', thus effectively making it illegal for the parish to support travelling poor in emergencies such as childbirth or broken bones, and reinforcing the reluctance of many parishes to dip into parish funds for strangers, even in an emergency. Probably if the parish did take emergency action in such circumstances the officers could readily obtain a retrospective justice's order, but technically such relief was *ultra vires* without one, and open to objection by a malicious or tight-fisted ratepayer. If a private individual charitably took care of a poor traveller he or she had no entitlement to claim the cost from the parish, although a petition to Quarter Sessions might be successful.

The law, settlement, and sick non-settled poor

'Casual poor' was and remains an ambiguous term, used by contemporaries and by historians to mean both settled paupers in receipt of only occasional poor law support, and non-settled paupers becoming chargeable; it is with the latter group of casual poor that this chapter is concerned. Some of these were travellers passing through, others resident in a parish but not legally settled in it.[1] The hypothesis here presented is that s. 25 of the 1744 Vagrant Act, by bringing under the act all women becoming chargeable by giving birth in a parish where they had no settlement, may well have furnished parishes with a model, illegal in the case of the non-settled sick, for shifting the cost from the parish to the county. It can be seen as an example of 'harnessing the latent energies of the statute book under the direction of a new philosophy' (Sweeney 1985, 57).

---

[1] My thanks to Joanna Innes for a copy of her unpublished paper 'Who were the casual poor?'

The Elizabethan poor law attempted to draw a clear distinction between the deserving poor, and to make provision for them, and the undeserving poor, who were to be punished and forced to work. These two aims were later divided, and in the eighteenth century the deserving poor became the subject of the poor law, the undeserving of vagrancy law. But there was always a grey area where the travelling poor and the idle and wandering poor overlapped, and it is chiefly with those in this grey area and with the stretching of vagrancy law to furnish a mechanism for coping with poor sick travellers that this chapter is concerned. The careless interchangeability, or the crafty deployment, of the terms 'poor', 'pauper' and 'vagrant' in the original documents bedevils attempts to establish to what extent, and in which cases, vagrancy law was being manipulated to serve particular purposes, and the argument advanced in this chapter is therefore somewhat speculative. Nevertheless it helps to explain the widespread contemporary belief that extensive perversion of vagrancy law by parishes was going on.

The chief aim of the 1662 settlement law was to clarify which poor were legally entitled to parish relief, and thereby to limit the liability of parishes while ensuring poor law provision for the deserving, and it was subsequently extended by further legislation to furnish additional ways of gaining a settlement. A number of unfortunate consequences resulted, however: one was that the obligation to relieve the settled poor led to parishes making every effort to avoid acquiring any more settled poor than they already had, with the result that those likely to become chargeable were unwelcome, often rejected and even driven into vagrancy, and the subject of much contention among parishes. There was no corresponding legal obligation to relieve non-settled poor. Anxiety to be rid of potentially expensive sick non-settled poor was an intrinsic flaw in a parish-based system of poor relief, which the law of settlement aggravated rather than alleviated.

Under settlement law poor immigrants without a settlement certificate could be removed if the parish officers thought them likely to become chargeable, or if they actually became so. In practice this meant large families, widows with young children, pregnant women, especially pregnant single women, the sick and old were removed, while able-bodied single men were not. The poor law pauper removal procedure was cumbersome, slow and expensive, requiring the order of two justices and a formal notice to the alleged settlement of intention to remove the pauper, and potentially involving expensive litigation to determine the legal settlement. The well-meaning addition of further grounds for settlement greatly complicated appeals, leading to long delays, to the summoning of witnesses from some remote county where the pauper might have been a hired servant years before, or ships' masters to say where the ship was berthed at the time the pauper was a sea-apprentice, and much more (Taylor 1989, 85–7). Settlement appeals became a lawyer's meal ticket.

Another unfortunate consequence arose because the Settlement Act was not sufficiently comprehensive. It was early decided that it did not apply to Ireland, Scotland or offshore islands. Persons born in those territories or abroad, unless they had subsequently acquired a settlement in one of several ways, had no legal entitlement to poor relief, including sick relief, anywhere in England. In the seventeenth century this did not affect many people, but by the eighteenth century large numbers of Irish and Scotch came to England in search of work or as a result of army service; having no settlement, they were irremovable under settlement law, which only permitted paupers to be removed to their settlements. If however they were apprehended as vagrants, they could be committed – when their sickness would be dealt with in the bridewell – and passed, and the parish would be relieved of the expense of their current sickness and of future liability for them.

Vagrancy law permitted vagrants to be passed to their place of birth as well as to their settlement; only where neither settlement nor place of birth could be ascertained was the county obliged to maintain the vagrant until he could maintain himself or be found a place as a servant or apprentice, a provision limited in practice to young stranger children and wandering lunatics. Thus even the Irish and Scotch could be passed as vagrants: the Irish were conveyed to one of the western ports and embarked, and the Scotch to the border where they were handed over to the officers of the nearest stewartry.

Vagrancy law from the point of view of parishes thus had significant advantages over the poor law: removal was far quicker and cheaper, requiring only the signature of one justice, and taking immediate effect. It saved the parish money by shifting the cost to the county, and it could be used for those without settlements. Thus in the eighteenth century a way opened up to cope with the non-settled poor using vagrancy law. By far the greatest increase in the numbers of vagrants passed from Middlesex later in the century was due to increasing numbers of Irish: parishes such as St Giles in the Fields were largely inhabited by Irish poor, most of whom survived by begging in neighbouring parishes, and who were so numerous they were generally ignored by the constables. But by the end of the eighteenth century Middlesex magistrates routinely passed as vagrants any Irish who became a serious financial liability.

Hitchcock notes that illness and disability were both reasons for begging and acceptable excuses for it, often evoked the sympathy of the public, and might even be encouraged by parishes (Hitchcock 2004, 12, 107–8). It seems likely that non-settled poor were often tolerated and a blind eye turned to begging, but if sickness or misfortune obliged them to apply to the overseers they might be apprehended and handed over to the county. Although the Middlesex bench officially deplored this practice it had great difficulty controlling its own members. After the Rex v. Ringwould decision declaring vagrant appeals by parishes illegal the substitution of vagrant passes for pauper removals may have increased, since henceforth there could be no comeback from the receiving parish; it might even have encouraged vagrancy, because the receiving parish, unable to appeal, would be very likely to 'persuade' the vagrant to move on by refusing relief.

Thus, because the poor law and settlement law left significant gaps in provision for certain groups and, as we noted in the case of women lying in on the road, were perceived as placing an unfair burden on certain parishes for the care of non-settled poor, it was inevitable that these gaps should be plugged by the use of vagrancy law, despite the fact that such a stratagem was illegal and much complained of by some counties, and despite attempts by parliament to stop the practice. It was a simple matter for a parish to refuse relief, leaving a pauper no alternative but to beg or steal, and then to apprehend him for begging and get him removed as a vagrant. Clearly the law itself had set up a situation where it was far simpler, quicker and cheaper to remove a sick vagrant than a sick pauper, and thereby also to shift the expense to the county. Some justices, notably those in Westmorland, evidently felt this was not unreasonable, but others objected strongly although the forbidding of the removal of both sick paupers and vagrants in 1795 suggests it had become a common practice.

The casual poor in this sense were those non-settled poor who were dealt with under vagrancy law for practical and financial reasons. They might be those poor travellers for whom no alternative system was in place, in particular discharged soldiers and seamen, and the families who accompanied them. Ann Bertram, for example, turned into a vagrant in 1768 when, having accompanied her husband for seven weeks from the time he was enlisted in Durham by a recruiting party, she could no longer keep up because of her pregnancy and two other small children. She applied for relief to the parish officers at Appleby, who promptly apprehended her as a vagrant and passed her to her husband's settlement at Whitby.[2]

A small number were non-settled resident poor who had met with misfortune, mainly children deserted or orphaned, deserted wives, or accident victims; yet others were casual poor in the sense that they had no settlements, and thus if they fell sick or became destitute had no legal claim to relief except as vagrants. Or they might be poor travellers who, falling sick, in labour or lame on perfectly legitimate journeys, had been found in distress by the roadside or in an outbuilding, had tottered to the nearest house or pub and asked for help, or had approached parish officers in desperation, and were then 'apprehended' solely to

[2] WRO WQSR 349/31–2.

make use of the mechanisms set up for conveying vagrants to their settlements or place of birth, and for paying any costs incurred out of the county rate rather than the parish poor rate. It is this group who are the focus of this chapter.

Attitudes to poor sick travellers

Relief of the sick was one of the traditional corporal works of mercy, and before the Reformation was seen as a Christian duty incumbent on all, whether the sick were neighbour or stranger, and especially on monasteries and parishes. After the Reformation, parliament adopted a more proactive role both in encouraging parish provision for those unable to earn their own living by reason of sickness, old age or disability, and in punishing the able-bodied poor who did not work – it was assumed they were all idle and undeserving. Although the repeated failure of attempts to set the poor on work might have alerted the authorities to the root cause of the problem in economic factors totally outside the control of the poor, this mindset, with honourable exceptions, dominated official thinking until late in the eighteenth century, and reasserted itself forcefully in the policies of the New Poor Law.

Parishes had always tended to be protectionist and reluctant to support strangers not obviously useful to the parish, and settlement law reinforced this tendency, stipulating that persons merely *likely* to become chargeable could be removed. The Settlement Act positively encouraged the hasty removal of sick non-settled poor, by enacting that if a person fell sick at work in another parish he might be removed, and if he refused to go or returned after removal, any justice might send him to the house of correction to be punished as a vagabond (13 & 14 Charles II c. 12 s. 3). Even parishes prepared to support their own undeserving poor were often reluctant to help strangers (S. King 2000, 188).

Sick poor travellers had always presented a financial problem to parishes, and some parish officers were so concerned to save expense to the parish that they might hustle the obviously sick and women in labour out of the parish rather than look after them (Dobson 1997, 273). The most protection the sick poor traveller had was that an individual, including a parish officer, could be indicted for manslaughter if a needy traveller died for want of relief, but cases where needy travellers did die for want of relief greatly outnumber cases where anybody was held responsible, let alone punished. The justices were often more sympathetic than parishes: the Buckinghamshire bench in 1700 condemned the inhumane treatment of a smallpox victim whom the parish officers had whipped, evicted and exposed to the cold despite her sad and languishing condition (Hindle 2004, 413). In the nineteenth century parishes accused of tolerating begging defended their practice of giving casual poor small amounts of money for a night's lodging on the grounds that they would be in trouble if a destitute person died of exposure during the night.[3]

Before the vagrancy laws opened up the possibility of coping with poor sick travellers by reclassifying them as vagrants they were often driven out of one parish to the next; even, or perhaps especially, those with infectious diseases might be treated in this way. Dorothy Marshall cites cases where a wanderer with smallpox was harried to the next parish, spreading infection, and where a parish officer in Towcester Northamptonshire 'Gave a woman and two small Children to Goe from Towne having the Small Pox on them ... 6d' (Marshall 1926, 11, 228). In 1698 William Allen of Halstead yeoman was prosecuted at Quarter Sessions by the overseers of Tilbury-juxta-Clare 'for sending Wm Barnard into Tilbury-juxta-Clare being very sick and full of the smallpox' (Smith 1987, 27). Vagrants were often blamed for spreading disease, but given the reluctance of parishes to help them they might have no choice but to keep moving on.

Snell pointed out that in the late seventeenth century the cost of burials rose, due to legislation such as the acts requiring burial in woollen and the payment of fees for registration of burials, and quoted a comment of Sir William Meredith: 'Coming up to town last Sunday, I met with an instance shocking to humanity: a miserable object in the agonies of death crammed into a cart to be removed lest the parish should be at the expense of its funeral' (Snell 1984, 36–7). Seventeenth- and early eighteenth-century parish accounts include small sums of money given to poor sick travellers 'to be gone'. Andrew Wear noted that charity in St Bartholomew's parish London in the seventeenth century did not extend to strangers: those who were fit were whipped out of the parish, the sick were put in the cage and given virtually no attention, and many deaths occurred in the cages of London parishes (Wear 1991, 52). Not only parishes were guilty of this brutality, nor did it end with the seventeenth century: some sick vagrants died under a pass in the eighteenth century, and the City of London passed many who were dangerously ill, some in the smallpox, a few of whom then died in the hands of the Middlesex vagrant contractor.

Stretching vagrancy law to include sick travellers

We have seen that travelling women lying in upon the road and becoming chargeable were *ipso facto* vagrants liable to the penalties of the vagrancy laws, although in practice very few were punished, that parishes commonly charged

---

3 1834 Report on vagrancy, 90E.

the cost to the county without necessarily going through the procedure specified under vagrancy law, and that some counties accepted these often dubious claims. It seems probable that an analogous method of shifting the cost to the county was not unusual in the case of sick travellers, although they were in quite a different situation legally in that falling sick and becoming chargeable in a parish where one was not settled was certainly not an offence under the vagrancy laws. Indeed, although no compulsion existed, it was assumed that in such cases the parish itself would bear the cost of the sickness and remove the pauper by the usual poor law procedure in due course, if applicable.

Because expenditure for women lying in on the road and wandering lunatics could legitimately be charged to the county under vagrancy law, it was not a great step to extend this idea to sick travellers. Counties were well used to paying for vagrants falling sick or dying under a pass, and for persons sick or dying in prison, whether awaiting sessions or serving a sentence. Peter King has pointed out that legislation was often stretched by local practice, and cites the extension of statutory provision for paying prosecutors' expenses in certain cases to apply to other cases not intended by parliament (P. King 2006, 10).

Similarly, counties themselves plugged gaps in the poor law provisions by paying expenses incurred by private individuals for sick travellers, and some, notably Westmorland, motivated by the same differences in the geographical and economic situation of the parishes as in the case of women lying in on the road, gradually extended the process to include expenses incurred by parishes. By an act of 1752 (25 Geo. II c. 29) coroners' fees and mileage for inquests, including inquests on unknown persons found dead, were paid by the counties, and by the second half of the century counties might also pay for the burials of unknown persons found dead, whose settlements obviously could not be discovered. Gilbert's Act of 1782 (22 Geo. III c. 83), applicable only within Gilbert Unions, legitimated this practice and also made some attempt to enable parishes to reclaim the costs of caring for sick poor strangers from their settlements, provided the settlement was known and in the same county.

Although it is often impossible to determine whether the parish or the county paid for the burials, in coastal parishes large numbers of unknown victims of maritime accidents might be washed up at the same time, particularly noticeable in Dorset and Lancashire. In Dorset in 1786 an unusually large number of people were drowned: the Wareham coroner dealt with six persons found drowned at Seacombe in the Isle of Purbeck and nine persons unknown at Chapman Pool, Worth and the Isle of Purbeck, and another coroner with nine unknown men at Abbotsbury. Traditionally the parish had buried them, but even before s. 38 of Gilbert's Act made the county responsible for the burials of strangers counties may have relieved these parishes of part or all of such extraordinary expenses; however, hard evidence either way is mostly lacking.

As early as 1758 Cambridgeshire allowed John Baker of Linton 15s towards his expenses about a poor man who was taken ill and died at his house.[4] It is not clear whether Cambridgeshire paid for the burial of a certain widow Roberts in 1756; the coroner's court heard that she had been begging in various places in Snailwell on her way from Fordham to Newmarket on 16 February, and 'being a very ancient woman either sat or fell down in a field near a place called Ditchways in Snailwell' and was found dead the next day about 12 o'clock. The court concluded she had perished from the cold.[5] She was a vagrant by virtue of her reported begging, but she had not been apprehended or examined as to her settlement, and like many of these cases occupied the grey area between vagrants and poor travellers – that is, poor travellers if they were not apprehended, vagrants if they were.

Cambridgeshire certainly did pay for the burials of poor men found dead at Bassingbourn in 1769, and at Coton in 1774, and for the burials of three other unnamed paupers who died in various parishes between 1764 and 1774 as well as for the burials of two vagrants. The Cambridgeshire bench does not seem to have objected on principle to paying for non-settled paupers' funerals, although we cannot be certain that these paupers were not vagrants, because the terms were so often used imprecisely, especially where an individual had died and could not be examined. There was some hesitation whether to pay two bills submitted by the Rev. Dr Plumptre in 1787 'respecting a Charitable Cause that happened at Arrington'; this charitable cause concerned a female pauper, evidently a stranger, sick of the smallpox. After respiting the matter to the next sessions the bench finally ordered the treasurer to pay £2 18s 9d to the overseers and £2 19s 6d to D. Crespin for relieving her. Cambridgeshire was not an over-generous county, but it seems that here too the bench might tolerate the payment of borderline or particularly costly cases on the county rate, possibly by this time bearing in mind the 1782 act; there is no evidence that this woman was ever examined or apprehended.

Although large numbers of people were found dead in Lancashire, including many drowned in the Mersey, it does not seem that the county was prepared to assist parishes with the cost: Steven King has described Lancashire as the most parsimonious poor law county in the country (S. King 2006, 73). Lancashire paid only part of the money when the overseers of Penwortham submitted a bill in 1757 for a post mortem and the funeral of an unknown woman found dead

4 CA Q/SO/5 21 January 1758.

5 CA Easter 1756.

in the boathouse in the parish, 'it being supposed that she was poisoned'. The total bill was £3 10s 3d plus court fees of 5s; the county allowed the two guineas charged by Dr Radcliff for opening the body, but left the parish to pay the rest, including the half guinea to the apothecary who assisted him, 8s 10d for drink for the inquest jury, and the expense of the burial.[6] Virtually all the sick poor paid for by Lancashire were vagrants under a pass, but in 1762 Windleton was allowed 12s 8d for 'Burying a poor Woman lately dead in their said Town as she was travelling through the same'.[7] But even the Lancashire bench, though rarely prepared to pay for the care of sick travelling poor, might pass them as vagrants as the cheapest option. In 1764 John Winter had been in Manchester for some ten months mainly working as a checkweaver but had recently broken his collarbone and could not work. An Irishman, and therefore irremovable under the law of settlement, he was 'apprehended' and passed home to Ireland, almost certainly to relieve both parish and county of maintaining him until he was fit.[8]

Although no statute authorized them to do so, county benches sometimes paid expenses necessarily incurred by individuals who had looked after sick poor travellers and who subsequently petitioned Quarter Sessions for redress (possibly on the advice of the parish to avoid paying the bill itself, or following the refusal of the parish to do so); they generally received at least part of the amount claimed, although the redress in some cases consisted of an order to the parish to pay. Cambridgeshire in 1745 ordered the overseers of Hauxton to provide proper relief for 'a poor Harvest man whose name is unknown ... and is at the point of death for want of Reliefe'; it is not evident who had brought the case to their attention, but very likely a person who had been relieving him and could not persuade the parish to reimburse the expense.[9]

Petitioners who had looked after vagrants, as opposed to sick travellers, were legally entitled to claim from the county treasurer, and it seems that the law was manipulated both by individuals and parishes to enable sick travellers to be claimed for, at first by the legal fiction that they had been 'wandering and begging', later with the tacit agreement of the justices without even bothering to pretend they were vagrants. The mayor of Dorchester allowed a bill for £2 8s 0d presented by William Garrett 'for taking care of a Vagrant, perishing for want, that was found in the Town of Dorchester',[10] but the 'vagrant' was clearly not under a pass since he or she was 'found' very sick and in great misery, neither

6 LRO QSO 2/126, QSP 1753/26.

7 LRO QSO 2/131, QSP 1825/33.

8 LRO QSP 1870/14–15.

9 CA Q/SO/5 12 September 1745.

10 DRO Epiphany 1752.

was any pass or examination filed, leaving it an open question what this person's legal status really was.

No doubt it could have been argued that any poor sick traveller who approached a member of the public, parish officer or justice of the peace for relief was technically begging, and therefore a vagrant. Indeed, many examples occur where poor travellers, falling sick or turning lame, themselves approached an innkeeper, parish officer or justice of the peace, and were then 'apprehended'. It is common to find the terminology referring to the sick person varies depending on the purpose of the document, and an individual may be described as 'a vagrant wandering and begging' in the pass, but 'a poor woman travelling through' in the bill for her treatment and maintenance or the entry in the burial register. Jane Tobias was on her way back to her settlement at North Chapel Sussex after an extended visit to her brother in Plymouth and fell ill on the road; she then went to William Denning, a victualler in Sherborne, 'asked charity', and was relieved accordingly. Quite what happened next is obscure, but she was passed home by vagrant pass. It is not difficult to imagine William Denning suggesting that the best thing to do was to send for the constable and get her passed, and her accepting the suggestion. She was examined but not committed, and there is no bill for medical treatment, so probably all she needed was a meal and a rest and some transport.[11]

Very likely most poor travellers on lengthy journeys relied on charity for food and drink, and possibly lodging in some outhouse, particularly if an emergency arose; at least, many of the sick poor travellers admit to that sort of subsistence begging. It remains an open question how ill they had to be before they could expect help from official sources: in most cases the actual ailment either is not specified, or referred to vaguely as fever or falling lame. Dramatic and visible problems such as broken bones, frank smallpox or fits do occur, but most of the sick vagrants were in a less obviously dire situation. It was commonly alleged that many of the claims to illness were bogus and served as a pretext for begging, but either the justices were a great deal more gullible than it seems reasonable to believe, or these allegations were exaggerated by propagandists keen to crack down on vagrancy.

Probably many of the vagrants who say in their examination that they were 'in distress' were ill, although it is not always possible, without other documentation such as a bill, to be sure. William Hulbert and his wife were apprehended as vagabonds in Shaftesbury in January 1785 and passed to Tetbury Gloucestershire. In his examination, besides details establishing his settlement, Hulbert said that 'being in distress' he had applied for and received relief. We

11 DRO Midsummer 1753 p&e 20 June 1753.

know that this distress was caused by illness because the constable was paid 8s for their maintenance four days 'being thro' Illness incapable of being removed' and a further 1s 8d for conveying them four miles on horseback. One John Cookney tailor was paid 10s reward for their apprehension. It seems more than likely that John Cookney was the person to whom they applied for relief, or in other words from whom they begged, who possibly with their agreement then called the constable to get them off his hands, looked after, and passed by the county.[12] The Dorset bundles contain many similar examples, including other cases where a reward was paid to someone other than a constable, perhaps someone who had relieved the sick traveller and then handed him over to the constable.

Although it no longer formed part of vagrancy law, the provision for sick, old or pregnant vagrants to be excused whipping apparently continued in practice, and they were rarely punished. Some were however sent to the house of correction or the workhouse, no doubt as the most suitable place for them to be looked after and, importantly, costs controlled. Workhouses in the eighteenth century were not entirely the punitive institutions they became under the New Poor Law, but often functioned partly as emergency hospital wards, some having a stretcher or a chair to transport the sick poor, and housing the bodies of those found dead pending an inquest (Hitchcock 2004, 133).

Michael Bray had been employed for some months to drive the artillery for Colonel Amherst's regiment of foot but was discharged in January 1757, no doubt unfit for work, and at the beginning of February 'having a Mortification in his Leggs' he was obliged to seek relief and put in Sherborne workhouse. In June he was examined and passed as a vagrant to Hitchin Hertfordshire, one of many cases where vagrancy law was used as the most practical way to get a sick pauper home again.[13]

Cambridgeshire sent Mary Hutchins and her three-year-old child, found sleeping rough and begging, to the hospital – that is, the old Addenbrooke's Hospital in Trumpington Street – before passing them,[14] and several of the sick vagrants passed through the vagrant contractor's hands in Middlesex were found places in St Bartholomew's Hospital. In 1788 Elizabeth Cope was sent in a coach from the City and left at the pass-house in his absence 'bad with a fever and a mortification coming on in her feet. She was got into the Hospital 12 March'.[15] One sick Irishman was sent first to the workhouse but not improving there was transferred to the hospital, where he stayed from July to November

12 DRO QDV box 4 bundle 10.

13 DRO Midsummer 1757.

14 CA Epiphany 1782 p&c 7 May 1781.

15 LMA MJ/SP/1788/04/021.

1785 before he was well enough to be sent home to Ireland.[16] In many of these Middlesex examples the bill from the workhouse or hospital to the county survives, but they were all vagrants under pass, and it is less easy to discover whether they were originally sick non-settled poor apprehended to make use of the passing system. Probably many of the homeless and destitute beggars, taken up quite legitimately under the vagrancy laws, but suffering from exposure and malnutrition, formed an ideological bridge to sick casual poor in similar need. Even Middlesex, where an exceptional number of penniless and homeless poor were taken up as vagrants, was sympathetic to the idea of passing the genuinely unfortunate, although Mary Lund, apprehended in Hammersmith in 1757 'laying in out houses very sick and almost naked' was nevertheless ordered to be publicly whipped.[17]

Parishes and individuals might recover the money spent on sick non-settled poor by a petition to Quarter Sessions. Long before Gilbert's 1782 act made it statutorily possible the court might make an order for the parish to reimburse an individual, and in settlement appeal adjudications the justices would often order money necessarily spent on a sick pauper under removal to be repaid by the settlement. In some counties both parishes and individuals appealed to sessions to make orders for the repayment of expenses incurred for sick non-settled poor. Although it may have been outside the statutory powers of the bench it seems probable they took it as a matter of justice and arrogated to themselves the authority to make such orders if they wished to do so. In 1741 Sherborne gave notice to Thornford of an intention to claim expenses from them for the sickness of William Short, his wife and child, taken ill of the smallpox in Sherborne; Thornford, although not disputing the settlement, was unwilling to pay Elizabeth Lester's bill for £5 0s 4d. The bill was mainly for food and drink, including an unusually large amount of meat – pork, a shoulder of veal, a breast of mutton, and beef. Other items were wine, physic, ointment etc. 7s 0d, Mary Hide for attending two weeks 10s, Peter Davis for attending four weeks £1 0s 0d, and a coffin and grave for the child 3s 0d.[18] A bill in similar circumstances for £2 14s 0d for relieving John Bayley and his family in the smallpox was presented by Stoke Abbas in a dispute with Rampisham over the bill the same year.[19] In both cases the court ordered the reluctant settlement to pay the bill for their absent sick poor.

These possibilities however did not apply, even after 1782, unless the settlement was in the same county; if it was not, the removing parish was left

16 LMA MJ/SP/1785/12/034, MJ/SP/1786/01/110.

17 LMA MJ/SP/V/01/009/01.

18 DRO Midsummer 1741, QSM 3/6 Dorchester 1741.

19 DRO Michaelmas 1741, QSM 3/6 Michaelmas 1741.

with the bill. Still, inter-parish reciprocal arrangements were developing, independently of parliament and county alike (Sokoll 1997; Taylor 1997). Counties were independent of each other and even capital felonies had to be tried within the county where the crime was committed. Yet it seems that in some cases the court, sympathetic to the plight of those who had spent large amounts in urgent cases on poor sick persons without a settlement, or settled in another county, issued an order for the money to be paid by the county treasurer, in whole or in part. Sometimes this was done by the legal fiction that any poor person who asked for help was 'begging', and therefore a vagrant, but gradually it came to be assumed that a power existed to give such relief out of county funds by analogy with that under vagrancy law.

The court however could and did refuse petitions relating to sick travellers, retaining ultimate control over the cost, but under vagrancy law the county was obliged to pay for a vagrant. By the late eighteenth century processing sick travellers as vagrants seems to have escaped the control of the court and become something parishes and individual justices assumed they could do, so that one of the main purposes of the 1792 Vagrant Act was to put an end to the practice. Yet where the pauper had no settlement, or where the settlement was in another county, there was still no mechanism for claiming back money spent, and a built-in temptation to parishes to treat them as vagrants to relieve them at county expense.

By the 1792 Vagrant Act magistrates were obliged to commit vagrants for at least seven days, or to order them whipped, but the house of correction was often the best place for them to be looked after anyway, and usually the cheapest, since bridewells by then normally had a surgeon–apothecary contracted to look after all sick prisoners, sometimes including the supply of medicines, and arrangements for bathing and stoving verminous clothing. Bills from other practitioners on the other hand might run very high. Any pauper sick enough to be in obvious need would probably have needed the seven days for food, shelter and treatment. By 1821 some witnesses to the parliamentary enquiry into vagrancy claimed vagrants sought commitment because they were better off in bridewells.[20]

It would have been grossly inequitable to deal with some of the cases that occurred in Westmorland as casual poor under the existing parish relief system. A poor stranger might be dependent for a long while and cost a great deal. In 1788 Thomas Harrison of Kirkby Stephen surgeon petitioned sessions for £18 for treatment and travel attending Reuben Coats, a poor miner who 'had his leg fractured bruised and lacerated in a most terrible manner with several large

---

[20] 1821 Report on vagrancy PP vol. 4, 64, 87, 90.

wounds and bruises on other parts of his limbs and body by the falling in of the roof of a coal pit on Stainmore where he was working'. On 23 October 1788 he had been sent for to the turnpike house at Molds Bar on Stainmore to attend this man, 'several of which Journeys were at the peril of your petitioner's own life owing to the inclemency of the Weather and the mountainous Situation of the place called Molds Bar'. Probably the parish had balked at paying such a large bill for a casual pauper and this petition was Harrison's only hope of getting paid. A total of £7 was allowed on the county account, although Reuben Coats was clearly not a vagrant but a working man, the victim of an industrial accident.

At the Easter sessions 1789 Robert Hastwell of Molds Bar, the turnpike keeper in whose house Reuben Coats was looked after, also petitioned the court for redress; he had applied to the overseers of Brough for Coats's maintenance, but they had refused, claiming that Molds Bar was not on their patch, and that anyway Reuben Coats was legally settled in Swaledale Yorkshire. No redress could have been claimed from Swaledale under the 1782 act because it was in another county. The magistrates ordered Brough to pay Robert Hastwell 5s per week, but the county also allowed a further £4, thus splitting the expense between parish and county. There was no pretence that Reuben Coats was other than 'casual poor'. These pragmatic arrangements were quite common in Westmorland, and in time the county assumed a large share of responsibility for sick travellers, so that the legal fiction that they were vagrants gradually ceased to be necessary.[21]

At least Reuben Coats kept his leg, unlike Charles Gordon, 'a Negroe man wandering and begging' who broke his leg in Lupton in 1767 and had to have it amputated. He was brought to Thomas Burn to be looked after and stayed nineteen weeks. Thomas Burn's bill came to £6 2s 2d, which the overseer of Lupton paid initially. John Parkinson the surgeon charged 7 guineas for the amputation, medicine and daily visits for three weeks, and a further 5s for a wooden leg and belts to hold it in place.[22] The county eventually paid both the surgeon's and the overseers' bills in full. Charles Gordon the vagrant was looked after exactly the same as Reuben Coats the poor miner. The overseers however were obliged to pay a substantial part of Reuben Coats' maintenance, whereas Charles Gordon's was paid in full by the county.

Although begging was an act of vagrancy, none of the poor sick travellers who turned to parish officers or nearby residents for help and were 'apprehended' as vagrants were whipped although several were sent to the house of correction, probably to be lodged and looked after. In other counties, better provided with

21 WRO WQSR 485/14–15.

22 WRO WQSR 341/7–8, 11. This was the standard charge – see Loudon 1985, 19.

public institutions, workhouses were often used for the purpose. Many of the sick poor travellers in Westmorland might equally well have been relieved as casual poor by a parish or as vagrants by the county – they were treated much the same and cost much the same. In several cases the sick traveller had gone to the parish officers or the nearest house for help and was therefore technically 'begging'. The net effect, as interpreted by the Westmorland justices, was to make them all vagrants, and the parish that looked after them eligible for reimbursement by the county.

In some cases where an individual was originally regarded as a pauper and later 'became' a vagrant a strong suspicion arises that the categories were interchangeable when it suited the parish. Elizabeth Sparrow, for example, had been lodging in several houses in St Clement's Cambridge for two months until she fell ill and became destitute. St Clement's was then compelled by a justice's order to relieve her, but in December 1763 she was apprehended in the same parish 'wandering and laying about' and destitute of necessaries, and given a cart pass to her settlement in Fulbourn. It is impossible to prove, but it seems extremely likely that she was 'apprehended' by the officers of St Clement's solely to avoid the expense and bother of maintaining her further under the justice's order or of removing her to Fulbourn under poor law procedure.[23]

Many sick travellers had survived for some time on the charity of members of the public until they became so sick they were obliged to risk the penalties of vagrancy law by applying to parish officers for relief. Sarah Phillips, wife of a soldier in General Howard's regiment of foot, was apprehended in Sherborne in August 1751; in her examination she said that she was with her husband on the march to Plymouth, but he left her at Salisbury some time in June because she was lame. Since then she had been living on the charity of various people, but was now 'in a deplorable condition, having a cancer in her right breast and several wounds in her right leg' making it impossible for her to travel to Plymouth. Their settlement was at Land Devisant Carmarthen and almost certainly she had given up hope of catching up with her husband and had got as far as Sherborne on her way back to Wales but wanted to be passed home, which she was.[24]

Both sick poor and vagrants under pass occasionally died on the road. Henrietta Smith, a vagrant originally taken up in Towcester Northamptonshire on 29 March 1764, was being passed to Branton Cumberland where her late husband was settled. She got as far as Brough Stainmore, died, and was buried there on 18 April. Brough paid for the funeral and the county reimbursed them.[25]

---

23 CA Epiphany 1764 p&e 3 December 1763.

24 DRO QDV box 6, August 1751–October 1753.

25 WRO WQSR 309/8–9.

Apparently these matters were to some extent negotiable: when the overseers of Bongate petitioned for their expenses in burying William Miller, who arrived at John Percival's house on 29 April 1773 and died there, the justices agreed to pay the 19s claimed 'upon Condition that the said Parish do pay unto the said High Constable their County rate now due'; probably William Miller was a poor traveller, for if he had been a vagrant being passed the county would have been obliged to pay.[26]

A parish might be put to considerable trouble and expense quite apart from the actual costs of the sickness. In 1770 Shap petitioned for money spent relating to Thomas Proctor, a dragoon of the 1st regiment of dragoons lying at Manchester, who died at Shap and was buried there.[27] The parish claimed no funeral expenses, but they had spent £1 8s 0d on several journeys to Orton to get Richard Burn's advice and to Kendal, in addition to letters to Lowther, Askham, Penrith and Manchester, presumably trying to find out who was responsible for Thomas Proctor. The petition described him as a vagrant wandering and begging who fell sick and died before he could be taken to a justice and examined. This may well have been a device to shift the cost to the county, but the magistrates evidently felt the parish had done the best it could and allowed the bill. Such cases were the greyest of the grey area, and Proctor, having died without being apprehended or examined, might equally well have been a vagrant or a poor traveller, a deserter or simply too sick to keep up with the column. There was no procedure for claiming expenses for sick or dead soldiers left behind on the march from the government, and certainly none for their wives and children.

Militiamen too might fall sick or meet with an accident on manoeuvres, and since many were serving as substitutes for men from other counties the question of who should pay might be complicated, and most counties where the men fell sick seem to have accepted the financial responsibility. Charles Snelling was apprehended in Royston and passed to Scarning Norfolk late in 1759; he had enrolled as a private militiaman in Norfolk and marched with the regiment to Portsmouth, where he fell sick and was discharged consumptive and unfit for service. Possibly he had reached Royston on his own, probably by begging, and was finally apprehended there and passed.[28] Cambridgeshire paid £3 5s 0d to John Plummer for looking after Thomas Smith, a private militiaman who fell sick on duty,[29] and bills to parishes in 1773 for several militiamen who fell ill of the smallpox, when there seems to have been an epidemic in the camp.[30]

---

26 WRO WQSR 332/9–10.

27 WRO WQSR 362/24.

28 CA Epiphany 1760 p&e 26 November 1759.

29 CA Q/SO/8 17 July 1778.

30 CA Q/SO/7 16 July 1773.

Because some cases were so expensive, and all were unevenly distributed, it may have seemed reasonable even to a miserly bench to help a parish financially; but often all the poor sick traveller needed was some help to get to his or her destination, which could only be done by providing a vagrancy cart or horse pass. Westmorland was again quite willing to oblige. Ann Lonsdale was married to a Scotchman who had been pressed about five months previously at Newcastle-upon-Tyne. She was now 'seized with the rheumatism and not able to travel further on foot', asked to be 'helped forward on horseback', and was duly given a vagrant horse pass.[31] Sarah Jackson, a Scotch soldier's wife, was going home from Leeds to Dumfries, and asked for and received a horse pass, 'her time of Reckoning with Child been up'.[32] Alexander Cowan had been at harvest work in the fen country for three months, contracted the ague and 'pissed blood', and needed a horse pass to get home to Scotland.[33] Another Scotchman, William Johnston, was taken ill after driving cattle down to Brough Hill Fair, and could not travel without a cart pass. He was 'apprehended' at Brough but had probably asked for help himself.[34] All of these were passed to Scotland, and there is no evidence that any of them was punished as a vagrant. Dorset constables regularly noted on their accounts that persons passed on horseback or by cart were sick and unable to travel any other way, and Middlesex magistrates also sometimes justified cart and horse passes by noting the state of health of the vagrant on the pass warrant.

Sick vagrants under pass

Given that poor sick travellers might be passed as vagrants and that a vagrant's total journey might be very long, it was by no means unusual for an individual to fall sick or die on the way; others were very sick to start with, yet others already dying when they were apprehended. The vagrant or poor traveller might literally be picked up off the road, like Ann Griffith, 'a Stroling Beggar who was taken up in a perishing condition laying in the Turnpike Road Gutter' in Ambleside in 1777.[35] Probably she would not have been taken up had she not been ill. Ann Griffith lived three and a half weeks, long enough to be taken before a magistrate in Kendal and examined, but died before she could be passed on. Ambleside petitioned for the £1 12s 10d they had spent, and the county paid £1 5s 0d

31 WRO WQSR 259/10–11.

32 WRO WQSR 271/7–8.

33 WRO WQSR 266/28–9.

34 WRO WQSR 390/24–5.

35 WRO WQSR 407/11.

towards the bill. Her case among many others exemplifies the overlap between the casual travelling poor falling sick and the wandering beggar. Sarah Gardiner was turned out of the watch house near Aldersgate on Monday morning 14 July 1757 and found in an open ditch in the fields in Hammersmith in a very weak condition, 'having the venereal disease, the itch and almost starved'.[36] Probably picked up by the watch as a streetwalker, she admitted having begged for the past year, but only when sick was she passed as a vagrant to Stonehouse Gloucestershire.

The Middlesex vagrant contractor Henry Adams stated he had often received vagrants passed from the City dangerously ill, some of whom then died in his hands. In 1785 John Barnfather Esq. reported to the vagrant committee that notwithstanding an order of sessions desiring justices not to pass vagrants unless in a fit state of health parish officers continued to pass them in numbers, many

> so dangerously Ill and Weak, that when in Bridewell they frequently dare not move them agreeable to the Pass but they remain in that Gaol in the most deplorable Condition of Filth, Vermin and Disease for Weeks to the great danger to the lives of the other Prisoners by the infection spreading over the Gaol.

Among specific examples mentioned, a vagrant called John Edwards was sent from Shadwell actually dying and expired shortly afterwards. His body after death was 'full of vermin and every disorder'. Mr Barnfather said this happened so often that it had become dangerous for any person to attend them and it gave the apothecary and nurses a great deal of extra trouble.[37]

Attempting to close the floodgates

The problem of dealing with the 'grey area' cases underlay much of the abuse of vagrancy law complained of throughout the eighteenth century. Parishes that lay on busy roads, and Middlesex parishes with large numbers of non-settled immigrants, felt especially aggrieved because many such parishes were by no means rich, and others nearby with more ratepaying inhabitants had far fewer needy casual poor. The practice of passing casual poor improperly under vagrancy law had been one of the issues that the 1714 Vagrant Act sought to address, following complaints from counties that felt oppressed by it; this it did by defining those persons who were genuine objects of the law. But partly because

---

36 LMA MJ/SP/V/01/009/01.

37 LMA MJ/O/C/011 December 1785.

there remained a grey area where the poor, especially the travelling poor, and vagrants overlapped, partly because of perceived inequities in the situation of different parishes, partly because of a lack of alternative legal provision, efforts to stop up the loophole were never wholly successful. Gilbert claimed that parishes frequently encouraged the poor to beg and then had them passed as vagrants to save expense, which he thought greatly increased the county rate and was a manifest fraud (Gilbert 1781, 124). Some counties were more tolerant of the practice than others, and some magistrates more ready to defy their colleagues than others, and the effect to some extent was to convert feelings of grievance and unfairness from a parish to a county level. Illegal 'walking passes' were commonly issued to travellers whose only offence was poverty despite renewed attempts to tighten up the rules in 1792. Middlesex for a few years obeyed the requirement to commit vagrants for at least seven days, but by 1810 the act was once again widely disregarded and the practice was more common than ever (P. King 2006, 19).

Individuals who permitted poor travellers to lodge in their outbuildings were brought within the 1740 Vagrant Act, citing the expense brought on parishes when poor travellers fell sick there, although the same act stated that parish officers could provide lodging and other relief to persons incapable of being removed by reason of sudden sickness or accidental misfortune, until they could safely be removed 'by a Pass, as is herein before directed' (that is, a vagrant pass), and were to be allowed the expense in their accounts. Parishes may well have interpreted this imprecise clause to mean they could pass sick poor by vagrant pass and claim on the county. Counties however saw it differently and it can hardly have been the intention of this act to shift the entire cost of sick poor travellers to the counties: even when some provision was made for recouping the cost of non-settled sick poor in 1782, it only shifted the cost to the county in very restricted circumstances. This poorly drafted 1740 act was rapidly replaced, and any mention of providing relief to sick poor lodging in outhouses and removing them by pass was dropped.

In 1757 the Middlesex bench, alarmed at the increase in vagrancy costs, attributed it in large part to the improper use of vagrant passes by some parishes 'to save the great expense of settlement passes [poor law removal orders] or maintenance of casual poor not settled whose settlements were distant, notwithstanding no act of vagrancy had been committed, more especially the Scotch and Irish vagabonds [sic],[38] unwittingly demonstrating that the justices themselves had trouble making a clear distinction between casual poor and 'vagabonds', and that the terminology of vagrant passes and pauper

38 LMA MJ/O/C/006, 21 April 1757.

removal orders scarcely made the matter clearer.[39] Vagrancy law itself blurred the distinction by lumping idle and disorderly settled poor together in the same statutes with wandering beggars.

Middlesex discriminated between sturdy beggars and the unfortunate by decreeing that the former must be whipped, and only the latter passed, but from bridewell.[40] Sick travelling poor and soldiers' dependents were likely to be coped with as vagrants even in Middlesex, but Middlesex magistrates were particularly careful to include some sort of acknowledgement of an act of vagrancy in examinations, often clearly framed in answer to a leading question. This is especially evident in the examinations of destitute poor sleeping rough, many of whom were 'weak and sickly', 'in a destitute and starving condition', and so forth. Apprehended as vagrants they said they were penniless or ill and 'obliged to ask relief' or 'forced to seek charity'; in most cases the magistrate would have been able to see the truth of this claim with his own eyes.

Henry Zouch, a Yorkshire magistrate, listed groups of legitimate travellers currently dealt with as vagrants at county expense for lack of other provision for them, including sick travelling poor (Zouch 1766, 34), but the issue was not addressed by parliament until Gilbert's Act of 1782 (22 Geo. III c. 83). This act provided that, if any poor person passing through a parish where he was not settled was delayed by sickness or accident, without means of subsistence or of proceeding to his settlement, the nearest guardian of the poor was to provide lodging, nourishment and assistance, and clothing if necessary, until the poor traveller was fit to proceed, and then take him to a justice to be examined on oath and an order made for his removal to his settlement. Charges were to be accounted for and paid by the parish of settlement if it could be discovered and lay within the same county, on production of the justice's allowance and certificate. If the poor person died before being examined or was found dead the guardian had to pay for the burial and claim from the settlement in the same way, but if the settlement was not known or not in same county, he could claim from the county treasurer. This provision enshrined in law a practice that we have seen had been followed in some counties. The same act also contained a clause tackling fraudulent enticement or conveying of poor children, pregnant women, or sick and infirm poor people from one parish to another without a legal order of removal; however, this clause (s.51) was specifically restricted to those parishes that adopted Gilbert's Act.

---

39 I have occasionally found pauper removals and vagrant passes wrongly catalogued in record offices; but the former are addressed to the overseers and churchwardens, the latter to the constables.

40 LMA MJ/O/C/006 Report of the vagrant committee 21 April 1757.

Serious ambiguities remained: it was not clear whether the act as a whole applied to parishes that had not chosen to join Gilbert Unions, nor what sort of removal order the act authorized – a pauper removal order required the agreement of two justices, but it is not clear that the order of a single justice described in this act was intended to be a vagrant order – it mentions no exemption from punishment, for example. This was of some moment to the parishes involved because of the 1777 ruling that no appeal lay against a vagrant pass.

How much effect the act had in protecting the sick travelling poor is debatable – probably not much, although counties did become more ready to pay after 1782. Nevertheless the 1795 act forbidding the removal or passing of sick poor and vagrants stated that they were often removed or passed 'during the Time of their Sickness, to the great Danger of their Lives' (35 Geo. III c. 101 s. 2). Examples of such callousness occur among the cases quoted in this and the previous chapter. Indeed, taken in combination with the 1792 Vagrant Act demanding the punishment of all vagrants, even the 1795 act did not end the problem. In 1825 Michael Nolan stated that a parish could not claim the expense of looking after casual sick poor from the settlement unless an order of removal had already been made (Nolan 1825 vol. 2, 161), leaving the parish no alternative but to pay the bill or to claim on the county fraudulently by using vagrancy law.

John Mance, keeper of Petworth house of correction in Sussex, argued in 1833 that many poor travellers falling ill were inhumanely treated as vagrants and punished or forced into a workhouse or gaol. He thought a sharper distinction should be made between the unfortunate and the guilty and that the magistrates should be empowered to make special relief orders including passes to such sick poor, as they had often done illegally despite all attempts to stop them. In support of his point of view he cited the case of a poor woman going through a town in Sussex who sat down in the street, too ill to go on. 'Unkind endeavours' to force her to get up and leave the town were made but to no avail and the parish officers were reluctantly obliged to put her in the parish workhouse; a few days later she was moved to prison (as a vagrant) about six miles away where she died nine days later and was buried at county expense. In his view the treatment she received from the parish had hastened her death. Mr Grove Esq. of Shenstone-park Lichfield, who passed many vagrants, thought the passing system would be less objectionable if magistrates paid more attention to the state of the persons removed, 'many being forwarded in a state of infectious and dangerous illness. Women, too, in the very last stage of pregnancy, and lying-in upon the road, become an additional charge upon the county, to say nothing of the cruelty and risk to their lives'.[41]

41 1834 Report on vagrancy, 84E, 65E.

It is also questionable whether the provisions of the 1782 act were still available in the nineteenth century. Nolan stated,

> Poor not settled in a parish becoming chargeable from accident, sudden calamity or any other circumstance are casual poor and must be maintained by the parish where they are. If an individual not being a parish officer takes care of a person e.g. with a fractured limb, he may recover from the parish officers, but the parish officers may not recover from his settlement nor from his master if he is a servant (Nolan 1825 vol. 2, 437).

In 1786 the Middlesex justices held an enquiry into the causes of the increased numbers passed, rising from 1,307 in 1775–76 to 4,244 in 1784–85. Questioned, the vagrant contractor said he thought it due to the ease with which passes were obtained from City of London magistrates, and added that 'many are passed as Vagrants who do not appear to be Objects of the Vagrant Laws'. The bench accepted this explanation and sought a meeting between William Mainwaring, the chairman, and the Lord Mayor, which led only to promises to investigate.[42] But the Middlesex justices themselves were not always more meticulous, as repeated admonitions from the bench demonstrate.

In July 1789 the Middlesex bench received a letter from Lord Montagu, president of the Proclamation Society, urging stricter enforcement of the vagrancy laws in all counties, and especially action against the abuse of granting walking or begging passes indiscriminately to any person applying for them. In this he was preaching to the converted; three years before this letter arrived the vagrant committee had asserted, not for the first time, that if no persons were passed as vagrants but true objects of the vagrant laws, and according to 17 Geo. II, it would decrease vagrant numbers and reduce expense.[43] Middlesex had made repeated but largely unavailing efforts both to pull its own maverick magistrates into line and to stop the City magistrates issuing passes willy-nilly and passing vagrants too sick to be moved. In the course of an enquiry into conditions at the Islington pass-house in 1790 three vagrants who had been passed from the City said they had neither begged nor asked relief, but because they wanted to go home they had been advised to apply to the Lord Mayor for passes 'and had them of course'.[44] Once a magistrate in another county had issued a vagrant pass there was nothing Middlesex could do but continue the passing process.

---

42 LMA MJ/SP/1786/03/106.

43 Ibid.

44 LMA MJ/O/C/012 January 1791.

Although many Middlesex magistrates were as culpable as any they did not protest when at the meeting of the Proclamation Society at the St Albans Tavern in 1790 passing persons as vagrants without following the instructions of the vagrancy law to punish them was identified as a common abuse. When in 1792 the revised Vagrant Act was passed, largely as a result of the Society's initiative, it was believed to have become so common that one of the chief objectives of the new act was to stop the passing of persons as vagrants who were not within the provisions of the vagrancy law. The act insisted that no persons were to be passed, and by implication paid for by the county, who had not been convicted under the vagrancy legislation and punished by a minimum seven days in bridewell or whipping. Middlesex magistrates themselves put down the high cost of vagrancy to the county largely to improper passing of persons who were not really vagrants.[45]

Sick travelling poor were by no means the only group aimed at: the very long-standing practice of passing service personnel as vagrants, and of passing Irish and Scotch poor as vagrants solely because they became chargeable, were also envisaged. As we noted, the 1792 act failed in these objectives because no alternatives were forthcoming, and indeed the passing of service personnel as vagrants, and the passing of Scotch and Irish poor as vagrants, were both later permitted legally.

In a sense, using vagrancy law to spread the cost of non-settled poor to the county could be seen as an extra-legal variant of the old rate in aid, whereby if a parish faced extraordinary expenses the justices could order other parishes in the same county to contribute (43 Eliz. c. 2 1601). Coggeshall Essex had such a severe smallpox epidemic in 1697 that it had to appeal for financial help and the divisional justices ordered a rate in aid from six neighbouring parishes (Smith 1987, 23–4). Rates in aid however had gone out of use in the eighteenth century, leaving a petition to Quarter Sessions the only alternative, with a distinct possibility that it would be rejected (Cockburn 1963–66, 507). But of course the manoeuvre of simply reclassifying sick and destitute casual poor as vagrants was in most cases unauthorized by the bench, although individual magistrates might consider it the most practical thing to do in a particular case, and the county might pay if the circumstances seemed to warrant it.

45 LMA MJ/SP/1786/03/106.

Chapter 6
The Prosecution of Vagrancy Crime

This chapter seeks to put some additional flesh on the bones of themes outlined in previous chapters. Vagrancy covered a multitude of sins and misfortunes and the vagrancy laws were a ragbag of minor offences, many of which can equally well be seen as survival strategies for the poor, and were so seen by some contemporaries, but which were nevertheless illegal. Record survival problems, the wide and flexible application of the law, and problems in interpreting the records make any attempt at quantification, either of the total extent of the problem or of the pattern of offending, highly problematic. The possibility of meaningful statistical analysis of crime trends before the Victorian period is questioned by contributors in Gatrell et al. (1980, 4–5, 46, 98–9), and Oberwittler (1990, 21) advances a cogent argument for scepticism even in the case of capital crime.

Estimating the size of the problem

Vagrancy seems to have been of more concern in the eighteenth century, at least to the ruling classes, than perhaps now appears justified; and probably the surviving records only reveal a small part of the problem as it appeared to contemporaries, partly because of the different attitudes taken by parliament and the public. The 1740 Vagrant Act seems to have been rushed through chiefly because of the sheer number of beggars impeding the way to the parliament buildings; this hostility on the part of the ruling class was due to the idea, considered self-evident at the time, that there was work for all, and for those who could not work a benevolent and generous poor law, and that idleness if not firmly dealt with led inevitably to theft and worse. Hogarth's series of moral prints 'Industry and idleness' (see Plate 7) represents these ideas visually. But there was also a great deal of sympathy for beggars, especially among the less affluent who knew how quickly a labouring man could come close to destitution. Most of those apprehended and sometimes even punished as vagrants were poor and unfortunate, although some were idle, drunken, feckless and immoral, and some were cheats, frauds and chancers of various sorts. Bearing in mind however that these were more likely to appear at Quarter Sessions, they were clearly a minority.

There was of course a 'dark figure' of vagrants never apprehended, mostly beggars, whose marginal existence and strategies for survival have been the subject of several recent studies on the 'economy of makeshifts'. Indeed, it seems likely that most poor travellers begged and could not otherwise have undertaken long journeys – discharged soldiers and soldiers' wives are particularly noticeable in this group, as are many itinerant entertainers, hawkers, and low-skilled tradesmen, chimney sweeps, tinkers and so forth (Hitchcock 2001, 175).

Jane Young may have been fairly typical of poor travellers: a singlewoman aged twenty-five, she had left Hampstead where she was settled and worked as a charwoman to go to visit a relation in Dorchester. She admitted she set out with no more than half a crown obtained by pawning her clothes in London, and that she had begged on her way to Dorchester, and also obtained food in return for needlework.[1] She had reached Dorchester without apprehension, and was only picked up then because of a local privy search. Often poor travellers seem to have been relieved even by officials who in theory should have apprehended them for begging; not a few said they had begged and been relieved by overseers and justices of the peace, and constables' lists are full of travellers with dubious 'walking passes' given a few pence. Probably much more research on parish records would shed some light on the extent to which poor travellers were relieved, although it would not be straightforward because both poor travellers and settled poor temporarily in need of relief might be described as 'casual poor'; and as we have seen, the justices suspected those without settlement were often refused help deliberately in order to shift the responsibility to the county.

There were also many vagrants apprehended elsewhere being passed through each county who appear, if at all, only in constables' lists as items of expenditure. Many Middlesex vagrants had been apprehended in the City, where their examinations would be filed, in theory. In Dorset at least five times as many were passing through as were apprehended within the county, whose examinations would have been filed elsewhere, or who had passes, mainly seamen.

Estimates such as those of Colquhoun at the end of the century are partly guesses and partly propaganda, since the relevant statistics had never been collected (Colquhoun 1806 [1], 38–43). It would be impossible to attempt any reliable estimate of the total size of the vagrancy problem using the surviving material, although it would be safe to say that Middlesex, counties through which Irish vagrants passed, and the West Riding had the worst problems.

Nevertheless, since survival appears to be random rather than due to any deliberate selection process, it may be that such matters as, for example, the sex ratio of apprehended vagrants, the pattern of offences they were committing,

---

1 DRO Epiphany 1753.

their backgrounds, and the punishments awarded for different offences may not differ greatly from the profile that could be obtained if all the documents had survived, although the 'harmless' beggar is undoubtedly under-represented. It is the best that can be done, but it must always be borne in mind that the whole picture can never be known.

Problems of record survival

Petty sessions records and justices' notebooks survive very sporadically and have not been used for this study. Oberwittler (1990) has analyzed five surviving justices' notebooks but finds poor law offences and vagrancy a very small part of their work. The Quarter Sessions records in several of these six counties also present problems of record survival. Little survives in Hampshire except a complete series of calendars, in addition to order and account books; the vagrant papers were apparently discarded when on two occasions in the eighteenth century the clerk was ordered to clear out old papers to make room for current records. In Lancashire the sessions rolls were discontinued in 1750; some passes and examinations were then filed with the petitions rolls, but not systematically, and they peter out around 1765 (*Guide to the Lancashire Record Office*). In Dorset one roll is missing, and several cannot be produced because of their poor condition. The Middlesex records are similarly much affected by poor storage: several years are missing from the sessions papers and there are no examinations bundles 1745–53.

Even greater problems arise from the failure of most justices to file passes and examinations as required by the 1740 and 1744 acts. For those committed the examination might be sent with the *mittimus* for the use of the court, or the examination was taken in court, and these examinations are found quite frequently among the court papers. But there was considerable shortfall: no duplicate pass and examination was filed for many vagrants whose names appear in calendars, order and indictment books, bills, informations and so forth. Examinations of disorderly parish poor as opposed to strangers are particularly poorly preserved, and may not even have been taken, since the chief aim of examination was to determine where the offenders should be passed, which was irrelevant if they had no other settlement. A few informations survive, and order books may give more detail, but disorderly poor seem to have been regularly committed on the mere complaint of the overseers, and many strangers on the unsupported evidence of a constable.

To indicate the sort of shortfall in Middlesex very roughly, in 1757 bundles of certificates for payments to constables survive for fifty-six vagrants apprehended, but only twelve of their examinations or passes were filed. In 1758 the constables of St George Hanover Square apprehended forty-three vagrants between December and May, yet only one examination survives; in 1757 no examinations were filed for any of the thirty-nine vagrants listed in the sole surviving turnover calendar for Tothill Fields Bridewell that year. Turnover calendars do include summary convictions, but are far less regularly found than court calendars and among these six counties for Middlesex alone. Summary convictions were supposed to be filed (P. King 2006, 37; Emsley 1996, 21–2) but are rarely found, especially for vagrants.

Examinations survive for roughly 30 per cent of the vagrants apprehended in Cambridgeshire, 21 per cent in Dorset, and in Hampshire and Lancashire under 10 per cent. At least 900 vagrants were apprehended in Hampshire 1740–95 and 254 in Lancashire 1740–70, but few examinations survive. In all counties it would seem that examinations were filed very erratically, certain magistrates being more methodical than others. It certainly cannot be assumed that those places with most surviving examinations are necessarily those with the worst problem.

The patchy survival of examinations and the probability of numerous unrecorded summary convictions make analysis and quantification of vagrancy crime of questionable value.

Problems of record interpretation

All counties present considerable difficulties in establishing the number of vagrants charged and in determining the pattern of vagrancy offences, partly because of the flexible use made of the law, partly because of obscurities in the wording of documents. In Hampshire particular problems arise from discrepancies between documents. For example, James Curtis was committed in July 1775 for breaking into a house and stealing a pair of shoes and a buckle; the calendar has 'whipped' crossed out, the order and minute books 'discharged and passed as a vagrant', leaving it doubtful whether he was prosecuted for theft or as a vagrant, and what the outcome actually was. In January 1782 against the name of Elizabeth Vaughan, vagrant, the calendar has 'severely whipped' crossed out and 'discharged and passed' overwritten. These may be administrative mistakes, or they may indicate the court changed its mind at some point, especially as the changes are usually substitutions of some milder penalty or discharge for a harsher sentence.

In other cases the charge is different in different documents. Charlotte Webb, according to the calendar for 14 January 1783, was committed for illegally returning to Kings Somborne after being removed, but the order book lists the charge as desertion; in July 1778 against Isaac Mills's name 'vagrant' is crossed out and 'misdemeanour' substituted, probably reflecting the existence of alternative legislation and the willingness of a victim to prosecute.

In the case of minor offences committed by the poor courts assumed wide powers and paid little attention to the wording of the charge or to the relevant legislation – if indeed any existed. Cockburn (1978) has shown that despite legal theory even assize indictments in the sixteenth and seventeenth centuries might differ from the facts. 'Rogue and vagabond' or 'idle and disorderly' could mean virtually anything the justices wanted it to mean, so that without other evidence it is often impossible to reach behind a charge to discover what the accused had actually been doing. A Haslingden labourer was fined 1s plus fees and imprisoned for three months for fraudulently getting a poor lame woman into Pilkington workhouse, 'she having no settlement there'. But how he had done so and what statute he had infringed is not stated.[2] Occasionally '17 Geo. II' is mentioned, but otherwise the procedure used may not be apparent.

The very loose wording of the charge in vagrancy cases and the tendency to throw the book at offenders by mentioning a whole range of actions, some proscribed by vagrancy law, some triable as misdemeanours or even felonies, some outside any law, can make it difficult to establish exactly what had led to the case and which procedure was being used to prosecute. For example, James Dean of Bourton was charged with illegally returning from Silton after being removed, being idle and disorderly applying himself to no manner of business, insulting and threatening people, and suspected of stealing sheep and robbing gardens around Bourton and Silton.[3] This ragbag of offences includes vagrancy crimes, misdemeanours and felonies. A vagrancy charge could usually be found to justify committing a problem individual, and if one accusation could not be proved another generally could. From the justices' point of view it hardly mattered as vagrancy could be punished in much the same way as any offence short of capital felony, at least if the offender was poor and financial penalties could not be used. Three people charged with obtaining goods with false tokens in 1770 were differently treated: Jane Major and Martha Cable were also charged as vagrants, idle and disorderly, and running away from their service, and discharged; Nathaniel Lee however was charged additionally with uttering false coin and ordered to be set on the pillory and imprisoned six months, presumably under 15 Geo. II c. 28.[4] William Muspratt was charged with desertion but also on suspicion of receiving stolen goods and detained three months.[5] Such

2 LRO QSO/2/120.

3 DRO Epiphany 1750.

4 HRO October 1770 calendar.

5 HRO July 1773 calendar.

multiple charges permitted the court to pick and choose what action to take and what punishment to use.

Where the charge is simply a description of offending behaviour, especially where immoral or threatening behaviour is concerned, it is impossible to be sure whether the prosecution was under vagrancy law or some other statute, but if challenged the justices could have claimed the accused was idle and disorderly and thus a vagrant. Edith Martin was committed in February 1775 as 'an Incorrigible bad Woman and a Person who offends the whole Parish of Milborne St Andrews', but why and under what statute? She was discharged for want of prosecution at the Easter sessions, and presumably the parish felt it had made its point.[6] Any mention of a jury rules out vagrancy, hence although there is no other indication that his master had charged him as a misdemeanant it would appear that John Price, accused of running away from his master, being an idle and disorderly boy, and found on top of one of his master's outbuildings, was tried by jury – at least, 'po. se' was marked against his name on the calendar.[7] Moreover, fines could only be imposed under vagrancy law for harbouring vagrants and for dereliction of duty by officers, casting some doubt on vagrancy statistics including vagrants fined (for example Hastings 1981, 153).

Vagrancy as a holding charge

Vagrancy could be useful as a holding charge pending further information. In Hampshire, for example, several people including Richard Belbin were committed as common vagrants on 10 December 1748, but when the case came to court a month later a second charge had been added, of assaulting Elizabeth Wareham and breaking her arm; probably all but Richard Belbin had been discharged since he alone appeared at the April sessions.[8] The group originally charged might equally well have been disorderly parishioners or strangers, but had clearly been involved in an affray, and were all held as vagrants while further enquiries were made, and possibly in case Elizabeth Wareham declined to prosecute. No outcome was recorded and it remains unclear whether the case was pursued, under what procedure, and whether Belbin was ever punished.

Similarly in Cambridgeshire a disreputable group was committed as vagrants lodging in outhouses but suspected of perjury in swearing the women to be their wives; they were to be examined separately and passed, but if any of the women

6 DRO Easter 1775 calendar.

7 DRO Easter 1754 calendar.

8 HRO Epiphany and Easter 1749 calendars.

contradicted the men's statements a charge of perjury was to be preferred at the next Assizes.[9] A charge of perjury was of course entirely unnecessary because giving false information, after due warning, was punishable under vagrancy law by up to two years' imprisonment and unlimited whipping, and a good deal less trouble than a case at the assizes. Perjury was very common in bastardy and matrimonial cases but very rarely punished (Checkland 1974, 264; Stone 1995, 243).

A most striking example of vagrancy law as a holding charge was the case of Charles Hamilton Mercer who came to official attention in Sherborne in 1751 when a soldier swore he had seen Mercer in the Pretender's army in Scotland during the 1745 rebellion. Mercer was apprehended and committed as a vagrant in July, despite being described as 'a gentleman of figure'. He admitted being low in funds, but in a lengthy letter to the bench indignantly denied he had done anything that could possibly bring him 'under the lash of a Vagrant'. Meanwhile the justices were busy making enquiries behind the scenes, which resulted in one of the king's messengers being sent to collect him and take him to London, where he presumably faced further interrogation (Eccles 2010 (2)).

Vagrancy as an alternative charge

Several historians have pointed out that minor crimes might often be prosecuted as vagrancy (Beattie 1986, 284–6; P. King 2000, 89–91; 2006, 26–31); this section also focuses on crimes that could be prosecuted under the 1744 Vagrant Act, but which it was not specifically designed to address. On the contrary, other legislation existed, but vagrancy law might be preferred because the evidence would not support an indictment and jury trial, because the victim could not be identified or was unwilling to prosecute, or because the perpetrator was indeed a wandering stranger. They include assault, threatening or suspicious behaviour, disorder and riot, and theft. Assault and threatening behaviour might equally well be prosecuted as a misdemeanour and theft as petty or grand larceny depending on the value stolen, but both might be bundled in with vagrancy charges. Henry Coleman was charged as a rogue and vagabond found in a cow house belonging to John Sabine Esq., but he was discharged without prosecution. He may have been suspected of 'feloniously milking a cow', as at least two other people were in Dorset.[10] The theft of food and drink, consumed immediately, could rarely have been proved. Theft of workhouse property might also be included in a general charge of idle and

[9] CA Epiphany 1774.

[10] DRO Midsummer 1774.

disorderly rather than indicted as theft: Jane Christie was committed for leading an idle, lewd and disorderly life but also for cutting up and converting to her own use part of the bedding lent her by Blandford parish, yet like so many Dorset poor she was discharged for want of prosecution.[11]

In Middlesex in particular large numbers of people appeared in bridewell calendars for evil fame, riot, assault and petty larceny, but it is impossible to tell whether they were prosecuted as vagrants or misdemeanants, since the complainant is not mentioned, and might be a victim or a constable, and the sentence not noted. Nor does the occasional name marked 'rogue and vagabond' mean that only those so marked were prosecuted as vagrants.[12]

The prison to which a suspect was committed is not a reliable indication whether the offender was to be tried as a vagrant, misdemeanant or non-capital felon, since all these might be sent either to the county gaol or to the bridewell. Some counties blurred the distinction more than others, notably Dorset and Lancashire (DeLacy 1986, 23), largely due to distance and poor communications; Quarter Sessions rotated to several towns in these two counties for the same reason. Sentences under vagrancy law nevertheless were normally served in bridewells since they were supposed to include hard labour, for which there was no provision in gaols until late in the century, but many other petty offenders were also sentenced to imprisonment in bridewells.

The punishment noted on the calendar may however be a clue that a vagrancy offence was *not* tried as such. The 1744 act prescribed only whipping, imprisonment and transportation as possible punishments, except for defaulting officers and persons harbouring vagrants, who could be fined. Thus fines and the pillory suggest other legislation was used; fortune telling was certainly a vagrancy crime normally prosecuted as such, but two women were sentenced to the pillory for fortune telling at Manchester in 1760, which suggests they were charged under the 1735 Witchcraft Act (9 Geo II c. 5) rather than vagrancy law.[13]

On the other hand, misdemeanants and those convicted of petty larceny might be whipped and imprisoned in a house of correction in the same way as vagrants (Beattie 1986, 18, 267; 2001, 23–32). Nor can we be certain the justices did not feel free to substitute some other penalty if they so wished: they certainly used impressment, which under the 1744 act could only be used for vagrants unable to provide for themselves (P. King 2002).

Capital charges all had to be referred to the assizes and thieves sentenced at Quarter Sessions would either be charged with petty larceny or as vagrants.

---

11 DRO Michaelmas 1784 calendar.

12 See Plates 9 and 10.

13 LRO QSO2/129. For other such cases see Morgan and Rushton 1998, 129–30.

Historians are generally agreed that petty larceny was treated very leniently in the metropolis, especially when committed by servants, apprentices or local poor, and not only in the metropolis (Emsley 1996, 184). This might be done by downgrading the value of the goods stolen: thus Grace Reynolds had stolen 14s in coin, handkerchiefs and 'Two Mobbs or Capps'; she pleaded guilty and was sentenced to one month in bridewell and to be whipped twice, but only for stealing the two caps 'of the value of ten pence'.[14]

Apprentices could be committed, whipped and kept to hard labour for a month on the mere say-so of the master (20 Geo. II c. 19 1747), and no doubt many were so punished for pilfering or suspected pilfering (Beattie 1986, 18, 267; 2001, 23–32). George Green, for example, a miller's runaway apprentice, was charged with defrauding his master of bread to the value of several pounds but was discharged after three months in bridewell between sessions.[15] James Hooper, whose master, a printer, claimed he had stolen printed material worth £3, backed up by several persons who said they had bought the paper, 'pleaded guilty' and was immediately whipped and discharged. Theft worth £3 was a capital felony, but probably he was charged as a misdemeanant; yet the outcome was exactly as if he had been charged under master and servant or vagrancy law.[16]

Peter Conlan, an itinerant Irish medicine seller lodging at a public house in Kirkby Lonsdale, stole some stockings; pursued by George Fisher, the owner of the stockings, who found them in his pocket, he at first said he had taken them by mistake and left his own, but later he 'pleaded guilty' and was whipped and discharged yet not passed – he was no doubt prosecuted for petty larceny by George Fisher.[17] Tamar Wiseman and Sarah Wilson were both sentenced to be whipped once in Kendal and once in Milnthorpe for stealing nine shifts from several bleaching grounds in Heversham. They were not passed and might have been strangers or parishioners, but it is not clear whether they were convicted as vagrants or for petty larceny. Nine shifts must have been worth more than the 1s limit for petty larceny, and in any case thieving linen from a bleaching ground was a capital crime (McLynn 1989, xii), so the punishment would have been regarded as lenient. Probably the owners of the shifts declined to prosecute and the culprits were whipped as idle and disorderly.[18]

14 CA Michaelmas 1750, Q/SO/5.

15 DRO Midsummer 1742.

16 DRO Michaelmas 1771.

17 WRO WQSR 336/5–7, 11.

18 WRO WQSR 471/6–7, 10.

Assault, threats and public disorder

Assault, threatening behaviour and public disorder were sometimes dealt with as vagrancy, whether committed by settled or wandering poor. Most assault cases never came to court but were dealt with by agreement before a justice, perhaps by the offender promising to behave better, paying some compensation, or being bound in a recognizance to keep the peace (Oberwittler 1990, 10–14). These methods were scarcely possible in the case of wandering poor, and vagrancy law was used, as it could be for settled poor unable to pay compensation or find sureties. It was much simpler to use vagrancy than to prosecute for misdemeanour, which required a jury and witnesses.

A few of those accused of assault or threatening behaviour were lunatics, who could be passed if strangers, or if parishioners or of unknown settlement committed and held indefinitely in bridewell under s. 20 of the 1744 act, but not whipped. The unfortunate Mary Williams however, whipped in January 1745 and kept to hard labour for refusing to tell her settlement, was by October found to be 'a mad woman'.[19] Alice French had been wandering about for some time when apprehended as a vagrant appearing to be lunatic. The constable stated that when people where she begged did not give her what pleased her 'she hath behaved very riotous Cursing and Swearing and threatening to kill people ... and still behaves in so outrageous a Manner that they are much afraid she will do some Injury or Hurt to such persons as may fall in her way'. The committal warrant confirmed this: 'being examined by me the said Justice she swears most prophane oaths and curses terribly and behaves in a most violent and outrageous manner and either is Insane and cannot or obstinate and will not give any account of herself'.[20] Who decided an individual was insane is obscure – it seems to have been a legal and practical matter, not medical. Such lunatics had to be 'furiously mad' and dangerous and might be committed on the complaint of a parish or a relative unable to cope, or apprehended exhibiting some 'outrageous' behaviour. Lunatics are a special case however and I do not propose to discuss the use of vagrancy law in coping with them in this book.

In Middlesex far more people accused of assault and riot are listed in the calendars than in other counties, reflecting the greater problems of policing the streets in an urban setting; many appear in calendars of persons to be prosecuted as rogues and vagabonds and these seem to have been dealt with as vagrants rather than as misdemeanants. Because Middlesex sessions were held eight times per year those awaiting sessions were rarely kept in bridewell the ten or twelve

---

19 CA Epiphany, Michaelmas 1745.

20 WRO WQSR 332/13, 23, 25.

weeks quite common in other counties, though they might be remanded for further examination. Tothill Fields Bridewell calendars are particularly useful in the mid century. They were turnover calendars and functioned as admissions registers, noting how long the person was to be detained and whether he or she was to be produced in court, and include those summarily convicted and hence often unrecorded. The Tothill Fields Bridewell calendar October 1757, sole survival for that year, lists fifty persons, thirty-nine of whom were charged as vagrants, mostly idle and disorderly, but one with wandering and begging and one lying out in a barn. Most were women, several also charged as streetwalkers, prostitutes or common whores. The eleven not charged as vagrants were charged with assault and theft, under unspecified legislation: for example, John and Winifred Coffe were committed as loose idle disorderly persons not able to give a good account of themselves and also charged with abusing a watchman and breaking his lantern, leaving it doubtful what legislation was used if and when their case came up.[21] In 1765 Ann Crawford was in the same bridewell charged as loose and idle coming to people's houses making a disturbance and threatening to strike them, and Mary Kirkland was committed for want of sureties for 'coming to the first Regiment Hospital of Foot Guards Insulting and abusing the Surgeons of the said Hospital Raising a great Mob and Disturbance and breaking the windows of the said Hospital'.[22] All these might have been settled or strangers since the calendars do not record which if any of them was passed.

John Cobley, 'a traveller' committed for want of sureties on the complaint of Jane Elson of Soham, was discharged with the victim's consent on condition he left Soham and did not come back; in his case vagrancy law does not seem to have been used, although he was obviously not a parishioner.[23] Katherine Samways on the other hand was a disorderly parishioner committed in July 1741 for assaulting James Lovelace yeoman of the same parish by throwing stones at his door and threatening and abusing his family; she died, still in bridewell, in September.[24]

Assault charges against vagrants often arose because they were refused relief. Thomas Selane turned nasty when he begged for beer at Thomas Otway's house and Elizabeth Otway told him she had none. He threatened to kill her and her children and broke the windows. He admitted breaking the windows and said he was 'in liquor' at the time; probably drink was a factor in many assault cases but is rarely mentioned. Selane was settled in Wetherall Cumberland and claimed to be going to harvest work but had no certificate. At the next sessions

---

21 LMA WJ/CC/B/188.

22 LMA WJ/CC/B/206.

23 CA Q/SO/7 October 1775.

24 DRO Michaelmas 1741.

he was ordered to be whipped through Kendal market.[25] James Tapper too was wandering and begging when he broke the windows of the Rt Hon. Lord Mountfort and threatened to blow up his house; he was committed and ten days later sentenced to be publicly whipped next day and passed.[26]

Breaking windows was common as an act of revenge; weapons are rarely mentioned, but Bernard Collis was committed as an idle dissolute and disorderly person having violently assaulted and threatened to do injuries to several inhabitants of Exbury, and also charged with carrying and using a gun in the manor of Beaulieu – possibly he was a local poacher with a reputation for violence whom no individual ventured to prosecute.[27] Michael Morgan had demanded food and drink from Sarah Robinet at knife point, but he was merely passed after two months in gaol at the request of the victim's husband, because she had lately given birth and was presumably not able to attend sessions.[28] Phineas Lara of Enfield, gentleman, handed George Butler over to the constable when he begged alms and attempted to draw a knife on Lara. Butler seems to have been unhinged: he was settled in St George Hanover Square, but had been wandering about the country four or five years sleeping in outhouses 'and explains the Scriptures as a Prophet by Figures and Signs' for a living. He committed a further vagrancy offence by refusing to sign his examination, but the outcome is unrecorded.[29]

Assault on constables or other officials such as workhouse staff appears to have been dealt with under vagrancy law because the authorities wished to signal their disapproval of such behaviour, and because although normally the victim prosecuted at his or her own expense, no satisfaction in the form of monetary compensation could be expected in such cases, as was usual with more affluent assailants. Richard Green was charged with riotously breaking the windows of the poor house at Cerne Abbas, Elizabeth Herdery with assaulting the mistress of Sherborne workhouse, and Ann Lawden was sentenced to one month for aiding and abetting her father and breaking the door of the prison at Wimborne Minster in an attempt to rescue her brother. Hannah Elliott conversely was committed 13 March 1767 for trying in a riotous manner to break *into* the workhouse at Blandford to see her two bastard children. These were all disorderly poor, but Richard Cochrane, an Irishman, was committed as a vagrant, found to be an idiot or lunatic, and moved from the bridewell to the workhouse but had to be moved back 'for breaking the windows at the work house in Sherborne

25 WRO WQSR 272/6–7.

26 CA Michaelmas 1762 calendar, Q/SO/6.

27 HRO Easter 1741 calendar.

28 CA Q/SO/7 Epiphany 1773.

29 LMA MJ/SP/1793/05/069.

and thretning to kill the poor'.[30] Elias Woodford was charged in 1792 as idle and disorderly for abusing and ill-treating several persons, including the master of Weymouth workhouse, but although it was his third offence he was discharged for want of prosecution.[31]

Most but not all vagrants came quietly: William Cummins was sentenced to be whipped and passed for beating the constable of Fen Ditton,[32] and William Lingard was charged with wandering and begging in Weymouth, beating and obstructing the constables in their duty.[33] The constable of Bourn Cambridgeshire had to enlist the help of four men to take a gypsy couple and their six children to the house of correction in 1760.[34] On 29 August 1765 the bailiff of Blandford Forum laid an information that on 27 August George Adams, a traveller whose pass he had signed the day before, came to his house and insulted and abused him 'in a most extraordinary manner' by threats and otherwise, whereupon Mr Marsh ordered him into the custody of the constables Arthur Rogers and George Street. Rogers testified that Adams then struck him with his fist, beat his hat off his head, and behaved so unruly he was obliged to take him to the town gaol.[35] In 1747 a large number of beggars claiming to be seamen terrorized Lowbarrow, extorting money with menaces; four were finally apprehended, but two broke custody and only one eventually appeared in court.[36] There were probably more cases than appear of assault and threats by vagrants that never reached court because the perpetrators escaped.

Threatening arson was another offence not mentioned in the 1744 Vagrant Act but often committed by vagrants and disgruntled poor parishioners and dealt with under it. Although deliberate arson was a felony, intent to burn a house was not, still less accidentally doing so. Threatening arson however was punishable by imprisonment if sureties could not be found, and if done by letter a felony under the Waltham Black Act (Burn 1793 vol. 1, 295–302). Joseph Tanner was 'charged with entering the stable of John Bear in the night time and taking therein a small paper of tobacco'. He was probably charged under the clause against lying out in the open, alehouses and outbuildings, although his real offence was endangering property.[37] Ann Lovell was imprisoned for six months, whipped twice, then passed for threatening to set fire to Beaulieu

---

30 DRO Easter 1765.

31 DRO Michaelmas 1792.

32 CA Michaelmas 1753.

33 DRO Michaelmas 1792.

34 CA Michaelmas 1760 calendar.

35 DRO Michaelmas 1765.

36 DRO Midsummer 1747 petition of inhabitants of Lowbarrow.

37 HRO January 1744 calendar.

parish; she was punished as an incorrigible rogue, although she had apparently not committed any of the offences liable to that penalty under the 1744 act.[38]

Vagrants did sometimes set fire to outbuildings by carelessness (Hardy 1905 vol. 1, 347, 375; Marshall 1926, 228–9), and even more frequently threatened to do so. Michael Bonebrook was convicted of vagrancy and sentenced to three months in bridewell for refusing to tell his settlement and threatening to set fire to the parish of Charminster.[39] Arson was a threat much favoured by the powerless poor, but Dorset may have been inclined to take such threats particularly seriously, since Blandford Forum had been completely destroyed by fire in 1730. Samuel Shepherd was charged with threatening to set fire to the parish of Oborne in 1767 but possibly charged as a misdemeanant: he was continued in the bridewell sessions to sessions for a year 'for want of sureties'.[40]

Public disorder often involved vagrants as well as locals, especially when it arose at fairs: we noticed vagrancy law invoked in dealing with a riotous bull baiting in Dorset. Middlesex had a serious and persistent problem with fairs, of which there were many. As the dates of May Fair, Goose Green Fair, Rag Fair and many others came round orders were sent out to summon constables to police them, and magistrates warned to brace themselves to read the Riot Act. A constable was once killed on duty at May Fair and undoubtedly these fairs attracted swarms of beggars, pickpockets and illegal entertainers.[41] Middlesex was particularly concerned about the bad influence of these fairs on apprentices and servants.

In 1763 the constables of Finsbury were ordered to apprehend 'loose idle and disorderly persons and vagabonds (chiefly Boys)' who frequently gathered at Pack Thread Ground in St Luke's parish 'in a riotous Manner Gambling and making various outrages as well on Sunday as other Days', disturbing the neighbours, and likely to cause unspecified mischiefs.[42] The magistrates were worried about crowds setting off squibs, rolling iron balls across footpaths, using wheelbarrows as mobile gambling tables, and so forth. Middlesex bridewell calendars in the later decades of the century included a significant minority charged with riot, but it is rarely possible to pursue the cases. In 1763 Ephraim Farebank was brought to court from the bridewell by the constable of St James Clerkenwell 'for breeding a Riot before the Smallpox Hospital', but the papers do not reveal whether he was settled or a stranger, or which legislation was used.[43]

38 HRO Q1/15 July 1751.

39 DRO Midsummer 1740.

40 DRO Epiphany 1767.

41 Middlesex orders of court *passim*.

42 LMA MJ/SP/1763/11/023.

43 LMA MJ/SP/1763/10/007e.

Suspicious behaviour

As long ago as the Statute of Winchester in 1285, suspicious persons could be taken up by peace officers. In 1737 the City of London obtained a local act empowering the watch to arrest 'Nightwalkers, Malefactors, Rogues, Vagabonds, and all disorderly Persons whom they shall find disturbing the Publick Peace, or shall have cause to suspect of any evil designs' (10 Geo. II c. 22 1737). The 1744 Vagrant Act, although it did not specifically authorize the arrest of suspicious persons, was prayed in aid by justices to deal with much the same persons as the City's local act, and in 1783 parliament brought suspicious persons within the vagrancy laws, claiming that the justices' powers to deal with persons found lurking about premises carrying housebreaking tools or weapons by demanding sureties had been ineffective.

This act only applied to the metropolis, but people, invariably men, carrying housebreaking equipment or weapons or behaving suspiciously were apprehended and tried long before the 1783 act, often as idle and disorderly or rogues and vagabonds. William Bolton was charged in 1765 with begging and 'putting an Instrument in ye keyhole of ye Back door of Mark West of Bradford Gent with ye intent to open it'.[44] Nicholas Myell was originally arrested for acting suspiciously, but after some behind-the-scenes manoeuvring he seems to have been eventually tried as a misdemeanant and imprisoned for want of sureties. He asked to speak to Mr Portman at the gentleman's house but was turned away because it was late. Mr Portman's coachman saw him lurking about the stable yard an hour later and apprehended him. He was taken before Mr Hutchings, a local justice, who committed him but on what charge is obscure – possibly as a rogue and vagabond, possibly for attempted theft. Evidently it was doubtful whether the case would stand up in court as a letter was sent to the undersheriff on behalf of Mr Portman:

> As there is no possibility of fixing any Thing on the Fellow what I would desire of you (as I can't attend the Sessions myself) is to prefer an Indictment of some kind or other against Miel, which of Consequence will not be found against him by the Jury and by that means the Prosecutor will be discharged from his Recognizance, which at present is all Mr Portman desires.

Whether this was done is not clear, but Myell was marked discharged. On the next calendar however he reappeared fined 3s 4d and required to find sureties; evidently *something* had been fixed on him at some point after the original

---

44 DRO Easter 1765.

discharge order. Hutchings petitioned the court to keep Myell in prison for threatening to be the death of him, and perhaps preferred a charge against him as a misdemeanant, leading to the fine and demand for sureties for the peace. Myell could not meet these requirements, and was still in prison when he died a year later.[45] The magistrates could always find ways to prosecute undesirable persons.

Predominantly an urban crime, after the 1783 act charges of carrying weapons and housebreaking tools occur more frequently in Middlesex, although 'evil fame' probably conceals many such before that date. In a revealing Middlesex case in 1787 John McNeal was apprehended for felony and committed to New Prison, but 'the case not being made out' although a pistol was found in his possession, he was detained as a rogue and vagabond in Clerkenwell Bridewell, probably under the 1783 act, illustrating the use of vagrancy law as a backstop if felony could not be proved.[46] The list of vagrants brought from Clerkenwell Bridewell in February 1788 included John Bayliss, accused by James Clerk of thrusting at him with a cutlass hidden under his coat as Clerk went his rounds. He was adjudged a rogue and vagabond and imprisoned in bridewell for six months.[47] John Vandersall, a vagrant aged sixteen settled in Greenwich, was apprehended in the high street in Shoreditch as a person of ill fame and reputed thief; a piece of wire found in his pocket was taken as conclusive evidence of intent to commit a felony and he was given a three-month sentence in bridewell. Probably this was a 'fishing' wire used to lift goods out of shop windows.[48] A group of three youths apprehended by the constables in Crow Street Shoreditch had 'sundry articles' on them, but whether these were the items specified in the 1783 act or things they were suspected to have stolen is not stated. The two younger lads aged thirteen and fourteen were discharged at the sessions, but Thomas Griffin aged eighteen apparently was not.[49] James Randall alias Richardson was arrested in December 1783 carrying a cutlass and imprisoned for six months as an incorrigible rogue but committed again in May 1785 for the same offence, this time carrying a pistol with intent to assault, and having a crowbar and a darkened lantern, with intent to break and enter. For this second offence he was sent to Tothill Fields Bridewell for two years' hard labour.[50]

Some did indeed make a poor fist at defending themselves. Thomas Kinman, examined at Bow Street in 1793, was apprehended lurking in one of the passages leading to the pit at Covent Garden Theatre. He claimed to have gone there

45 DRO Easter, Midsummer, Michaelmas 1748, Midsummer 1749.
46 LMA MJ/SP/1787/03/001.
47 LMA MJ/SP/1788/02/001.
48 LMA MJ/SP/1793/12/037.
49 LMA MJ/SP/1793/02/019, MJ/SB/B/0398.
50 LMA MJ/SP/1785/06/014.

merely to escort his sister, not to see the play. He also claimed 'it is totally out of his power to produce his sister to prove what he says'; this and the fact that he was with three other men who promptly ran off when approached by the constable of St Clement Danes, plus a previous conviction for felony, probably led to his conviction although the verdict was not noted.[51] James Good, aged fourteen, arrested carrying an iron hook of the sort used in housebreaking, was sentenced to six months,[52] and so was George Bailey, who was not carrying anything suspicious but was found in a yard with intent to steal.[53]

John Armstrong said he believed Moses Chivers and Francis Thomas were rogues and vagabonds 'within the Act'. He apprehended them in Kingsland Road Shoreditch, and Chivers let something fall that was afterwards found to be an iron crow; he also had a screw gimlet in his pocket. On searching Francis Thomas's lodgings Armstrong found a centre bit, and in Moses Chivers' apartment an iron hand-vice, implements used in house breaking – or possibly carpentry. The headborough of St Leonard Shoreditch confirmed Armstrong's statement.[54] Joseph Harrington, a soldier in the Tower Hamlets Militia, was spotted by a passing neighbour in Thomas Jones's yard in Union Row with his arm in the fowl house and suspected, not unreasonably, of intending to steal the fowls.[55] Others were carrying the picklock keys mentioned in the 1783 act, and all charged as rogues and vagabonds. Unfortunately the judgment is not recorded consistently enough to calculate a conviction rate, but it was probably high.

An interesting letter to the Dorset clerk of the peace suggests justices may have passed more information about suspects among themselves than appears in most sessions records. The letter concerns Thomas Bassett of Gittesham, who enlisted in the Guards under Col. Kingsley but deserted and came home ostensibly to see his parents, and by pleading ignorance and a desire to return to the regiment persuaded a local justice to give him a pass. The Colonel had now written to say he had not returned and it was reported he had broken into a shop in Coombe. He was last seen in a little alehouse in Dorchester,

> the Ostler at the Antilope Knows the House where he was and Knows the Fellow he believes so I beg the Most Strict Search may be made for him. ... PS The fellow is Tall thin hath Straight Black Hair of Yellow Complexion about one and

51 LMA MJ/SP/1793/12/038.
52 LMA MJ/SP/1794/04/067, MJ/SP/1794/04/088.
53 LMA MJ/SP/1783/10/022.
54 LMA MJ/SP/1793/05/063.
55 LMA MJ/SP/1798/09/080.

> Twenty years old and I Cannot Say he is Indow'd with a great deal of Sense he had on Soilders Cloath and Lether Breeches.[56]

In all counties the justices occasionally reported suspicious persons to the Bow Street office to see whether they were wanted for some felony (Styles 1983, 127–49). Writing to the Dorset bench in 1773 Sir John Fielding promised to send an officer promptly if any offender on the wanted list were apprehended 'to see the Prisoner and to take every other necessary Step which the Nature of the Case may require'.[57] When Thomas Iverson, apprehended as a rogue and vagabond in Ickleton in 1785, appeared in court the clerk was ordered to send his description to Bow Street and the gaoler to get him some clothes; nothing further was recorded and his lack of clothes suggests he was destitute.[58] In Hampshire John Brown was committed to Odiham Bridewell in May 1792 as a rogue and vagabond wandering in Pamber not giving a good account of himself; at Winchester in July the court ordered him to be advertised with his description in the newspapers, but apparently no further information was forthcoming and he was discharged in October.[59] Even in remote Westmorland John Nelson, although apprehended as a vagrant wandering and begging, was ordered to be notified with his description to Bow Street and advertised in the Leeds and Newcastle papers; he was sentenced to twenty weeks' hard labour in a solitary cell but whether because of further information does not appear.[60]

Moral offences

Although there was no provision in the 1744 act for the use of vagrancy law to discipline offenders such as fornicators, adulterers and prostitutes, and there were specific statutes to deal with bastardy and bigamy, the original Bridewell had been used to deal with moral offences (Innes 1987, 58). In some counties bastardy was treated as idle and disorderly, in others using s. 7 of the 1609 Vagrant Act, whereby the woman could be imprisoned for a year, a clause retained when the vagrancy laws were amended. Ann Grimshaw and Ann Atherton were sentenced to be whipped and imprisoned for twelve months for having bastards

---

56 DRO Michaelmas 1751.

57 DRO QSM 3/9 Michaelmas 1773.

58 CA Q/SO/8 October 1785.

59 HRO Q3/11 July 1792.

60 WRO WQSR 494/21.

likely to be chargeable to Abram; no statute was cited, but the sentence suggests the 1609 act was used.[61]

It was therefore no great step to use the same sort of penalties under the 'idle and disorderly' clause to deal with other kinds of immoral behaviour, most often prostitution, especially in Middlesex (Shoemaker 1991, 185). Vast numbers of Middlesex prostitutes appeared in court calendars as of 'evil fame', which may suggest they had been around long enough to acquire such a reputation, or it might be shorthand for 'seen in a notorious locality at night'. Cambridgeshire also had a noticeable prostitution problem, dealt with usually by the university authorities but occasionally at Quarter Sessions. Mary Hunt was sentenced to six months' hard labour as an incorrigible rogue for persistently returning after being passed to her settlement by one of the doctors of the university, and had been apprehended yet again wandering in King's College walks.[62] In Dorset too such matters arose: Mary Rabbitts was charged with keeping a common bawdyhouse in Shaftesbury in 1787;[63] keepers of brothels could be charged either under 'evil fame' or the Disorderly Houses Act, but calendars may not indicate which. In Dorset however John Petty was charged with maintaining a disorderly house in Gillingham on an information by three men who said they each lay with Ann Wrizzle at his house, and that he later 'endeavoured to treat with them' to lie with her for sixpence.[64]

The demise of the church courts left a gap in legislative powers to deal with immoral behaviour, partly filled by civil actions such as 'crim. con.' for adultery for the better off. Moral offences were also dealt with under vagrancy law for want of any alternative, but courts felt under no obligation to cite particular statutory authority and it is frequently difficult to identify when vagrancy law was used and when some other legislation. Sessions felt free to use charges not specified by any law: William Kirkham was fined £2 for causing 'certain lewd evil and wicked disposed persons as well Men as Women in a certain Room in the Castle of Lancaster to assemble and come together and then and there with Whores casually to lye', although it could hardly have been a disorderly house.[65] Possibly he was charged as a misdemeanant under 'nuisance'. Lancashire and Middlesex felt free to charge women as 'common whores' without citing any particular statute. There was indeed no statute to cite as prostitution itself was not illegal, nor was adultery, but such offences could nevertheless be prosecuted without specific statutory authority.

---

61 LRO Midsummer 1762 calendar.

62 CA Easter 1765.

63 DRO Epiphany 1787.

64 DRO Epiphany 1784.

65 LRO QSO2/127.

'Evil fame' could be used to apprehend couples suspected of fornication (Burn 1793 vol. 3, 98), but they were then supposed to give sureties for good behaviour; vagrancy law could be used against those who either could not or would not do so. William Bromley wrote to his father from Lancaster Castle agreeing to enlist 'for Am Werey of my Sitaytion and think it is the Best Way'. The parish officers of Bolton-le-Moors had managed to keep him in prison for some time presumably as 'idle and disorderly'. They consented to his enlisting 'provided Care be taken that he be swore and no tricks play'd us but we are Determined he shall not Live with Elias Mather wife in the Unlawfull manner he has done if possible we can help it'.[66] In a similar case in Dorset both parties were arrested in March 1758, continued to July, and then discharged. A woman charged with infecting several men with venereal disease and keeping a bawdyhouse, and another with criminal conversation with some of the soldiers quartered at Sherborne and found in bed with one by the constable were also discharged.[67]

Mary Edge and Esther Porter were committed for want of sureties on the complaint of George Campbell Esq. They 'lately without any lawful Occasions wandered about his House, from whence divers Goods have been lately stolen; and were detected in a lewd Posture with his black Servants', but whether suspected theft or their immoral behaviour or both was the problem is an open question.[68]

Although much of the argument put forward in this chapter is necessarily open to question due to the inconclusive nature of the evidence, it seems clear that vagrancy law was often used to cope with offences, either as a simpler option than other legislation or as the only option to plug gaps in the statute law.

---

66 LRO QSP1996/8.

67 DRO Midsummer 1758.

68 LRO Michaelmas 1766 calendar.

Chapter 7

The Punishment of Vagrancy Crime

The range of punishments available to the justices for vagrancy offences was extremely limited. The single justice could commit the idle and disorderly to bridewell for up to one month, and could also order rogues and vagabonds whipped, but justices seem to have passed vagrants very freely, and it is unlikely that vast numbers were whipped by order of single justices, since relatively few of those appearing in court were whipped by order of sessions; county practice varied quite widely however, and changed perceptibly over time. According to Cockburn vagrants in the North Riding were generally whipped before being passed (Cockburn 1963–66, 492). Quarter Sessions in Cambridgeshire seem to have handed down a higher proportion of sentences of whipping than in other counties, but what justices sitting alone did in any county is unknown. Courts had greater powers and could order repeated sentences of whipping and longer prison sentences for more serious offences; vagrants with no ascertainable settlement could be placed out to some work or if male sent into the army or navy, a sentence sometimes stretched to apply also to troublesome settled males.

Transportation was a possible sentence, but was extremely rare, perhaps because it was an expensive option. Catherine Clark, convicted as a rogue and vagabond for false pretences and several other acts of vagrancy, unspecified, was sentenced in Hampshire to transportation.[1] Legally only incorrigible rogues escaping from prison or offending again could be transported, and it is not clear whether this sentence was legal and actually carried out. She is the only case I have found, but George Baillie was sentenced at the Old Bailey to transportation for seven years for repeatedly escaping after conviction as an incorrigible rogue under the 1783 act.[2] A few border gypsies were transported early in the century (Morgan and Rushton 1998, 89), but the sentence was so seldom imposed for vagrancy that we may safely ignore it.

1 HRO Q1/16 July 1756.

2 Proceedings of the Old Bailey reference o17860222-1.

Whipping

In Elizabethan legislation sentences of whipping were directed to be 'until his or her body be bloody by reason of such whipping'; this phrase was not common in eighteenth-century sentences, but in 1777 James Driver was ordered to be publicly whipped twelve lashes at Fulbourn the next Monday 'until his body be bloody'.[3] Evidently twelve lashes was normally enough to produce this result. Elizabethan woodcuts show a bundle of birch twigs being used, but although the type of instrument was not specified either in the law or in Quarter Sessions sentences, the cat o' nine tails was used in Dorset – the gaoler was paid 1s 6d for whipcord and making it in 1787.[4] Hogarth's 1747 engraving of the idle apprentice sent to sea shows him being prophetically threatened with the cat, used in the navy from about that time, and further away on the shore the gallows (*Industry and idleness* 1747 Plate 5, Brereton 1786, 28). Vague words such as 'moderately' or 'severely' attempted to indicate the level of severity the justices intended. However repugnant such punishments may be to a twenty-first century sensibility, they must be regarded as fairly light compared with the scores, even hundreds, of lashes handed down by courts martial in the army and navy, or to transported convicts in Australia. In the navy twelve lashes was the maximum a captain was permitted to order under admiralty regulations; any more serious crime had to be dealt with by court martial, but in practice this limit was widely ignored (Rodger 1988, 218–20; Hughes 1988, 454, 464–6).

In a society accustomed to corporal punishment and where the prisons were particularly unpleasant, whipping may not have been seen as a harsher sentence than imprisonment, and might be quite perfunctory. Obviously the severity of the sentence depended a great deal on the person doing the whipping: Jacob Ilive described whipping in Clerkenwell Bridewell as often 'a mere Ceremony' (Ilive 1757, 38). Mary Saxby in her autobiography claimed the keeper took care not to hurt her, and a correspondent to *The Times* in 1786 considered public whipping a ridiculous farce, 'the punishment being of itself so trifling, as to be only a matter of merriment' (Saxby 1806, 16; S. King 2000, 351). Perhaps when Matthew Broome was sentenced to be whipped at the cart's tail twice in different places the admonition of the court 'and the person who whips him is required to do his duty' suggests they doubted it would amount to much.[5] Cambridgeshire used whipping particularly often for men deserting their families, probably because, from the point of view of the parish, imprisonment prevented a man

3 CA Easter 1777 calendar.

4 DRO Easter 1787.

5 LMA MJ/SB/B/0105.

from working to support his family, which whipping followed by immediate discharge did not.

These sentences were usually carried out publicly, as specified in the 1744 act, although later in the century vagrants were increasingly whipped privately in the prisons; the reasons were not stated but may have been related to lack of public support. Sentences were normally carried out on a market day at a time when most people were moving about, as part of the theatre of deterrence. Sometimes the vagrant was ordered to be taken back to the parish of apprehension to be whipped there, although Hampshire and Dorset expected the parish in question to pay the expense of doing so. In rural counties offenders were usually whipped at the post, in Cambridge at the market cross. In the City sentences of whipping were more often at the cart's tail than at the post, although that changed over the eighteenth century, possibly because it caused disruption to increasing traffic (Beattie 2001, 307; Shoemaker 2004, 80). In other counties too a few were sentenced to be whipped at the cart's tail over a specified route, indicating roughly the duration of time the process was intended to take: for example, in July 1784 William Welsh and his wife were sentenced to be publicly whipped at the cart's tail from Gosport beach to the upper end of Middle Street on three occasions, in July, August and September, although they were charged only with vagrancy.[6] It seems possible this severe sentence was not actually carried out, since the order book of the same date marked their names 'discharged'. The sentence was usually carried out within a week followed by immediate discharge unless combined with a period of imprisonment, in which case the whipping usually came at the end of the sentence just before discharge. When the culprit was whipped more than once the interval between the punishments varied from later the same day, but at different places, to several weeks with periods of imprisonment in between.

Cambridge justices often specified the number of lashes, usually twelve. This was not done in the other counties, where the conduct of the punishment seems to have been left to the constable or keeper, and not even in Cambridge where the charge was simple wandering and begging. It probably represents an attempt to tailor the punishment to the gravity of the offence, so as to produce 'a just measure of pain', although since we cannot know what was said in court it is not possible to explain the variation in the number of lashes, except in the minority of cases where it was clearly linked to repeat offending or to prolonged absence.

On the other hand repeat offenders were occasionally simply discharged for unstated reasons; a defendant who managed to find sufficient sureties would normally be discharged, though few on vagrancy charges were likely to do so.

---

6 HRO 14 July 1784 calendar.

Probably the sentence was influenced by a combination of the defendant's attitude (a promise not to offend again often worked), local reputation as reported by the parish officers, sickness or some other acceptable excuse, or the length of time already in prison awaiting the sessions.

Although legally a justice was only allowed to pass a vagrant after the vagrant had been either whipped or committed it is unusual to find any note whether the vagrant had been punished, unless perhaps by implication if the pass sent him via the house of correction. Certainly very few passes note the vagrant had been whipped, although in Dorset an order of 1753 for payment of the reward to Richard Stone of Sherborne for apprehending Sarah Lacey notes she had been whipped pursuant to the act.[7] A single 1740 pass from Weymouth for John Harris to go to Castleton via Radipole notes, 'we do hereby allow the Space of Three days for his passing to the said parish of Castleton. The said Vagrant hath not been whipped in this Borough and Town on account of his Ill State of health', but these notes are rarities.[8] After the 1792 act notes of punishment become common in Middlesex, but they always certify the vagrant had been confined seven days, or 'dealt with according to law', which might either mean imprisoned or, if male, whipped.

Counties varied considerably in their use of whipping (Morgan and Rushton 1998, 73–5). According to Slack (1974, 361) all Salisbury vagrants were whipped 1598–1638 unless pregnant, disabled or under seven, and in the first decades of the eighteenth century over 50 per cent of prisoners in Westminster and Middlesex were whipped on admission to the house of correction (Shoemaker 1991, 188). But in 1764 Richard Burn observed that, although 'Almost all severities have been exercised against vagrants, except scalping', nothing had worked (Burn 1764, 120). Possibly the perceptible decline in the use of whipping during the eighteenth century was due to a loss of faith in the effectiveness of the punishment, not by parliament but by the justices who actually administered the law; even the Proclamation Society thought it had no good effect. Occasionally counties tried to insist their neighbours whipped vagrants, but often without success (Clark 1979, 84–5).

Historians of eighteenth-century capital crime have noted that despite the growth of capital statutes this increased severity was in practice more apparent than real. Shoemaker notes an increasing reluctance to use violent public punishments as the eighteenth century wore on, and we have seen that the 1792 Vagrant Act abolished whipping for female vagrants. The sheer imprecision of the sentence, depending very much on the individual who carried it out, may also

7 DRO QDV box 6 Sherborne 1753–54.

8 DRO Easter 1740.

have contributed to its increasing disuse. The Middlesex bench was informed in 1757 that the punishment provided in the Vagrant Act was 'too often' dispensed with thus making the passing of the vagrants illegal,[9] and Nottinghamshire wrote to Middlesex in 1786 to inform them that they had resolved to pass no vagrants who had not been whipped or imprisoned as laid down in the 1744 act and had appointed a proper person to check the passes of vagrants brought to the county vagrant carrier.[10] Not everybody saw this trend away from rough punishment as progress: in the early nineteenth century a perceived rise in juvenile delinquency was attributed to the decreasing use of summary procedures – 'I remember in former days, persons were taken and pumped upon, or something of that sort; but now they are handed over to the Police, and tried on it.'[11]

The repeated exhortations of county benches, Middlesex in particular, urging justices to whip or commit vagrants and not simply to pass them suggest such reminders were frequently needful. The exemption of the 1714 Vagrant Act for pregnant women and others where the justice deemed the vagrant unfit to undergo such punishment, although omitted from later acts, seems to have been almost universally continued in practice, and liberally interpreted, no doubt because most vagrants were indeed objects of compassion. Warrants for whipping vagrants are conspicuous by their absence in Quarter Sessions records, but the form of one was included in Burn's handbook (Burn 1755 vol. 2, 502–3). It is impossible to prove a negative so that the absence of written evidence that they *were* whipped does not prove they were not, but whatever the law said and intended it seems enthusiasm for the wholesale whipping of vagrants was by no means universal, and becoming less so. Every market town had its whipping post and courts did sentence a minority to be whipped, but not usually for simple wandering and begging, at least after the mid century. Long before the whipping of female vagrants was forbidden there was a marked reluctance to whip women unless they were suspected of offences other than wandering and begging, and where women were taken up in company with their husbands almost always the man was whipped but not the woman.

Whipping vagrants as opposed to thieves was not always supported by the public. By mid century there were complaints that the public failed to appreciate the necessity for this severity. Middlesex vagrant committee reported in 1751, 'The Committee being informed that it will be dangerous for the Constables to whip vagrants in the publick streets, are of opinion that the vagrants who shall be apprehended should be ordered to be whipped in Bridewell.'[12] In a drive to

9 LMA MJ/O/C/006 21 April 1757.

10 LMA MJ/SP/1786/04/118.

11 1828 Report on criminal commitments and convictions, 4.

12 LMA MJ/SP/1751/5/37.

tighten up observance of the vagrant laws the Middlesex justices decided in 1757 to put up a public notice 'as the common people have not a proper Idea of the offence of begging and have in many instances by their Obstruction rendered it very dangerous for the Peace Officers to whip Sturdy Beggars'; the printed notice included the clause in the 1744 act imposing a £5 penalty on persons hindering its execution, and urged the public to assist the peace officers in apprehending and punishing vagrants.[13] Tim Hitchcock notes the effectiveness of physical infirmity in eliciting public support (Hitchcock 2004, 113). In 1775 the committee was again urging the justices to enforce the vagrancy laws more strictly and to 'distinguish the pretended from the real objects of distress by ordering the former to be publickly whipped according to the Statute'.[14] When the new Middlesex Sessions House was built in Clerkenwell in the 1780s a mobile whipping post was erected on an apron of ground in front of it, but it may have been used more for other offenders than for vagrants.[15]

In the nineteenth century even apprehending vagrants had become unpopular: the clerk to the Lord Mayor of London told the 1815 parliamentary enquiry into mendicity that in the City beggars were rarely arrested unless they were also pilfering – 'It is a very disagreeable office for an officer to undertake, for he is sure to get a crowd about him, and to be ill treated; there is generally a serious struggle before any of those common beggars can be taken into custody.' The beggars would fall down and scream 'and then good-natured people interest themselves, and desire he will not pull the poor creature about.'[16] Shame was certainly part of the intention in public punishments (Beattie 1986, 463–5; Shoemaker 2004), especially whipping and the pillory, and may have been a factor in such cases as the numerous Cambridge men deserting their families, although most vagrants so punished would have had no local connections.

Bridewells

In 1609 the establishment of houses of correction was required in every county, intended to provide work and maintenance for the destitute and also punishment for the disorderly. There the idle were to be set to work and vagrants punished; the master was given power to punish both rogues and vagabonds and idle and disorderly persons by putting fetters and gyves on them, and by moderate whipping (7 James I c. 4 s. 4), apparently at his discretion. How far these powers

13 LMA MJ/O/C/006 21 April 1757.

14 LMA MJ/SP/1775/12/063.

15 LMA MJ/O/C/011 October 1786.

16 1815 Mendicity report, 16.

remained in use in the eighteenth century is debatable, and probably varied in different places. The bridewell was a sort of penal workhouse, and some were prison and workhouse combined (Burn 1764, 201–2; Chalklin 1998, 151). It is uncertain which of these functions predominated in the seventeenth century, but in the eighteenth- the idea of the workhouse as a place in which labouring paupers might both be provided for and compelled to work so efficiently that the institution would show a profit became popular and the house of correction was seen more as a prison for petty offenders including vagrants. But the multiple functions of the early house of correction as penal establishment, workshop and poorhouse ensured that it was resented by the poor, who saw it as a penal institution, unprofitable as a workshop because it housed too many impotent persons, and impossible to manage because keepers were expected to cope with all these different objectives. It was neither fish, flesh, nor good red herring, and throughout the period of the Old Poor Law some overlap of functions persisted.

Although the house of correction ceased to be a poorhouse, inevitably many disorderly poor and vagrants sent to it, often with children, were incapable of work but still had to be maintained, if only slightly above starvation level, and given some minimal medical attention. The idea of hard labour as a penal sentence evolved from the earlier idea of setting the idle poor on work and was eventually embodied in the treadmills and stone breaking of the nineteenth-century prison and vagrant casual ward. The workhouse likewise might be essentially a poorhouse full of the old and orphans, with little if any work going on, but it might also be carceral, with paupers forbidden to go out without permission, denied alcohol and tobacco, and obliged to wear distinctive clothing, a development of the idea of badging the poor that spread to the prison uniforms issued in the late eighteenth century.

Workhouses were often used as temporary prisons for sick vagrants, particularly before the 1774 Health of Prisoners Act (14 Geo. III c. 59) required prisons to set up sick wards and employ surgeons. In 1755 Mary Harris, an idle and disorderly person and common streetwalker, was arrested for making a riot and disturbance in Newgate Street and sentenced to two months' hard labour in bridewell; 'Nevertheless it being alledged by Mary Harris that she's infected with the venereal disease it is therefore ordered that the case be subject to the control of the Rt Hon. the Lord Mayor if it shall be found expedient to send her elsewhere in order to her cure in the mean time.' She was committed to the London workhouse, evidently for treatment, and sent back to bridewell to finish her sentence.[17]

---

17 LMA WJ/SP/V/01/005/01.

Carceral institutions in the eighteenth century thus tended to shade into each other and overlap, a confusion often reflected in the nomenclature – all might be referred to as prisons, and although the county gaol was always the gaol (unless it actually was also the bridewell, as in Dorchester at the end of the century), the bridewell might be referred to as bridewell (especially in the south) or house of correction or prison or even gaol. In Cambridge Hobson's workhouse served as the town bridewell for part of the century, while the county bridewell was at the other end of the town at the Castle, where the county gaol and the gallows also stood; a 'workhouse calendar' listed the prisoners brought from the town bridewell to the sessions alongside the usual gaol and county bridewell calendars.

For purposes of dealing with prison breaking, prisons were held to include stocks, the house of a constable or private person, anywhere a person was under lawful arrest (Burn 1793 vol. 4, 49). However, although inmates might escape from any of these places it has been rightly pointed out that, whereas escapes from workhouses resulted in little official action, far more notice was taken of escapes from houses of correction, reflecting the greater level of security expected (Morgan and Rushton 1998, 176).

The county gaols were the king's prisons under the sheriff, and their upkeep was originally the responsibility of the crown but shifted to the county in the sixteenth century. The sheriff also originally appointed the gaoler; until the reforms of the late eighteenth century the gaoler's office was an office of profit – that is to say, his income came from fees the prisoners were obliged to pay for all sorts of things from 'turning the key' to discharge fees, fees for the privilege of wearing lighter irons, or for having a separate cell or a bed. Prisoners bought food and drink from the tap, which was run for profit by the gaoler, or had it brought in by friends or by a turnkey – for a consideration, naturally. County gaols held criminals on the more serious charges and, in a separate part of the gaol, debtors; in the metropolis there were also numerous compters, which were specifically for debtors. There were debtors' prisons elsewhere too – there was one in Southampton called Cheyney Court.

With the exception of refractory prisoners, who might be put in an underground dungeon, and prisoners awaiting execution held in specially strong condemned cells, prisoners were kept under lock and key, herded together and usually in irons. There is little sign that any attempt was made until the 1770s to separate male and female, juveniles and old lags, sick and healthy, or those awaiting trial from those serving sentences. Paul remarked, 'Confinement is, at best, a Degree of Punishment' (Paul 1784, 11), hence the large numbers of vagrancy offenders confined for a very short time.

Gaols were not meant to hold felons long term, although they sometimes did. Until the last quarter of the century imprisonment in gaols was not much used as a sentence: punishments ranged from fines to whipping, branding, and the pillory, transportation and hanging. Imprisonment did not include hard labour, although debtors might work at their own trade where practicable. The original purpose of bridewells on the other hand, 'prisons for the poor' in Joanna Innes's felicitous phrase, *was* hard labour – to 'correct' the disorderly poor by work, by force if necessary. The keepers were meant to find work for the prisoners and keep them hard at it. Bridewell keepers were appointed by the county justices and paid a salary, although they might also receive fees, and the justices, at least nominally, supervised the management. The authority of the keeper to iron prisoners and whip them given in 1609 continued in law well into the nineteenth century, although late in the eighteenth century the visiting justices in many cases limited this *carte blanche*, preferring restricted diet and segregation as punishments, and whipping to be used only with their approval.

As vagrancy law developed to encompass a mixed bag of minor delinquents the houses of correction became more prison than workhouse, and it has been doubted whether much hard labour was done in many of them (Cockburn 1963–66, 495). Returns to parliament in 1776 revealed that out of 113 bridewells hard labour was done in only fifty-five.[18] In 1773 Hampshire ordered bridewell prisoners to have the same bread allowance as gaol prisoners, 'there being no work to be found for them to do'.[19] Certainly some of the smaller bridewells, such as those in Appleby and Kendal, held so few inmates and had so little space they can never have been anything but lock-ups. Enthusiasm for both bridewells and workhouses waxed and waned over the centuries, with the emphasis shifting from punishment to deterrence to economic productivity and back.

Unfortunately they never succeeded in turning the idle and vagrant poor into model workers except in the short term in a few places, partly because there plainly was not enough work available producing anything marketable for those with no particular skills: 'it simply was not possible to provide profitable work for workers whose skills were the very ones not required by commercial employers' (Kumar 1988, 144). Yet even experienced magistrates such as Richard Burn still clung to the belief that it was possible to set up 'some easy manufacture if there shall chance to be none', which, he optimistically declared, though it had failed in Elizabethan times, might work now (Burn 1764, 215). Although, once the bridewells became more frankly prisons for petty offenders with the emphasis on punishment, hard labour was still intended to form part of that punishment,

18 1776 Report on houses of correction.

19 HRO Q/1/18 April 1773.

the very short time most vagrants were in bridewell and the fact that so many were women with children, the old and the sick, meant that they could seldom earn their keep.

Sir George Onesiphorus Paul protested, 'it is inconsistent with the Humanity and wide Discrimination of the Spirit of our Laws, that the *Unfortunate* should share a Common Fate with the *Infamous*, or that the barely *Accused*, without Distinction, be classed with the *convicted* Prisoner' (Paul 1784, 5). The concept of remand prisoners did not exist at the time, and prisoners awaiting sessions were treated exactly the same as those serving sentences of imprisonment, so that anyone who had spent ten weeks or so awaiting trial had effectively already served a sentence. Naturally this was only the case for vagrants and paupers who had not the means or contacts to obtain sureties for their future appearance. Warrants for committing those charged as rogues and vagabonds usually commit them 'to hard labour' even though they were referred to sessions for further action. Reforms requiring the classification of prisoners began to be implemented late in the century so that men and women, felons and minor offenders or prisoners awaiting trial were kept separately.

Apart from these limited reforms there is no evidence whether, or in what way, prisoners awaiting trial or further examination, or even simply held for want of sureties or as witnesses, were differentiated from those who had been sentenced to a period of imprisonment. Very probably the only difference was that they were not kept to hard labour. In such circumstances it seems reasonable to suppose that *any* period in the house of correction was an unpleasant experience and might well have been seen as sufficient punishment; conditions might be such that a few weeks in bridewell could turn out to be a capital sentence (Eccles 2010 (1) 30).

Poor prisoners in both gaol and bridewell were allowed water and a daily bread ration at county expense, usually about a pound weight, but officially nothing else unless they earned it, or could pay for it themselves. Hugh Willcocks and Robert Harding, committed to Sherborne Bridewell for vagrancy in May 1747 and sentenced to twelve months as incorrigible rogues, petitioned the bench in October for release under a recent act of indemnity (possibly 18 Geo. II c. 28 for smugglers) because since their committal 'their state of health is greatly impaired'.[20] Willcocks had then been on the county bread list 144 days and Harding 133. Keepers sometimes gave prisoners vegetable soup from the prison garden, and some prisons received charitable donations of 'broken victuals'. George Hoskins's petition for release from Dorchester Gaol in 1757 acknowledged the kindness of the gaoler: 'I your poor petisnor ho have abeen

---

[20] DRO Michaelmas 1747.

Confind hear for twelve Month and nothing to supsest on but one penny Lofe aday but the Charity of Mr Chaffey Good Fammeily outher wise I must abeen misable'.[21]

In 1753 Middlesex enquired into the fees received by William Pentlow, keeper of New Prison, because he had no allowance for poor prisoners such as the keepers of Newgate and the City Bridewell had, and was frequently obliged to subsist them himself to prevent their perishing for want. The upshot was that the bench made an allowance for subsisting poor prisoners in all three Middlesex prisons.[22] On the other hand prisoners in Bury St Edmunds House of Correction in 1588 were fed two meals per day, each consisting of 8oz rye bread, a pint of porridge (probably a stew of cereals or root vegetables), a pint of beer, and either 4oz meat, a herring, or a third of a pound of cheese (Sharpe 1997, 49). Such a diet would have met with the approval of Howard, except for the meat, which he did not think prisoners should have. Even in 1784 he found some bridewells had no bread allowance (Howard 1784, 4). It is difficult to know what the prisoners ate in most bridewells until the end of the eighteenth century, when the justices took an interest in the diet as part of their supervisory role. Beattie noted that little is known in detail about the gaols and houses of correction in the eighteenth century, in particular what proportion of prisoners had only the county bread (Beattie 1986, 288, 301).

It seems conditions in most prisons before the 1774 Health of Prisoners Act were squalid and filthy, although vagrants were often already in a desperate condition on commitment. The master of Appleby house of correction was paid 7s 6d for cleaning and clothing John Hopkinson, a vagrant committed September 1769, 'who is at Present in a most sad Condition and a great Object of Charity'.[23] Gaols might be even worse: when Edward Farguson, convicted at Appleby Assizes in 1767, arrived at Whitehaven to be transported, Joseph Deane petitioned for £1 13s 2d spent clothing him. The ship's captain added a note to his receipt for the £6 passage money, saying otherwise 'I woud not have taken him for three times the sum, he was such a sight naked and run over with lice and further if Mr Deane had not clothed him from top to Towe not one Sailour woud have gone with the Ship and he might have stayed'.[24]

Keepers often reported problems finding suitable work. Beating hemp and picking oakum were the most common forms of hard labour, both of which met the punitive and practical requirements that the work should be disagreeable drudgery but need no particular skill, and both met genuine needs for the navy

21 DRO Epiphany 1757.

22 LMA MJ/O/C/005 6 September 1753.

23 WRO WQSR 347/22, 350/31.

24 WRO WQSR 342/15–17.

but produced little income. The hemp was used for ropes and the oakum was tarred rope recycled and used for caulking, after soaking and pulling it apart into strands. At times even hemp and oakum were hard to come by, leading Surrey justices in 1784 to substitute the pointless shifting of large piles of sand and gravel (Beattie 1986, 604–5).

In the last quarter of the century imprisonment to hard labour was introduced in county gaols for felons, in the search for alternatives to hanging and transportation. More imaginative work schemes were tried and taskmasters who practised some trade were appointed. Dorset prison produced hats (a consignment of these hats was bought by Middlesex for the prison uniform), installed a corn mill, and baked its own bread instead of buying the bread on contract from outside. But even there in the 1790s most of the male prisoners worked either shifting soil or 'at the engine', probably some sort of capstan or treadmill, although shoemakers might be set to their own trade making inmates' shoes and clogs. Most of the women did no work at all, although a few did domestic work, sewed linings for the hats, or made shifts and shirts.

Prisoner labour was used in many prisons for cleaning and rubbish clearance and sometimes cultivating the prison garden while female prisoners made shirts and did the prison laundry. Prisoners were often given extra food as an incentive, or a small sum of money for work such as whitewashing the prison, or for acting as nurses to the sick. The keeper of Clerkenwell Bridewell listed in his sundries bill six weeks' extra subsistence for three poor convicts who had whitewashed the prison, and an extra 10s 6d to Joseph Spencer 'as a reward for his industry he being by Trade a plasterer and the Principal Hand in the above work'.[25] The eighteenth century expected the work to be useful or productive if at all possible.

Most bridewells had a 'dark hole' where refractory inmates could be shut up for a while. In Clerkenwell Bridewell in 1757 there were twelve blocks and beaters for beating hemp, and new irons for the posts were ordered 'to hold the hands of those that won't work'.[26] Hogarth's engraving of the harlot in bridewell shows a man with his hands in stocks bearing the inscription, 'Better to work than Stand thus'.[27] Until the later eighteenth century prisons were little fiefdoms run by the gaoler or keeper as he saw fit, with virtually no interference from the justices, and lacking reports it is hard to establish exactly what went on in them. Keepers' bills include fetters, 'a collar to go round a man's body', and other such ironmongery, but in bridewells irons may have been used only for refractory prisoners and those thought likely to escape. When the justices began

[25] LMA MJ/SP/1779/09/073.

[26] LMA MJ/O/C/007 January 1760.

[27] See Plate 8.

to supervise the bridewells the rules either do not mention whipping as a form of punishment or permit it only with the approval of a visiting justice (Paul 1790, 37), and the governor was allowed to put a prisoner in the dark hole or on a bread-and-water diet for only a short period, an action that had to be reported in a book kept for the visiting justices to inspect.

In the City Bridewell however the keeper was permitted to punish prisoners of both sexes with up to thirty lashes with the cat at his discretion as late as 1817, although he claimed no more than fifteen or sixteen prisoners of either sex, out of two thousand passing through the prison, had been so punished in that year. Whipping was abolished altogether for women in 1818 (Henderson 1999, 136), a step anticipated in vagrancy law in 1792.

Impressment

Impressment, although permitted for vagrants with no settlement, and for incorrigible rogues, was of questionable legality when used in other vagrancy cases, although it sometimes was, especially in wartime. Recruiting officers might even be in court ready to take away suitable men.

Naturally impressment could not be used for women or manifestly physically unsuitable men, which limited its usefulness. It is likely that many cases never appeared in court, and that magistrates simply tipped off a press gang or a recruiting party in the neighbourhood. Periodically the admiralty issued directives to Lords Lieutenant to take up straggling seamen and send them on board a man of war, and magistrates might use the opportunity to send local undesirables away. It could backfire, however: Dorset was left with a bill for £1 14s 6d when Mathew Powell, 'a man thought fit to serve his majesty', was taken to Weymouth under guard but refused by the receiving officer.[28]

The magistrates would impose heavy sentences of whipping and/or imprisonment and propose enlistment as an alternative; it was hence 'voluntary' and invariably accepted. In Cambridge three men apprehended in 1776 were each given the harsh sentence of three months' imprisonment and three public whippings unless they joined the navy. One was 'not giving a good account of himself', the other two were beggars. Derk Credelo indeed was a pretty successful beggar, and had two large bags of halfpence on him when he was arrested. He was a Dutchman and the magistrates were prepared to send him back to Holland via the nearest seaport after the third whipping unless he enlisted, although it is not

[28] DRO Michaelmas 1755.

certain that he did.[29] The other two however were received by an officer of the 60th Foot a few days later (Conway 1985, 47). The severity of these sentences may have had more to do with a contemporary drive to apprehend straggling seamen and recruit than with their actual offences; they were not the only men to be made 'an offer they couldn't refuse' of this kind, but they were the only ones charged merely with begging to receive such a sentence in Cambridgeshire.

Robert Towell indeed volunteered in desperation after serving part of such a sentence. An incorrigible rogue, Towell was sentenced at Michaelmas 1744 to two years' hard labour in Sherborne Bridewell 'and to be Publickly Whipp'd in the Town of Dorchester on Satturday the thirteenth Instant and afterwards to be Whipp'd in the Town of Sherborne once every Month on the Market Day there during the Said term of Two Years.' At the Easter sessions 1745 he petitioned the court either to suspend his sentence or to allow him to enter the navy, pleading that he was now in a bad state of health due to his imprisonment and inability to earn his keep and the severe whippings. He was duly discharged to enter the navy.[30]

29 CA Q/SO/7 2 February 1776.

30 DRO Michaelmas 1744, Easter 1745.

Chapter 8
Offences within the 1744 Vagrant Act

This chapter presents evidence for those offences most often dealt with under vagrancy law and specifically included within its tripartite division, with some indication of their relative incidence and the punishments most usually imposed, bearing in mind the difficulties of quantification and the limitations of the sources already described. These must be regarded as the offences parliament saw as crimes and sought to control by means of the act, but not necessarily those that most concerned the justices, still less the people, in a particular locality.

The idle and disorderly

Poor people appeared at sessions more often for offences clearly specified in the 1744 act than for the offences we have already discussed that could be prosecuted under vagrancy law but were not actually part of it. It was mainly the settled poor who were prosecuted as 'idle and disorderly', although bracketed with 'wandering and begging' it sometimes formed part of the multiple charges so common in vagrancy offences. In the case of the settled poor the complaint of the overseers usually sufficed, in the case of strangers the statement of the constable. Those who appeared in court, and perhaps neighbours or an aggrieved wife, were probably questioned there, leaving no record; verbal statements or demeanour in court could explain some of the apparent inconsistency in sentencing. Written informations occasionally survive, and in most cases of neglecting or refusing to maintain dependants the wife or whoever was left to cope with the children was the original complainant, although the parish prosecuted.

Since magistrates had a range of options such as master and servant law as well as vagrancy law for dealing with troublesome poor, in many cases, probably most, the matter never came to court. Under the 1744 act a single magistrate could commit a person as idle and disorderly for up to one month, yet the settled poor also appeared at sessions charged as idle and disorderly, and presumably the examining magistrate, perhaps under parish pressure, was not satisfied that one month would be an adequate punishment, although there is rarely any indication why. Some were persistent offenders, others were lacking in proper deference. The act did not include whipping in the punishments available to the single justice for the idle and disorderly, although it did for rogues and vagabonds. No cases of begging in the parish of settlement came to court, and either these people were tolerated or dealt with out of court, or few settled poor begged in their own parish; but the fact that there is no record of the prosecution of particular offences is not proof that the offences were never committed. On the other hand, certain offences appear to have been included in the 1744 act less because they were still a cause of concern than because they were a hangover from previous vagrancy legislation; thus there were no fencers, bearwards or end gatherers.

There were very few cases of persons refusing to work, except where such refusal left a family chargeable; these were quite common and dealt with as desertion and will be discussed below as such. But Hannah Cousins was sentenced to be whipped and imprisoned for one month for refusing to work or go to service, and thereby chargeable to Papworth Everard,[1] and Priscilla Mullens was committed charged by Hampreston with refusing to work for usual and common wages, although the parish sent nobody to prosecute.[2] Persons threatening to leave dependants chargeable were also included in this clause as idle and disorderly and in Lancashire Ann Bell widow was committed 'having carried her two Children to the Dwelling-house of Alexander Leigh, the overseer, and left them there, declaring she would keep them no longer, and threatening to knock their Brains out if they followed her, and want of sureties', but discharged at the sessions.[3]

In the case of the settled poor, parish opinion was crucial: demanding sureties that could not be found was a simple way of keeping an undesirable parishioner in bridewell indefinitely 'for want of sureties', and might function as a quasi-sentence. These quasi-sentences might be a good deal longer than the maximum of two years (for incorrigible rogues) under vagrancy law. Vagrancy law did however tacitly allow open-ended imprisonment for poor with no discoverable settlement or for those not able to provide for themselves, mainly lunatics. Francis Tollerfield of Hillfield was originally committed for theft, and sentenced to one year in prison and to pay a fine of £5; at the end of his time a spokesman for the parish wrote to John Hutchings Esq. asking him to vote to keep Tollerfield in bridewell because he was 'an old and great Offender', and the principal parishioners, fearing someone would try to have him released, would rather pay for his maintenance there than have him come home. The court ordered the parish to pay 1s 6d weekly but obliged, and Tollerfield was still in

1 CA Q/SO/9 July 1787.

2 DRO Epiphany 1790 calendar.

3 LRO QSP 1908/12.

prison when he died three years later. Possibly he had never paid the fine and this served as grounds for his detention.[4]

On the other hand, the parish might be equally vital in obtaining a prisoner's release. J. Callard of Ford parish wrote to Robert Ring the bridewell keeper in December 1753,

> I have show'd your Letter to the Gentlemen of the parish and talked with them about poor Deane and they are willing to give him his liberty provided he will come home and take care of his Wife and Family. They won't prosecute him at the next sessions so I suppose Mr Hutchings (who committed him) will discharge him if you'l shew him this letter.[5]

The bridewell keeper had probably written to Callard because of worries about Deane's health – certainly this concern seems to have led to the release of John Berd, who was committed in April 1761 for refusal to maintain his family and continued for want of sureties to January 1762. John Hutchings Esq. wrote to the justices just before the sessions,

> I was this Morning to see the condition of one John Berd of Wareham now in Sherborne bridewell committed by the Mayor on 14 April last, he appears to be very weak and Lame and not able to go or ride to Blandford unless in some carriage which the Master of the bridewell hath inconveniency of getting, there being no carriage that goes from here to Blandford. If he is not discharged I believe the County will be at the Expense of burying him, he being not likely to survive the winter.[6]

In this case it seems probable the justices overrode any objection by the parish, which may not even have been consulted, since there is no further record of John Berd. The parish sprang to the defence of Robert Hames when he was accused of fathering a bastard in 1766. A letter signed by the parish officers and fourteen parishioners stated that he 'was never known to be Guilty in all his Youthful Days of any such Crime as keeping any Woman Company. He have been a very Sober Careful Man and hath bred up a large Family'; his accuser was 'a Common Whore that have had Four Bastards born to life and three Miscarriages we do think her Oath not fit to be taken in a Court of Justice'.[7]

---

4 DRO QSM/3; Easter and Midsummer 1757, Midsummer 1760.

5 DRO Epiphany 1754.

6 DRO Epiphany 1762.

7 DRO Midsummer 1766.

In a bizarre case in 1754 the parish of Martock Somerset defended William Prior, charged with travelling in disguise in Child Okeford (about forty miles away in Dorset) wearing women's clothes and therefore suspected of diverse misdemeanours. Nine parishioners signed a statement, almost certainly in reply to an enquiry by Dorset justices, that he had worn women's clothes for several years in his own parish not out of any ill intent but out of poverty.[8] He may have been a beggar, a harmless eccentric or a transvestite, but he could have been whipped as an impostor under vagrancy law or even charged with capital felony under the Waltham Black Act (9 Geo. I c. 22 1723).[9] Such letters were rarely kept, but no doubt similar activity behind the scenes took place in other counties.

Illegally returning

Illegally returning after removal was another offence included in s.1 of the 1744 act, interpreted in practice to mean removal either under settlement law or after passing as a vagrant. Although this offence was classified under idle and disorderly, repeat offenders were treated as rogues and vagabonds, or even incorrigible rogues. This clause was more often used against women than men, probably reflecting their restricted earning opportunities and their likely dependence on connections, perhaps cohabitation with a man, in the 'adopted' parish. Women and young boys were also more likely to return repeatedly.

One of the limitations of vagrant examinations is that they rarely reveal the reasons for return, sometimes persistently. A Middlesex committee report in 1774 cited several cases where illegally returning was due to abuses in the passing system and the failure of parishes to receive those passed.[10] The unfortunate Ann Waterlow and her child were a case in point: removed three times from Alverstoke to Shoreditch, they were turned out of the workhouse and refused relief each time. She was alleged to lurk up and down and lodge in outhouses, but if both parishes denied her settlement and relief she had little alternative.[11] How many such victims of settlement disputes were charged with illegally returning is impossible to tell. Middlesex examinations in these cases regularly note that the parish to which they had been previously passed had not appealed,

8 DRO Midsummer 1754.

9 See Hitchcock (2001, 168) for a case in 1708 of a man begging dressed in women's clothes and pretending to be lame; and Hitchcock (2004, 112) for Isaac Fairbrother charged in 1742 'pretending to be an old woman and begging'.

10 LMA MJ/SP/1774/10/125.

11 HRO Q9/2/6/15, /31.

and this seems to have been taken as implicit acceptance of the settlement, but the examinations do not indicate what action was taken; most likely they were passed back, especially after the receiving parish lost the right to appeal in 1777.

In Cambridgeshire ten women were charged with illegally returning, but only one man, and a couple with their daughter. Cambridgeshire sentencing policy was noticeably tougher than in other counties. Martha Daff was whipped in 1758 but was back again in 1765 and sentenced to six months as an incorrigible rogue for returning 'several times'.[12] Mary Edgly was whipped for returning to Cambridge from Royston after being passed by the mayor, who noted 'shee toor her pas at Royston and threwett a way thayr'.[13] At least four of the Cambridgeshire women charged were 'lewd', probably prostitutes making a living in the university area; six were whipped, some more than once or imprisoned as well; and only three discharged or passed.

In Hampshire and Lancashire the same gender pattern appears: in Lancashire eight women to four men, in Hampshire fourteen women, a boy aged fourteen, and only four men. In Lancashire none of the twelve people charged was whipped, but nine were imprisoned for short periods. In Hampshire all were discharged or passed back; the boy, who returned illegally at least four times, was passed back every time and apparently never punished. In Middlesex William Lowers was whipped once and imprisoned twice for returning and came back at least eight times, but the poor man was 'little better than an Ideot'.[14]

Rogues and vagabonds

All other crimes under the 1744 act came under s. 2, rogues and vagabonds, or s. 4, incorrigible rogues. The most common charge of all was wandering and begging. Rogues and vagabonds were 'required' to be either publicly whipped or imprisoned until the next sessions, or for some shorter period as the justice saw fit. If sessions then thought it appropriate they could order stiffer penalties than the single justice. We have already noted that whipping was used less and less, and that very few of those who were simply wandering and begging were punished after the early decades of the century. Those charged under other heads – for example, those deserting their dependants, illegal entertainers, cheats and impostors – were more likely to be committed and dealt with by the courts, and might be subject to these stiffer penalties.

---

12 CA Q/SO/6 October 1759, July 1765

13 CA Epiphany 1759 calendar, Q/SO/6 January 1759.

14 LMA MJ/SP/1792/07/020–21.

Desertion

By far the greatest number of settled poor charged as rogues and vagabonds were charged with deserting, refusing or failing to maintain families; clearly passing was not applicable in these cases, which were invariably brought by the parish officers. Very few people who had deserted their families were apprehended elsewhere, and in such cases the individual was passed back to the settlement, which then prosecuted. But threats of prosecution might have been used effectively by parish officers and magistrates to head off incipient desertion; on the other hand, too severe and inflexible an approach might keep a man on the run once he had deserted. Some men vanished while the family was travelling, and their wives then appear wandering and begging. Parishes did pursue deserters, generally by means of newspaper advertisements, but not always (Ashby 1912, 95; P. King 1984, 41; Hollen-Lees 1998, 71). If a man enlisted, went to sea, or somehow got far enough away, the parish usually failed to force him to honour his obligations. Desertion might alternatively be dealt with by obliging the offender to give security for the future support of his dependants and find sureties to guarantee he did so. Lancashire seems to have relied heavily on demanding sureties, and relatively few were detained for want of them. If a family was resident but not settled, the desertion or enlistment of the husband was often followed by the prompt removal of the family, suggesting the parish officers had no great hope the deserter would return.

Where men of some means actually absconded, which they rarely did having property and connections that acted as a brake, the justices issued a distraint order and vested the property not in the wife but in the parish officers to administer on her behalf; this was the procedure even when the property was originally hers, since she was still *femme couverte*. This process could be unsatisfactory, and we find a few of these women in the ranks of the destitute. Wealthier men did desert, however: for example, a surgeon in Westmorland and a tinsmith owning property worth £100 in Sussex, whose wife was apprehended as a vagrant in Middlesex.[15] In Cambridgeshire very few absconders had any goods: only six cases were dealt with by these methods including a schoolmaster who had run away leaving a bastard chargeable, although the inventory of his goods suggests he was by no means on the breadline. Francis Carter of Swaffham Prior owed the parish 13s 6d for his family's maintenance, 'he being then run away and left his said Wife and Children chargeable', but presumably back again; the court ordered his goods to be sold unless he paid up.[16] Similarly in 1762 Soham

15 LMA WJ/SP/V/01/007/16.

16 CA Q/SO/5 July 1741.

obtained a warrant against John Hawlett, a Soham farmer, for £3 3s 6d spent on his wife when he turned her out of doors and refused to maintain her. Richard Colley was ordered to enter into a bond to pay 2s weekly to his wife and child until the child reached five years old; he had gone into service with a gentleman and not allowed his wife any maintenance.[17]

Cambridgeshire clearly had a particular problem with men deserting, refusing or neglecting to maintain their wives and/or families, especially in the last quarter of the eighteenth century. Of the 387 men dealt with at Quarter Sessions as vagrants, 122 were charged with failing to maintain their families or running away leaving them chargeable (34 per cent), and the prevalence of the offence may explain why the justices were especially hard on them. Half the Cambridgeshire men who deserted their dependants (63) were whipped by order of the court. Of these, one was whipped on two occasions for separate offences and eight were sentenced to a period in the house of correction in addition. Fourteen were sentenced to be whipped twice plus a period varying from two weeks to three months in the house of correction, three to be whipped three times with imprisonment, and William Kidd four times with six months' hard labour.[18] This last sentence was the most severe handed down in Cambridgeshire for simple desertion. In only four cases were fewer than twelve lashes specified, the lightest sentence being six lashes. But even in Cambridgeshire 30 per cent of these men were discharged without further action, ten because they promised to mend their ways, two because the parish did not pursue the prosecution, the others for unrecorded reasons.

In Dorset on the other hand although much the same proportion (32 per cent) of men charged at Quarter Sessions as vagrants were charged with desertion, only four were whipped, at least two of whom were repeat offenders. Men charged with desertion were often committed and discharged at the next sessions without further action in Dorset because the officers did not appear to prosecute; the spell in bridewell before sentence seems to have been regarded as punishment enough, or at least as an effective shot across the bows. Nobody was whipped in Lancashire for desertion, not even the 'very idle, drunken, wicked and disorderly' Edward Bury, who was merely discharged.[19] The offence was common, however: at least ninety-one people were charged with failing to maintain dependents, some as idle and disorderly, others committed for want of sureties, and a small minority sentenced to short terms of imprisonment.

---

17 CA Q/SO/6 May 1764.

18 CA Q/SO/8 July 1785.

19 LRO QSP 1921/2.

Very few women were charged with desertion in any county, and only one of the five committed in Cambridgeshire was whipped; but unsupported mothers were likely to get parish help. Ann Whitbread refused to work to maintain herself and her family and misbehaved when she was before the magistrate, but she was nevertheless discharged after two months in the house of correction awaiting sessions;[20] Mary Wilson on the other hand was whipped at Haslingfield in 1757 for deserting a female child there.[21] In Dorset thirteen women were charged with desertion but only one was whipped, in 1748, although she herself had been abandoned in Horton some six months previously, pregnant and with two small children, one of whom had since died.[22] Later in the century a noticeable reluctance to sentence women to whipping for any vagrancy offence gradually becomes apparent, long before it was forbidden by the 1792 Vagrancy Act.

In 1777 James Bye, who had been committed five weeks previously for deserting his wife, 'very forward with Child of which she has since been delivered and are both now Chargeable', offered to go for a soldier. The parish officers consented and the court ordered 'that the said James Bye be immediately discharged on in Listing which he immediately did in open Court and went away with the recruiting Serjeant'.[23] The case was unusual, although not unique, because he was charged with desertion; in all counties male vagrants charged with other vagrancy offences could be and were sent into the army or navy. Why the parish officers agreed to his enlisting, and therefore committed themselves to the continued support of the wife and baby, is not clear. This was perhaps a case of a forced pauper marriage to deal with incipient bastardy and the parish had no hope of James Bye ever fulfilling his obligations, or he might have been such a bad lot the parish wanted rid of him even at a price (Radzinowicz 1948–68 vol. 1, 24). Practically the only respectable reason a man could have for leaving his family was to join the army or go to sea (D.A. Kent 1990).

It might not have helped the ratepayers since soldiers were paid so little that their families almost always ended up on the poor books, and although militiamen's families could legally claim maintenance from the county in whose militia the men served, there was no such provision for regular soldiers (Western 1965, 269–70). Possibly the parish was paid the bounty for his enlistment; under the Press Act of 1779 (19 Geo. III c. 10) a parish was paid a 40s bounty for any fit man convicted of deserting his family who enlisted instead of punishment as an incorrigible rogue, and the practice may have been longstanding. The money

[20] CA Q/SO/9 July 1789.

[21] CA Q/SO/5 April 1757.

[22] DRO Epiphany 1748.

[23] CA Q/SO/8 April 1777.

then partly compensated the parish for the inevitable expense of supporting the pressed man's family, and may well have improved the recruitment rate.

Anyway James Bye would not have come back, if he ever did, years later to face a charge of desertion. Parishes could have an elephantine memory: for example, Thomas Barfoot came back to Swaffham Bulbeck in 1782 and was promptly committed for desertion 'for these ten years past'. The court sentenced him to six weeks' imprisonment in the house of correction, and then to be publicly whipped at Swaffham Bulbeck.[24] Parishes could also respond very promptly; the overseer of Evershott reported that Thomas Bartlett had absconded the previous day, as he discovered when Bartlett's wife sent one of the children round to his house for relief. He gave her a shilling and immediately applied for a warrant.[25] Bartlett was discharged for want of prosecution at the sessions however, perhaps because the fifteen miles to the sessions and back would have taken the overseer at least a whole day, possibly more.

It is noteworthy that in Cambridgeshire almost all the more severe sentences were handed down in the decade 1780–90, when over a third of all the cases 1740–99 were heard. It was a period of severe economic distress, especially in the southern counties, with galloping increases in bread prices. These prosecutions probably reflect the uphill struggle of labouring men to support their families rather than any great upsurge in marital discord. The occupations of the men are not given in the calendars and order books from which most of the cases are taken, but probably they were mainly agricultural labourers.

By the spring of 1795 the Cambridgeshire justices had become sufficiently aware of the problem of poverty among agricultural labourers to order Speenhamland-style supplements of 3d per head weekly for poor persons in husbandry, and to consider a rise in wages for the labouring poor expedient, in line with measures taken in other counties.[26] At the next sessions they were resolving to make economies in the use of fine flour in magistrates' own families, to discourage millers and bakers from grinding or baking fine flours, and to take steps against illegal exporting, forestalling, and paying above the market price for grain. They further resolved to encourage charitable subscriptions for the labouring poor to provide meat or other food instead of flour.[27] Conceivably the slacking off in prosecutions and severe sentences after 1790 reflects a growing awareness among the justices that the desertion cases they had been attempting to stem by repressive sentences could not be countered by such an approach.

24 CA Q/SO/8 July 1782.

25 DRO Easter 1790.

26 CA Q/SO/9 April 1795.

27 CA Q/SO/9 July 1795

In Middlesex, on the contrary, very few men were charged with desertion, although a large number of women had been deserted, some so recently it must have happened in Middlesex. The uninformative nature of the calendars may conceal many cases, but deserters were more likely to escape arrest in a large conurbation because they could lose themselves relatively rapidly without going far afield. The law caught up with Edward Dacon in 1768 however. He was an Irishman with a wife and two children born in England and had lived in England twenty-seven years but never acquired a settlement. Now living in Harrow, he was charged with desertion by the overseers, and admitted he had indeed run away and had since been wandering about the country lodging in barns or outhouses, sometimes in employment and at other times begging. He was committed and passed; legally the wife and children had to be passed with him, but their future seems precarious.[28] Robert Wedderburn deserted his wife in May 1794 and was brought up for trial in October 1795, though whether he came back voluntarily or was taken up elsewhere is uncertain.[29] Simon Robinson on the other hand had only been gone three days when he was taken up.[30]

There is little evidence that Middlesex deserters were treated with the harshness so evident in Cambridgeshire, although Mary Williams was certainly taken from Clerkenwell Bridewell to be whipped at Kingsbury for desertion in 1761, and then referred to the local magistrate to decide whether she should be released or sent back to bridewell,[31] and Joseph Chatterton was sentenced to two years' hard labour for deserting two children and refusing to state his settlement.[32]

Those deserters who had means, as in other counties, were subject to distraint orders, but few such orders occur. Jesse Eyles, a collar maker, was twice the subject of distraint orders for deserting his wife and three children, in 1765 and again in 1769, when an order was made for payment of £18 3s 6d.[33] Other deserters were committed at the behest of parish officers, either as a punishment, or to exert pressure; the overseers of St Giles petitioned the court to keep Alexander Fenton in bridewell until he promised to compensate the parish for leaving his pregnant wife and two children chargeable.[34]

28 LMA MJ/SP/1768/09/053.
29 LMA MJ/SP/1795/10/034.
30 LMA MJ/SP/1793/12/039.
31 LMA MJ/SP/1761/06/002.
32 LMA MJ/SB/B/0106 1749.
33 LMA MJ/SP/1765/10/08, MJ/SP/1769/09/091.
34 LMA MJ/SP/1778/06/061.

Lying out in alehouses, barns, outhouses or in the open air

This group includes many of the most destitute and desperate vagrants who, along with the families of soldiers and seamen, even the authorities in the eighteenth century acknowledged were 'genuine objects', and who were rarely punished but might well be committed as the best way to access food, shelter and medical help. But others, especially gypsies, tended to live a long-term vagrant lifestyle, and it is with this minority that we are concerned here. The Elizabethan law against gypsies, not abolished until 1783, seems to have fallen into abeyance. Nobody was charged as a gypsy in Lancashire, Middlesex or Westmorland, but Cambridgeshire, Hampshire and Dorset all apprehended gypsies from time to time, who were charged with lying out, as did Kent (Rickard 1995). It seems quite possible that the Hearns and Boswells found in Cambridgeshire in the 1770s were part of the same extended clan also picked up in Dorset about the same time. Hearn, Boswell, Scamp, variously spelled, are characteristic gypsy names, as are Smith and Lee (Floate 1999, 76). Nineteen gypsies apprehended in Hampshire in 1742 were all called Lee and Boswell, and in July 1744 a group of Scamps and Stanleys were charged with lying out in barns and outhouses and continued until further order.[35] At least forty-five gypsies were committed in Hampshire.

Connections in these large groups are very difficult to disentangle as they defied convention and tended to include women cohabiting with men by whom they had numerous bastards. Ruditia Boswell and Lucretia Green had seven bastard children between them and both said the father was Francis Hearn, a tinker. Lucretia Green had previously been apprehended with Francis Hearn and privately whipped; she said she had had twelve children by him, all born in different places on the road, but only four now living.[36] Francis Hearn, 'one of the people called gypsies', was in court for beating two gypsy women in 1783 and under sentence of transportation in 1790. Any settlement gypsies had tended to be derivative by birth, since their lifestyle precluded the gaining of any subsequent settlement. They might claim to be tinkers, rat catchers, sieve bottomers, or suchlike itinerant trades, but were widely suspected of thieving fowls, crops, linen drying on hedges, and indeed anything they found lying about, although there was little hope of successful prosecution for theft.

Four gypsies travelling together, John Skempt and his wife Angelette, Kesiah Price, who seems to have been related to them by a previous marriage, and George Lovell, Angelette's twelve-year-old brother, were apprehended in Litton Cheney

---

35 HRO 10 July 1744 calendar.

36 CA Q/SO/7 October 1775.

in 1748 and charged with lying out in the open, Kesiah also with fortune telling. The adults all spent a year in bridewell,[37] but George was passed to Dulwich where his father was born. In 1764 a group of Stanleys apprehended in Wiltshire was passed through Shaftesbury to Fivepenny Okeford.[38] A group of Boswells, Skempts and Smiths charged as gypsies was held from one sessions to the next and then discharged in 1767,[39] and in 1777 a group of seven Hearns and Boswells was apprehended in Morden but discharged for want of prosecution. The following year Robert Boswell, one of this group, was sentenced to four months in bridewell for vagrancy; Kissy and Leonard Boswell were charged with theft from a dwelling house and continued in custody, but the case does not seem to have been heard at Quarter Sessions.[40]

Gypsies were undoubtedly a nuisance to the authorities and probably conformed to the vagrant stereotype more than most people prosecuted as vagrants, which may explain why the women in particular seem to have been whipped rather more readily than other females, but often there is no record to show what happened to them.

Gypsies like Kesiah Price were by no means the only ones charged with fortune telling. Jean Bald confessed to telling fortunes to finance a journey to London to claim wages due to her late husband, who had died in the naval hospital at Gibraltar some years previously.[41] Fortune tellers were not always women: William Fobzey was whipped twice for telling fortunes in 1754,[42] three men were charged with fortune telling in Hampshire at various times, and there were several male fortune tellers in Middlesex also.

Illegal entertainers

Minstrels and jugglers, and persons playing and betting at illegal games, specifically included as rogues and vagabonds, were represented chiefly by ballad singers and fiddlers, and by people entertaining crowds at fairs. Most of these activities, although illegal, formed part of the economy of makeshifts for many travelling poor. How likely they were to be apprehended cannot be known, but probably not very likely: at least, not many appeared at sessions.

---

37 DRO Midsummer 1748 and 1749.

38 DRO QDV box 4 bundle 5.

39 DRO Epiphany and Michaelmas 1767.

40 DRO Midsummer 1778.

41 DRO Easter 1755.

42 DRO Epiphany 1755.

Middlesex justices were much concerned with illegal games, which were prosecuted both under vagrancy law and as misdemeanours. In April 1783 two cases of illegal gambling with EO tables came up: one Porter was apprehended in December 1782 and sentenced to a fortnight's imprisonment, and Thomas Nelson according to his defence brief was indicted for a nuisance on the same charge.[43] Neither of these was dealt with under the 1744 act, but Colquhoun listed gambling with EO tables as a vagrancy matter by the end of the century (Colquhoun 1806 (1), 41). Thomas Heming appealed against his conviction and a fine of 40s for knowingly permitting gaming for halfpence by two apprentices at a certain game called Justice Jarvis,[44] and there were more prosecutions for illegal games than in the provinces, although illegal games were not unknown there. Illegal entertainers included female ballad singers scraping a living by entertaining and probably unlucky to be apprehended. Tim Hitchcock included them among the poor subsisting by the economy of makeshifts (Hitchcock 2001).

Fielding in 1770 wanted ballad singers brought within vagrancy law, observing somewhat disingenuously, 'no Person being a Vagrant now but who comes within some One of the Descriptions of Vagrancy in the Vagrant Act', although Fielding himself no doubt had committed many and a high constable stated he had often had warrants for taking up ballad singers (House of Commons Journals' vol. 32, 880b). Probably there were some among the various disorderly poor listed in the Middlesex bridewell calendars, but further detail is lacking.

Ballad singers often sold copies of the ballads, which Fielding claimed were usually obscene, although his chief objection was that they gathered crowds and thus afforded opportunities for pickpockets. One of the common sights of London, they were not an urban phenomenon alone. Elizabeth Field, apprehended in Hampshire, said she had been travelling the country as a ballad seller for nine years, and admitted begging for beer.[45] Elizabeth Massey too had lived by ballad singing for some years; she had been lodging in an alehouse in Puddletown for some time, and said she had no licence. Her examination was filed, but there is no further record; she was the widow of a soldier of Queen Anne's wars and probably discharged by the examining magistrate.[46] On the other hand, two ballad singers, mother and daughter and both widows, taken up during a general search in the same county, were whipped and imprisoned for one month for singing ballads and begging in 1753, although the mother was married thirty-eight years previously and must have been nearly sixty.[47] If these

43 LMA MJ/SP/1783/04/048–9.

44 LMA MJ/SP/1791/04/106.

45 HRO Q9/2/2/3.

46 DRO Michaelmas 1745.

47 DRO Epiphany 1753.

three women were indeed treated differently, the reason is inexplicable from the surviving evidence.

Some parishes encouraged blind poor to learn the fiddle and beg with it, others bought a few small items and sent the poor out as hawkers (Ashby 1912, 152; S. King 2004) – in neither case does the parish seem to have bothered with a licence, although both unlicensed entertainers and hawkers risked apprehension as vagrants. In 1797 Edward Blaney was apprehended as a minstrel in Shadwell, convicted and sent to Clerkenwell Bridewell for the mandatory seven days, and then passed to Ireland.[48] Samuel Bennett begged at the door of Nathan Gundy labourer in Sherborne, and next day went into Bartholomew Webb's inn and played the fiddle there. The landlord said he was asked to leave but refused and abused the company by calling them blackguards and scoundrels. Bennett admitted playing the fiddle in the inn, and although the papers were filed by John Hutchings Esq. it is unclear whether he took any other action.[49]

Middlesex several times ordered action against illegal players of interludes. In 1744 their motives were explained; being informed

> that Several Common Players of Interludes have for several years used and accustomed to assemble and meet together at or near a certain place called ... Tottenham Court in the Parish of St Pancras ... and to erect Booths and Act and Exhibit Drolls and other Shows, and use and exercise unlawful Games and Plays whereby great Numbers of his Majesty's Subjects have been encouraged to assemble and meet together and to commit Riots and other Misdemeanors in breach of his Majesty's Peace, and to the disturbance of the Neighbourhood of that place, And that some of the Said Players of Interludes and other evil disposed Persons are now seeking out and contracting for Ground in or near the place aforesaid to build Booths for showing and Acting Such Plays and Drolls and other Shows and for carrying on and encouraging of divers kinds of unlawfull Play and Gaming And Whereas all Such Players of Interludes are deemed and declared Rogues and Vagabonds, and the acting of Such Plays Drolls and other Shows and the keeping of Publick Gaming Tables or Gaming houses are contrary to the Laws and Statutes of this Realm and do manifestly and directly tend to the encouragement of Vice and Immorality, and to the debauching and ruining of Servants Apprentices and others as well as to the disturbance of the Publick Peace by occasioning Quarrells Riots Tumults and other Disorders.

48 LMA MJ/SP/V/01/040/11.

49 DRO Midsummer 1753.

The justices of Holborn Division were therefore urged to issue warrants to apprehend all such and proceed against them according to law, and notices were to be posted up and printed in newspapers.[50] The same order was repeated periodically in respect of other fairs; a general privy search was ordered in September 1750 at the New Wells in Clerkenwell, where many illegal players of interludes were reported to be active, but playing of interludes seems to have been a problem peculiar to the metropolis.[51]

Unlicensed hawkers

Unlicensed hawkers able to pay could be fined under the 1698 Act (9 & 10 William III c. 17): James Mackdonald was fined £20 in 1797 for selling goods in Linton without licence, and Thomas Anderson £10 for the same offence in Soham in 1793. The licensing of hawkers was first instituted to raise money for William III's wars, and in the eighteenth century seems mainly to have been used to protect local market traders, who were probably unaffected by the sort of subsistence pedlar taken up as a vagrant. An order was published in the Salisbury and Sherborne papers in 1786 threatening unlicensed hawkers trading in the town with £10 fines, but few appeared in court; part of these fines went to the poor of the parish where the goods were sold, and parishes may have preferred this charge.[52]

Alternatively they could be convicted as rogues and vagabonds. Dulcibella Parker was merely passed when apprehended in Soham in 1757, as was William White in 1771, 'he having confessed, not being able to pay the forfeiture incurred thereby, being sorry for his offence and promising to leave town immediately'.[53] Andrew Gibbon was sixteen, his father and grandfather both dead, and had been in Kirklinton poor house for a week and then got some buttons and other trifles to sell and went travelling with them for about a year, but he had fallen lame and was now destitute. Such hawkers and itinerant traders often begged food and drink as well, and formed part of the 'economy of makeshifts'. Gibbon was the sort of pedlar who was left unmolested unless he offended the locals by disorderly behaviour or needed help because he could no longer manage.[54]

50 LMA MJ/OC/005 10 May 1744.

51 LMA MJ/SP/1750/09/04.

52 DRO Michaelmas 1786.

53 CA Q/SO/7 July 1771.

54 WRO WQSR 328/48–49.

False papers, false pretences, impostors

Middlesex in 1757 complained of swarms of beggars, some in real distress, others who by 'artfull Disguises of Wretchedness' lived idle,[55] and in 1805 the Bath Society for the Suppression of Vagrants estimated impostors as high as one fifth of beggars (Radzinowicz vol. 4, 45). Many individual examples were given in evidence to the committees on mendicity in 1815 and 1816. But despite these claims they are scarcely to be found in the records of those coming before Quarter Sessions in the eighteenth century, except for those using false documents. A few were charged as impostors, but no further detail given.

'Dummerers' occur occasionally, like Elinor Molineux. Two women laid an information against her stating that although she claimed to be deaf and dumb they had heard her speak 'in an articulate and audible voice'. They said she 'pretends to have skill in many crafty sciences and in fortune telling' and told their fortunes for 6d by writing in chalk on a board. She answered the questions put by the magistrate by writing, but she did not sign her examination. Both the informants however were illiterate, suggesting the wording of their informations had been supplied by the magistrate, and the court merely discharged Molineux, who had been in bridewell two months already.[56] James Read said he had been persuaded to appear deaf and dumb by William Mitchell, and they had been begging together for the past week; Mitchell was sentenced to one month's hard labour, but it is not clear what happened to Read.[57]

In 1755 Thomas Larking was whipped and sent to Liverpool to be put on board a man of war for pretending to be dumb and carrying a false pass.[58] Three dummerers appeared in Westmorland: two were whipped in the 1760s, one of whom later spoke but refused to tell his settlement, and Mary Robson was sentenced to twelve days in the house of correction and then passed in 1800. She too was apprehended claiming to be dumb and telling fortunes by writing, and wrote in her examination that she was settled in Leeds by birth.[59] Henry Fielding claimed, albeit second hand and not from his own experience as a magistrate, that bogus cripples were common:

> Nothing, as I have been well informed, is more common among these Wretches, than for the Lame, when provoked, to use their Crutches as Weapons instead of

55 LMA MJ/O/C/006 21 April 1757.
56 DRO Epiphany 1783.
57 DRO Midsummer 1742.
58 LRO QSO2/124.
59 WRO WQSR 564/10.

> Supporters; and for the Blind, if they should hear the Beadle at their Heels, to outrun the Dogs which guided them before (Fielding 1751, 35).

Although in the nineteenth century men pretending to be disabled seamen were said to be common among the impostors, only one such was found in these six counties.[60] Middlesex calendars often noted vagrants as sick or lame, but they seem to have been genuinely so; John Ward however was apprehended begging in Hackney with his arm wrapped up, claiming to be a disabled seaman. The constable examined his arm and found he was not lame; it is not clear what the magistrates did with him though, since he was an American and had never gained a settlement.[61]

Richard Collings was a more creative impostor, having spent some days at the Chequer alehouse in Gamlingay entertaining a crowd of young people with conjuring tricks and music. He was charged with

> fraudulently endeavouring to trepan several young Men, under pretence of having enlisted them into his Majesty's Service; and with demanding, and by threats and false Pretences obtaining, from the Constable of Gamlingay aforesaid, Billets for quartering himself and two others, whom he pretended he had enlisted, although he was not himself a soldier, nor had any legal Authority to enlist Men.

He was sentenced to six months' imprisonment and then to be whipped at Gamlingay, and the county repaid the three guineas the parish had spent on the prosecution.[62]

Cases of persons begging with false briefs claiming losses or falsely claiming to be soldiers or seamen are also fairly rare in most counties, with the notable exception of Dorset. There was no statute against forgery in general (Emsley 1996, 251), only statutes making the forgery of particular documents felony, mainly various financial instruments but including lottery office licences and hawker's licences. Middlesex prosecuted George Graham for felony for forging the signature of one of the justices on an order for reward for apprehending vagrants.[63] Fake passes and petitions however were more easily prosecuted under the vagrancy clause against giving false information, or pretending to be soldiers or seamen; these offences were invariably committed by wandering strangers. Some military passes were genuine documents but issued by magistrates imposed

60 1815 Mendicity report, 63; 1821 Report on vagrancy, 108–9.

61 LMA MJ/SP/1793/04/137.

62 CA Easter 1771 calendar.

63 LMA MJ/SP/1778/12/093.

upon by plausible tales (Burn 1755 vol. 2, 490) and hence undetectable; others were forged, some very obviously so.

In Dorset no fewer than fifty-one people were suspected of using false papers, far more even than in populous Middlesex. Dorset was bedevilled by men claiming to be seamen, some to be victims of shipwreck or fire. The illiteracy, begging tone, or romantic claims of some of these papers make them obvious forgeries, but others were much more plausible, and had sometimes been signed by several unsuspecting magistrates. Dorset constables and justices were clearly alert to the possibility of fakes, which may account for the high number of recorded cases there, and they did take pains to establish the facts despite the obvious communication problems of the period – the only trace of a discharged soldier called Robert Dyer is a certificate addressed to the bridewell keeper from the secretary's office, Dublin Castle, stating that Robert Dyer, formerly a soldier in General Wade's regiment, had a pass dated 19 January for himself and child to go to Medust Kent. Evidently Dyer had been taken up either because he had lost the pass or it was suspected to be false, and was released on receipt of this letter.[64]

The semi-literacy of some forged passes probably led to discovery. To give only one example, the constable of Blandford Forum apprehended John Baker in 1764 suspecting his pass to be false, and he was committed to Dorchester Gaol. The pass, stitched to the usual coarse grey paper cover, read,

> These are to Certify the Persons beriers [*sic*] hereof Thos Holland Jno Baker Seafaring Men Latley belonging to ye Rose Marchant Ship belonging to Liverpool in Lancertershire Outward bound to Jameca was Lost of ye Cape Saint Vincent in a Viliant Storme At Sea All hands perished Exepting six poor Soules Master & Mate was Saved and they poor Soules As had the Good Luck to be saved is Verry much bodely Wounded one in the thigh & otheres in their Leggs and Armes which is in a Verry Unhappy Condition. And I Jno Herring Master Proving this before one of his Majesty's Justices of the peace for the County of Dorset Doe therefor Recommend these poor Soules as Objects of Pitty To All Gentlemen or any Other Parsons Whatsover Bayleys Constables & other Officer whome it may Concerne Or Any other Gentlemen as will Concider these poor Soules Great Callamity and In So Doing they will Allways be In Duty bound to pray. Signed by Me One of his Majesty's Justices of ye Peace for ye County of Dorset J. Hanning.

Dorset justices checked with John Hanham Esq. of Corfe Mullen, who wrote stating that the signature on the pass was not his. In fact the signature on the pass is a fairly good imitation of Hanham's real signature, although evidently

64 DRO Easter 1747.

a mishearing of his name, and arguably the least telltale feature of this bizarre document, yet Baker was discharged by the court.[65]

Richard Burn experimented in one year by getting a sample of the handwriting of the mayor of Newcastle upon Tyne and comparing it with the passes of sailors said to be landed there that year 'and out of eleven passes of that kind which came into my hands, the mayor's own proper hand writing was but set to two, and the other nine were forged' (Burn 1755 vol. 2, 490). In other cases claims of having been captured by Barbary pirates and tortured by having their tongues cut out probably aroused suspicion. Barbary pirates had indeed been a scourge in the late seventeenth century (Anderson 1956), but hardly by 1752 when Charles Oneale and James Burch, among others, made the claim, which was surely easy to verify or refute.[66] They were both publicly whipped and imprisoned three months.

Genuine passes do not survive since the bearers, even if apprehended, were allowed to keep them and the passes were only usable for a specific journey. John Macdonald however was committed as a rogue and vagrant wandering and begging in Sherborne with a pass after the expiry date for his journey and 'wandering backward out of the way directed by the pass' – evidently a pass specifying the route and limiting the time, as they were supposed to do.[67] Maybe he had a good excuse as he was discharged at the sessions three days later.

One of the first cases involving a charge of carrying false documents was that of Timothy Downing, a seaman taken up in Sherborne in 1745 as a deserter from a man of war suspected of carrying a false pass. Examined in April he said he was Irish by birth, and that at the age of sixteen or seventeen he bound himself apprentice in London to the master of the *Biddlecombe*, a merchant ship trading to the West Indies. There the entire crew was pressed except for the master, the mate, the boatswain and seven apprentices including himself. The skeleton crew nevertheless took on their cargo of rum, sugar and cotton, and sailed for home, but about 150 leagues west of Cape Clare they were attacked and captured by a French privateer and taken to Bayonne. They were kept prisoners there about seven months, and then exchanged as part of a group of some 250 prisoners and landed at Falmouth.

Downing said his pass was given him by the mayor of Truro and he was going back to London. Two days after this examination was taken he appeared at Shaftesbury sessions and was probably continued awaiting further information. Many of those who actually were carrying false passes told very

65 DRO Epiphany 1765.

66 DRO Epiphany 1752.

67 DRO Midsummer 1762.

similar circumstantial stories, and without doubt tales of sea adventure were recounted in many a seaport alehouse and could be imitated without too much difficulty. But in June his master Richard Brown wrote from Falmouth that Timothy Downing had written to him about his plight, saying that his pass was 'insufficient', and confirmed his story that they had been landed from a French prison. Brown said Downing had been an honest lad, but for some unknown reason had stolen away with some of the other prisoners the day after they landed, but he had no idea where they were going. He had been told by other members of the crew that Downing had been given a pass by the mayor of Truro, but since the mayor was in London at the time Brown wrote he could not get a new pass for Downing but would send one from London on his arrival there. In July John Everett of Longbredy, clerk to the committing justice, wrote sending the informations of two men about the *Biddlecombe* crew and enclosing a copy of Downing's examination that he happened to have – he had given the original to his master, who had mislaid it. Presumably Downing was discharged on the strength of this supporting information since he did not appear in the following calendar.[68]

William Davis's story on the other hand was not confirmed. It was possible for persons who had suffered financial losses by fire, storm or shipwreck to petition Quarter Sessions and obtain a brief allowing them to ask charity, or to get back taxes paid on malt or salt. He was taken up 9 June 1766 lodging at an alehouse in Sherborne. John Hutchings Esq. wrote to the clerk of the peace in July explaining that on 7 June Davis had brought him a pass that he claimed had been given him by two Welsh justices certifying a loss of £600 by a ship being burned at sea, which he signed, not suspecting any fraud. However, later that day a fellow magistrate called on Hutchings and told him that Davis had been begging at his house the day before, so they began to smell a rat, and had him apprehended. Hutchings took Davis's examination, of which he enclosed a copy, and wrote to the overseer of Battle Sussex to check his story.

Davis claimed in his examination to be born and settled at Battle and brought up in the woollen manufactory. With his wife and two children and one Samuel Johnson of Battle he had gone to London in November 1765 and boarded a merchant ship, the *Brilliant*, to go to New England; they took with them all their goods, worth £600, of which Davis's share was worth £60. After they had been at sea about nine days the ship caught fire by the captain's servant drawing rum from a firkin, but they were rescued by the *Elizabeth*, a Liverpool merchant ship. They were on board this vessel nearly six months, but on 20 May 1766 they were in Swansea and the captain of the *Brilliant* obtained the pass from two

68 DRO Midsummer 1745.

local justices for Davis, his children and Johnson to go to Battle; they were in Yetminster on 6 June, where John Vincent Esq. gave them 3d relief but refused to sign the pass, saying they were not going on the right road. Johnson and the children had gone ahead on the road to Cerne, but Davis fetched them back and they slept at the Black Lion alehouse at Holnest on the Friday and came to Sherborne on the Saturday, when Mr Hutchings signed his pass. Davis admitted begging in Sherborne, and said the overseer had given him a shilling. He was apprehended the same night at the Boot alehouse, where he stayed because he had the rheumatism, while Johnson and the children went on towards Wimborne taking the pass. He added, probably in response to a question, that his wife died in the fire at sea.

All this sounded plausible, and the dates and places fitted, but when Nicholas Palmer, overseer of Battle, replied to Hutchings's letter of enquiry he said the only William Davis of Battle was the son of William Davis and his wife Anne. He was thirty-five and in 1758 had enlisted a dragoon in Mordant's regiment. He had two sisters Anne and Mary, and a brother Thomas who had heard from some soldiers of the regiment that his brother William had died in Germany of fever. Palmer added that there had been nobody called Johnson in Battle, a shopkeeper or of any other trade, for forty years; 'We believe the Person you have committed to Prison to be a Cheat ... so Sir you may ask what Questions you think proper from this Information. We have no other family of the name of Davis But the above in the Town.' Armed with this information, and no doubt after further questioning, the court sentenced Davis to be whipped and discharged; whether Johnson and the two children ever existed is unclear. Two other men arrested at the alehouse with him, probably during a privy search, who seem to have had nothing to do with Davis, were also whipped and discharged.[69] Vagabonds taken up during a privy search were 'required' to be whipped (1744 act s. 7), but if the court had been inclined Davis could have been sentenced to up to two years as an incorrigible rogue under s. 9.

Owen Bready was sentenced to four months in the house of correction and to be whipped once a month for begging in Liverpool with a false petition,[70] but in Middlesex Walter Dobben was in Tothill Fields Bridewell in 1769 charged with writing a fictitious letter to the Rt Honourable the Lady Sondes imploring charity for a supposed object and thereby attempting to defraud her ladyship of money and was discharged.[71] Rose claims that 'screeving' or writing begging letters was highly developed by 1815, and that such non-highway begging was

---

69 DRO Midsummer 1766.

70 LRO QSO2/129, QSP 1801/23.

71 LMA MJ/SP/1769/01/039.

outside vagrancy law, but it seems unlikely that he was discharged on those grounds; more probably Lady Sondes declined to pursue the case (Rose 1988, 33).

John Graham, apprehended in Cambridge with a forged petition, gave an unusually circumstantial account of how he came by it. He said he formerly had a hawker's licence, but admitted he had since sold goods without licence. He had several times called and lain three or four nights at a time at the Bankers Arms at Eye in Northamptonshire, and a few months previously told the landlord he needed to raise money to buy some goods, whereupon the landlord told him that he was formerly a schoolmaster in London and could help him. The landlord then drew up a paper headed County of Northampton purporting to be a letter of licence in the name of Thomas Pattin to collect and receive voluntary contributions for £800 lost on the tenth of July last at Newton near Oundle by thunder and lightning. The document said Thomas Pattin lived in Newton Northamptonshire in very great credit until a storm of lightning set fire to his stable and spread to the rest of his outbuildings and house and that he had a wife and six small children. The landlord added the names and seals of Samuel Moone and James Gorman as Northamptonshire justices and the names of John Graham as curate, Peter Gibbon churchwarden, Thomas Carr and John Read as overseers of Newton certifying his loss. The landlord made the licence in about two hours in his parlour and told Graham he might collect money by it, which he had since done in Northamptonshire. Several justices, presuming his letter of licence was genuine and his loss real, had given him permission to collect money in different places and counties until he was taken up in Cambridge and committed as an impostor. Graham admitted he had been collecting with it when he was apprehended; he had collected a total of £1 2s 0d from four people and had used it in Cherry Hinton a few days before. Unfortunately the sentence was not recorded.[72]

John Elmer was less fortunate. He was committed in July 1759 with his wife Catherine charged with begging in Okeford Fitzpaine using a false certificate of losses by fire at Stoke Wiltshire. From an army background and born in the East Indies, he was no longer a young man – indeed if his examination is to be believed he must have been nearly sixty – and had been travelling about picking up occasional work ever since his discharge from the army after Culloden. He confessed to begging with the certificate, which a stranger at the Angel in Shaftesbury gave him to help him on the road. He was sentenced to six months,

72 CA Epiphany 1772.

although his wife was most likely discharged – at least she does not appear in the bridewell bread bills with him.[73]

Although there is little evidence that the justices in other counties were either as vigilant about false representation as those in Dorset or as meticulous in gathering information, on at least one occasion the Dorset justices were the recipients of the enquiries. James Wadham of Imber Wiltshire wrote to the Dorset clerk of the peace for further information about a William Hancock, who had been committed to Devizes Bridewell for begging with a false certificate of losses of £340 and upwards by a fire at a farm he rented at Langton on the Isle of Purbeck. Mr Wadham had made enquiries there and had been told by the minister of Langton that Hancock's whole account was not true, and that such a man lived at Wimborne Dorset and had been taken up about a year before and flogged for the same thing. Wadham asked for information about this conviction and punishment for use in prosecuting Hancock at the next Quarter Sessions; 'I think such Rogues ought to be made Examples of'.

Wadham reported Hancock's statement that he was seventy, born at Dunsborne Abbot Gloucestershire, and discharged from Dorchester Gaol in 1737 under the Act of Insolvency. He also gave a description of Hancock, who was about five foot six or seven and lame in the right hand, which was shrivelled and had two or three holes in it now healed. Hancock had said it was healed by Queen Anne touching it while she was in mourning for the death of Prince George, implying it was caused by the king's evil, but on another occasion that it was caused by a fall when he was about seventeen. He wore a brown cloth coat, serge waistcoat with yellow buttons, dark brown plush breeches with white buttons, and a brown cloth greatcoat. He wore no wig but his own hair, grey and a little curling. The petition and certificate suspected to be false were signed by William Freeman of Corfe Castle and John Gill of Bridport, who according to Hancock signed them at Wareham petty sessions. Mr Wadham particularly wished to know whether these gentlemen were Dorset justices and where they lived.

The clerk was ill, but a reply was sent on his behalf 6 April 1751 confirming that William Hancock was indeed released from Dorchester Gaol in 1737 as an insolvent debtor, charged as William Hancock of Dunsborne Abbot Gloucestershire yeoman, at the suit of seven named persons for debts amounting to £920 13s 0d. Mr Templeman, the clerk, had also learned that a William Hancock, who seemed to be the same person, had worked as a mason at the stone quarries near Langton on the Isle of Purbeck but left about seven years ago, entered himself on board a man of war, and had not been heard of since.

---

73 DRO Michaelmas 1759.

The description fitted, but as to the losses he must be an impostor: there were no justices in Dorset called Freeman or Gill, nor had there been any fire in Langton for many years past. Mr Templeman also sent Mr Wadham a letter he had found among the sessions records mentioning a Mr Freeman, who seemed to be a confederate of Hancock, and which he thought might be useful for the case.[74]

Incorrigible rogues

Any person who had been previously punished as a rogue and vagabond and repeated the offence became an incorrigible rogue, as did those apprehended as rogues and vagabonds and refusing to go before a justice, resisting arrest or refusing to be passed, or knowingly giving false information in their examinations, provided warning of their possible punishment was given them at the time. Anyone resisting arrest for begging or escaping the person apprehending him was punishable as a rogue and vagabond; a rogue similarly escaping was punishable as an incorrigible rogue, as was anyone escaping from a house of correction. Thus an incorrigible rogue was often related less to a particular offence than to repetition of previous offences and is better discussed under the offence repeated. It may be noted that some persons were prosecuted, or sentenced, as incorrigible rogues without any further information about the particular offence appearing.

False examinations

The punishment of this offence depended on local knowledge at the alleged settlement to detect the falsehood once the person had been passed to the overseers on arrival. These were more often women, although John Mott was charged with being carried by a vagrant pass to Wimborne from Corsham Wiltshire on a false examination, but discharged, either because he was cleared, or in consideration of the three months he had already spent in bridewell.[75]

Jane Dear on the other hand was convicted and sentenced to six months in bridewell. She was passed from St Mary Islington to Lyme Regis late in 1773 claiming she was the daughter of Matthew Dear deceased of Lyme, and had lived one year as a yearly servant with her uncle William Dear in the same parish. If this examination had been true she was certainly settled there, but the parish

74 DRO Easter 1751.

75 DRO Epiphany 1783.

prosecuted and on the motion of their counsel she was adjudged a vagrant under the act, although the grounds for contesting the examination do not appear, nor is it clear where she actually was settled. Possibly she had acquired a subsequent settlement in Islington, but wanted to come home and conveniently 'forgot' to mention it. But as is so often the case, it is only possible to guess at the underlying circumstances.[76]

Mary Holmes was committed in 1759 for obtaining a vagrant pass by swearing her settlement was Lower Lytchett but later declared the oath was false. She was continued from the Easter sessions to July, when she was discharged. She was originally apprehended in Maidenhead charged with wandering and begging and lying out in the open air and this pass notes she was to be 'first publickly whipped', which may explain the relative leniency of her treatment in Dorset, although again it does not emerge where she actually was settled or if and where she was then passed.[77] Mary Jenkins was committed to Winchester Bridewell charged with being an idle and disorderly person, 'being found in a ditch near Gosport pretending she had been robbed', but discharged; it could hardly be proved she had not been robbed.[78]

Ann Fox said she had obtained a pass to Bristol from the Mayor of London by falsely swearing it as her settlement at the instigation of her husband, an Irishman, who said he might get work there, and she had used it to get money in several parishes in the City and Westminster. She was given money in St James Westminster and next went to St Giles, where she fell in labour and was delivered of a child in the workhouse, since dead. Her husband disappeared while she was in the workhouse. What happened to her next is not recorded, but she had evidently had no trouble getting the pass, and had been given money using it after the expiry date, implying no very great difficulty in practising such frauds, at least in the metropolis.[79]

If the magistrates in the parish of apprehension suspected a vagrant of knowingly giving false information they were obliged to warn the suspect of the possible punishment before conviction, so as to allow an opportunity to retract the false statement, but these suspects were more often charged as rogues and vagabonds accused of various forms of fraud and imposture. Remarkably few of those practising various forms of deceit and imposture seem to have received the harsher sentences possible for incorrigible rogues.

---

76 DRO Epiphany 1774.

77 DRO Easter 1759.

78 HRO July 1757 calendar.

79 LMA MJ/SP/1751/4/027.

Escaping custody

Among those charged with assault several were attempting to escape or help others to escape, interpreted widely in practice as meaning anything from the county gaol to a workhouse. Sometimes these escape attempts were successful: John Gough was apprehended in December 1769 wandering about Newmarket at unseasonable hours of the night not giving a good account of himself, but he broke out of the bridewell a fortnight later and had not been retaken by the next sessions.[80] Sometimes the escapee got off lightly: Sarah Wilding of Inskip with Sowerby appeared in court in Preston for breaking out of the poorhouse and going wandering and begging, but was discharged, perhaps for want of prosecution.[81]

Escapes from bridewells were taken more seriously than those from poorhouses or workhouses and any prisoners retaken were often treated more severely than if they had not tried to escape: Richard Murfit, committed in April 1785 for deserting his family at Soham, escaped a week later but was retaken in August and sentenced to receive twenty-four lashes at Cambridge, and the same again at Soham a month later.[82] Martha Major an idle and disorderly pauper was whipped at Isleham in 1764 for running away from Isleham workhouse.[83] On the other hand, Thomas Hankey and Sarah Frost, accused of running away from Newmarket workhouse taking with them several items of apparel, were discharged because Newmarket did not pursue the case.[84]

John McNeal escaped while being taken from Clerkenwell Bridewell to court; Benjamin Nash, one of the governor's servants, was directed to fetch him. According to Nash the prisoner said he was faint and wanted a drink, so Nash and another turnkey Markwick took him to the Bell. Nash then left McNeal with Markwick while he went to make water; Markwick 'being sent for the Night charges' turned his back and McNeal slipped out. Nash told the court he had been out eight nights in pursuit and felt sure he could retake McNeal; the justices gave him until next sessions to do so, but there is no further mention of the case.[85]

Advertisements appeared from time to time in local papers for the apprehension of persons escaped from prisons; keepers could be fined or

---

80 CA Epiphany 1770.

81 LRO QSP 1900/13.

82 CA Q/SO/8 October 1785.

83 CA Q/SO/6 October 1764. Lynn Hollen-Lees however states that paupers escaping from workhouses were not pursued (1998, 71).

84 CA Easter 1789 calendar.

85 LMA MJ/SP/1787/03/001.

dismissed if prisoners escaped due to their negligence, and it was usually they who inserted the advertisements. Five men escaped from Sherborne Bridewell in 1787 and a reward of two guineas was advertised for each one retaken; at least two were retaken and the keeper's sundries bill included his expenses and two guineas for retaking one of them.[86]

Harbouring vagrants

Harbouring vagrants was one of the few offences included in the 1744 Vagrant Act (s. 23) but not included in the tripartite division of vagrancy offences. Punishable by a fine it was invariably committed by a member of the community, most often an alehouse keeper or farmer. Prosecutions for harbouring are however rare: even where a privy search found vagrants staying in alehouses or in outbuildings, who were promptly punished or passed, the person harbouring them was seldom prosecuted, let alone fined the 10s to 40s specified in the act. Probably most were alehouse keepers paid a small amount in the course of trade; it could rarely be proved that they had harboured vagrants 'knowingly'. Thomas Reynolds however agreed to pay the expense of passing a group of vagrants he had harboured in his outhouses, presumably pursuant to a court order, although he was not formally prosecuted.[87] Several vagrants were taken up in the houses of John Harvey, Elizabeth Bulpin and Mary Dobson following a general privy search in the Dorchester area in 1753. All the vagrants were passed (six immediately by the examining justice), four appeared in court, and two women were whipped, but there is no sign of any action against those harbouring them. Several of the vagrants had indeed paid small amounts for their lodging: for example, Jane Young had paid 6d a week and did sewing for Harvey's wife in exchange for food.[88]

Nobody was prosecuted at sessions for harbouring vagrants in Lancashire, nor is there any evidence of quarterly privy searches. A warrant was issued in 1768 for the arrest of Robert Breckell of Singleton for disturbing the peace by entertaining vagrants, but no further action seems to have followed.[89] Michael and Hugh Crawford were taken up in the house of Alice Watkinson, 'a person of evil fame and behaviour', and Flora Macneill was 'harboured' in John Cletherall's house at Barton for about a week, but Alice Watkinson and John Cletherall do not seem to have been prosecuted.

86 DRO Easter 1787 John Gerrard's account.

87 CA Epiphany 1774 calendar.

88 DRO Epiphany 1753.

89 LRO QSP 1920/14.

Middlesex did carry out privy searches, which netted at least twenty-four vagrants and a number of straggling seamen, but the justices seem to have targeted the lodgers rather than those who harboured them, who may have been dealt with either by withdrawal of their licence, or if unlicensed by presentments for disorderly houses or for nuisance. The orders of court reveal a constant battle against disorderly places of entertainment, especially in the Clerkenwell and Finsbury area. The existence of alternative procedures makes it impossible to quantify the incidence of many such offences that *could* come under vagrancy legislation.

Chapter 9
The Causes of Vagrancy

This chapter will suggest some additional causes of vagrancy emerging from the records to illustrate other reasons why so many mobile poor found themselves falling foul of vagrancy law.

Vagrancy examinations, although not primarily designed to do so, sometimes shed light incidentally on the reasons underlying an individual's plight, and may illustrate a long struggle against various forms of adversity. The details are not necessarily true, but if the magistrate before whom the vagrant stood detected no fraud we can hardly do better: as Alcock remarked, 'you are oftentimes at a Loss to know, whether a Man's Wants be real or pretended, and whether you ought to relieve him as a Pauper, or punish him as an Impostor' (Alcock 1752, 8). Hence some writers believed most vagrancy was voluntary and down to personal failings, and that most vagrants were impostors, others that structural social and economic problems were more important. Unfortunately, while it was easy to blame the victim and demand stricter enforcement of the law, it was far harder to suggest remedies for endemic poverty and the failures of the existing welfare system.

Economic causes

Although it may well be true that some beggars were 'professionals', it seldom seems to have occurred to those who complained about the bad example set by vagrants to the labouring classes that begging was attractive chiefly because wages were too low to live on and work erratic or unavailable in their parishes (Rule 1981, 49–52; Schwarz 1985; Kumar 1988; Wrightson 2000). Superabundant harvests produced unemployment because prices fell so low farmers could not pay decent wages, dearth because there was little to harvest and fewer workers needed. Outdoor trades might be laid off for weeks in bad weather, textile trades suffered by changes in fashion, overstocking by pauper apprentices, and competition from foreign imports. Burn pointed out that many were idle only for want of work they were able to do, or of work at sufficient wages to support them, especially if they had many children (Burn 1764, 143–4).

Clearly aggressive beggars with suspicious stories or dubious passes aroused more hostility and were more likely to be arrested than a poor woman in rags with small children who knocked on a kitchen door begging food and drink, and it has been noted that to some extent older traditions of hospitality to the poor persisted. Parliament itself spoke with forked tongue, forbidding begging but making large exceptions rather than charge the exchequer, and many vagrants' examinations show they had been living for months or years by 'makeshift', by begging or a combination of begging and an itinerant trade, apparently without coming to the notice of the authorities (Eccles 1989, 253; Hitchcock 2001, 174–5).

Many of the components of welfare, such as parochial relief, local charities, co-residence with family or other poor, the pawnshop and credit, were largely unavailable to the mobile poor, and many reasons, by no means all reprehensible, led to the poor being on the road. Henry Zouch observed,

> Want, curiosity, the prospect of bettering their condition, or a desire to visit distant friends (for they have their friendships and their feelings) doth frequently carry them from home: and when, if sickness or some unavoidable accident shall happen to befall them, so that their slender stock of money and cloathes is gone, they may be driven to commit some act of vagrancy to sue for a morsel of bread. (Zouch 1786, 2, 12)

Sickness often led to unemployment. Elizabeth Ridout, taken up in Shaftesbury, had been in Salisbury Infirmary for six months and then in different places seeking service but reduced to begging by distress.[1] William Piercey was over seventy and had been injured falling from a scaffold in his previous job in Plymouth; he begged from James Hoor in Sherborne, who refused to relieve him and had him apprehended.[2] John Tilley had been a seaman and was put ashore at Minehead Devon unfit for duty; he had been forced to sell his clothes for maintenance and had since been begging his way to his settlement at Christchurch. Many had been travelling in search of employment, and must have subsisted by begging while they looked for work. William Lodge admitted there was weaving work in Darlington, but he was seeking work elsewhere because of a quarrel with his master.[3] Richard Jellycott, a scribbler in the wool industry, was born in Wilton; he had worked several years in Bristol and three months in Devon, and had since been wandering in search of employment; on his way home he begged in Wootton Glandfield and was turned in as a vagrant.[4] Peter Jackson, apprehended

1 DRO QDV box 4 bundle 11.

2 DRO Epiphany 1753.

3 DRO Easter 1753.

4 WRO WQSR 228/13–14.

in December 1764, was a bricklayer looking for work, 'the trade of a Bricklayer having for several weeks last past been very bad', no doubt because of the winter weather.[5]

Some had tried in vain to make a living. Paul Gowling was seventeen, apprehended in Kirkland singing and selling songs and small books. His father was dead and his mother was in the poorhouse in Norton North Yorkshire where he was born. He had tried travelling selling hardware, but the box was taken from him because he had no licence, and he was now intending to go to sea.[6] Andrew Gibbons aged sixteen had been on the parish at Kirklinton following the death of his father and grandfather until he was hired to a shepherd at Haltwhistle for six months, then in Kirklinton poorhouse. After a week there he got some buttons and little articles to sell, possibly provided by the parish, and went travelling but had fallen lame and was now destitute.[7] Vagrants themselves reported they had begged on the road and been given money, food or drink. John Burch had been at sea for some years, then did husbandry work in Lincolnshire and had been wandering since just before Christmas (when there would have been little casual husbandry work); he had run out of money by the time he reached Shaftesbury early in March and admitted begging his way from there to Blandford.[8]

They are typical of many vagrants describing problems finding work. A pattern of constantly changing employments tends to be common among men, many of whom had been in and out of the army and navy. John Tarrbrook had enlisted in the Duke of Richmond's regiment of foot at sixteen, then was drafted into the Welsh Fusiliers and discharged at Plymouth just before Christmas 1764. He first went to Carlisle, presumably begging his way, and finding no work went to a colliery in Haltwhistle where he worked about four months. His wife was then taken ill and they returned to Carlisle and got books of songs printed, which they sang about the streets and sold; they then went to Sleadale and did the same, and on the way back were apprehended at an alehouse, probably during a privy search.[9]

There are many such examples, and occasionally other reasons for being on the road emerge: George Tilley had been in business but failed,[10] Edward Burrows had got himself deeply in debt and left home to avoid prosecution by his creditors,[11] Samuel Bennett left Ipswich to avoid arrest for breaking a bond

5 LRO QSP 1870/17–18.
6 WRO WQSR 393/17.
7 WRO WQSR 328/48–9.
8 DRO Epiphany 1752.
9 WRO WQSR 319/8–9.
10 LMA MJ/SP/V/01/035/18.
11 DRO Epiphany 1748.

to another person,[12] and Richard Frewin absconded to avoid prosecution for stealing a spade.[13] A few had gone on the road to avoid the press gang.

The destitute and homeless

Although the great majority of vagrants were beggars, those charged under s. 2 of the 1744 act for 'lying out' were mostly either picked up in alehouses during a privy search, or found sleeping rough in the open or in some outbuilding. These rough sleepers may reasonably be assumed to include the most destitute and desperate, and to be largely an urban phenomenon. Very few were apprehended lying out in the more rural counties, except for some of those sick and in labour we met in previous chapters, and gypsies who were more often seen in rural than urban areas; probably it was easier to find a remote farm building in the country and to escape official notice.

Nobody was charged with lying out in Westmorland or Lancashire and only gypsies in Dorset, but there were nineteen in Hampshire excluding gypsies, and in Cambridgeshire at least twenty, almost all found in farm buildings, although many rough sleepers there were in groups of long-term wanderers, rat catchers, tinkers and so forth including gypsies. These may have chosen a wandering lifestyle, adopted it to make a living, or been born and bred to it. Jane Miller was born to parents who travelled selling hardware, married a tinker, and was now on the road with another tinker. She said she had no other way of making a living than by gathering rags and casting spoons.[14] A child born to travellers could have had almost no chance of ever acquiring a settlement. A temporary itinerant job might also turn into wandering and begging: John Spence, apprehended in Newmarket, came to Suffolk from Rugby in 1758 as a cattle drover, and had been 'strolling about' for two years since.[15]

But others were certainly not lying out by choice: some were sick and had collapsed. William Page, a lad of thirteen or fourteen, was taken up in Histon lying in the snow 'in time of hard weather'; he had been orphaned a year before and had wandered about ever since seeking employment.[16] Two boys aged ten and eleven picked up the same day in Fen Ditton were given cart passes, which suggests they were sick. Some of the Middlesex rough sleepers were probably also sick, since they too were given cart passes.

---

12 DRO Easter 1753.

13 HRO Q3/8 January 1763.

14 WRO WQSR 397/13, 26–7.

15 CA p&e 18 August 1760.

16 CA Easter 1789.

Examinations survive for 239 individuals apprehended in Middlesex as rough sleepers, almost all lying in the streets or in the open air, although a few had found shelter in outbuildings. Two men found in a barn during a privy search were sleeping off a pub crawl and have not been counted among them. Late in the century a few admitted squatting having found an empty room somewhere; none were sleeping under bulks like the group in our cover illustration, although many such references have been noted (Hitchcock 2001, 172). A group of boy thieves slept in glasshouses when the woman who received their stolen goods shut them out (Hitchcock and Shoemaker 2006, 180–85).

The Middlesex coroner recorded that Thomas Philips died 'choaked, suffocated and stifled' while sleeping in a brick kiln,[17] which was alleged to be the last resort of gin drinkers who had nothing left for lodgings.[18] Lime kilns were also used for warmth, and were similarly dangerous: an unknown man was found dead in a lime kiln at Warrington in 1754,[19] and the Middlesex coroners sat on at least five unknown men who died sleeping in lime or brick kilns. One of the more unusual, and unpleasant, boltholes was used by Susannah Watts, who 'voluntarily saith that she has been oblidged to lodge in the passage and Necessary of the Infirmary of Chelsea Hospital several nights'.[20]

In Middlesex 68 per cent of all rough sleepers were female. Although many of them claimed to be in distress and homeless, examinations shed only incidental light on the reasons why they were in this situation since the magistrates were not interested in the reasons, only in whether the person before them was a vagrant within the act, and where the person was settled. Some of the reasons however emerge by the way, especially where the reason has a bearing on settlement.

Child vagrants

Noteworthy among the rough sleepers were child vagrants, although some of these may have been cases of a parish ridding itself of a liability the easy way by using vagrancy law. Eight per cent of the female rough sleepers whose age is given were sixteen or under, and four per cent of the males, but others of both sexes whose age was not recorded were certainly children. For children the examination of a beadle or neighbour was commonly taken, who clearly knew the background because the child was resident in the parish but now orphaned or deserted and hence 'destitute

17 LMA MJ/SP/C/E/383.

18 1815 Mendicity report, 31.

19 LRO QSP 1705/8.

20 LMA MJ/SP/V/01/035/24.

of habitation'. This may not have been literally true, but it enabled the parish to remove him or her cheaply and promptly as a vagrant.

Girls of fifteen or sixteen had often been servants and were probably now out of place, but a few had gained a settlement by apprenticeship. More boys than girls had been apprentices; runaway apprentices, especially parish apprentices, are not unusual among the destitute, and their position was particularly sad because neither their father's (or birth) parish nor the master's parish wanted them. Their brief apprenticeships had settled them in a strange parish but had taught them no trade. The motive behind the apprenticeship in the first place was often to shift the settlement, and since forty days was enough to secure a new settlement most parish apprentices could not come back to the parish where their old contacts were.

Parish apprentices might be as young as seven and had often been foisted on a reluctant master under pain of a fine, or had been taken merely for the minimal premium, after which the master could treat the child so badly he (less often, she) would run away, leaving the master with the money and no further obligation. The abuses of parish apprenticeship were well known (Webb and Webb 1963, 197–201; J. Lane 1996, chapters 4 and 10), but little was done until an act of 1792 made abusive masters give up the apprentice's clothes and pay £10 to the overseers to bind him out again (32 Geo. III c. 57). In 1797 William Wright was fined £100 for cruelty to Edward Goale, a poor boy from Weyhill 'who from the Ill Usage he had received is likely to be a Cripple for Life'. The lad himself was awarded £30 of this.[21]

Richard Roberts although not an orphan was probably a parish apprentice and was committed in 1780 for running away and refusing to serve his master any longer. His father claimed he had been obliged to keep his son at home and pay a doctor 1s on one occasion and 4s 6d on another. He alleged the master kicked and stamped on the boy as well as beating him about the head with his fist, and would have thrown him downstairs if the journeyman had not prevented him. A Mr Gray of Stalbridge wrote to the court that 'led by Motives of humanity (knowing him to be a poor and almost Friendless Boy)' he had been to see him and found by the marks on his body that he had been beaten to 'an unmerciful degree'.[22] In such a case the court could discharge the apprentice from his indentures, although it is not clear whether the Dorset justices discharged Richard Roberts.

If the apprentice died however the full weight of the law might be brought to bear, too late to save the hapless apprentice. The cases of Elizabeth Brownrigg

---

21 HRO Q1/24 April 1797.

22 DRO Michaelmas 1780.

in 1762 and Sarah Metyard and her daughter in 1767 were notorious: all three women were hanged for torturing and starving their female parish apprentices to death (J. Lane 1996, 225; Herber 2002, 10–11).

Although most apprenticeships that ended prematurely did so by the apprentice running away, in some cases the master absconded, died or failed in business; occasionally the parting was mutual. James Clinch, apprenticed by St James Westminster six months previously to a master in Shoreditch, had apparently come back because his master had absconded, but St James sent him back to Shoreditch by vagrant pass, having successfully shifted his settlement.[23] Little Shelford however was stuck with Sarah Head, who was almost blind when she was apprenticed to a sack weaver who had since enlisted, but the court refused to discharge her, since the master knew of the problem when she was indentured.[24] Lydia Hesket, aged thirteen, had been apprenticed by St James to a cook in St Pancras for some five months when 'her said Master was Shot in Belfond Lane in an attempt to Rob the Exeter Coach about one Year since'. She was apprehended in St Paul Covent Garden, and had probably been living rough since the dramatic end to her apprenticeship.[25] Margaret McCullough aged twelve had been apprenticed by St Giles in the Fields but ran away after six months because of ill usage, and had been fending for herself for a year; she too was apprehended in Covent Garden, but her brief apprenticeship had settled her in Surrey, and to Surrey she must go.[26] She was by no means the only apprentice to run away because of ill usage.

Female vagrants

Sixty-eight per cent of the adult Middlesex rough sleepers were female, reflecting the economic vulnerability of any female unsupported by a husband or father. Seventeen per cent of these were widows, some very recently, and the same percentage were married, although none currently with their husbands. Although possibly not all deserted wives are noted as such, nearly three quarters of the married women said they were deserted, some only a short time ago; a few were married to seamen or soldiers, which might have the same effect. Most female rough sleepers however (67 per cent) were singlewomen. Singlewomen were mostly settled by derivation from their father, but a minority had gained a settlement by apprenticeship or hiring. Bastards of both sexes were of

23 LMA WJ/SP/V/01/093.

24 CA Q/SO/6 July 1759; see J. Lane 1996, 84 for a similar case.

25 LMA MJ/SP/V/01/026/23.

26 LMA WJ/SP/V/01/016/3.

course settled by birth, unless born on the road. Mary Moore knew nothing of her parents or birthplace but said she had been 'dropped' in Lambeth and had lived there four or five years, so she was passed there for want of better information, although it would have been hard to prove she was legally settled there.[27] Increasing numbers as the century wore on were settled by birth, had no settlement, or claimed not to know it, although settlement as a concept remained even after the New Poor Law.

In several cases bigamous marriages, generally involving soldiers, came to light when the 'wife' was passed to the man's settlement, only to discover she was not really married, that her (occasionally his) examination was false, and her children bastards. Soldiers enjoyed certain legal immunities: a soldier could only be arrested for a criminal matter, and it had been ruled that a soldier who deserted his family could not be taken up under the vagrancy laws, nor could he be taken up for bastardy or committed for sureties or maintenance (Burn 1793 vol. 4, 241). Escaping such situations or debts was indeed the motive for enlistment in some cases (Skelley 1977, 248; Snell 1985, 362; D.A. Kent 1990).

Lancashire justices issued numerous affiliation orders against soldiers and mariners, and at least one distraint, but it is not clear whether they could have been enforced. Even bigamy, although a felony until reduced to larceny in 1795 (35 Geo. III c. 67), rarely seems to have been pursued in cases involving soldiers, despite the obvious wrong done to the woman and any resulting children, not least by the impact on their settlement. These bigamously married women, like those married to Irishmen or Scots, were most often passed to their maiden settlement, which was unlikely to welcome with open arms a woman with several bastards, however blamelessly acquired. Women too might commit bigamy presuming a long-absent husband was dead; examinations sometimes mention a husband 'if living gone from her'. In a century of repeated wars and poor communications many soldiers and mariners disappeared leaving the wife unable to prove whether she was wife or widow. Ann Holland was perhaps one such, committed for illegally returning to Overton after removal and also charged with marrying Thomas Horne of Overton, her first husband still living, but she was merely discharged.[28]

Catherine Dullingham, born in Cork, married Christopher Dullingham in 1757 when he was a soldier in Ireland. In 1764 she was passed with her infant daughter from St Albans to Newmarket, having sworn her husband had deserted her and was settled in Newmarket; she was then committed by the overseers for making a false statement in her examination. Dullingham was indeed settled in

27 LMA MJ/SP/1769/02/021.

28 HRO Epiphany 1771 calendar.

Newmarket and had been in prison earlier in the year for deserting his real wife. Catherine was passed to Ireland under her former husband's name of Collins after two months in Cambridge Bridewell while the whole thing was sorted out.[29] There is no further trace of Dullingham himself.

In 1743 a woman was passed from Berwick-on-Tweed as the wife of Edward Larcomb of West Stour Dorset, a soldier in Brigadier Howard's regiment, but the parish claimed she had no right to a settlement because Larcomb already had a wife in the parish whom he married many years before.[30] A similar case arose in the same parish in 1755, when Elizabeth Gray was passed from Liverpool by virtue of a settlement statement by her husband James Gray, a soldier in the Royal Irish regiment of foot then on the march, stating that he was unable to support his family and was settled at West Stour by hiring and service. Arriving in West Stour with her two children she discovered he already had a wife: the real wife Ann Gray stated she had married him in the parish church there fourteen years previously, he had absconded about eighteen months later and she heard had enlisted but had never seen him since, and that Elizabeth had turned up in West Stour claiming to be his wife and to have parted from him about three weeks before. Unfortunately it is not clear what then happened to Elizabeth, but presumably she was passed to wherever her maiden settlement was.[31]

Women, although more likely to get parish support than men, could be in a tricky position if deserted. In 1750 Cherry Hinton was granted an order to receive the rents on an estate for life of £20pa belonging to Sarah Carter. She was a widow who had then married one Henry Maine, who had deserted her and was keeping the profits of her estate for himself, although able to earn a guinea per week.[32] This case illustrates the unfortunate position of women who married ne'er-do-wells: since in law a wife's property became the husband's (unless safeguarded by jointure rights or family trust arrangements), she could be left without an income if he absconded or refused to maintain her. The wife had no direct redress, although her settlement could claim on her behalf, and if she was not in her own parish she had to be sent back there first. In another case Richard Colley was ordered to enter into a bond to pay 2s weekly to his wife Sarah and fifteen-month-old son until the child was five, having entered into a gentleman's service several months previously and not allowed her any maintenance.[33]

It is a limitation of the sources that with the few exceptions we have noted where the parish either refused to receive the vagrant or claimed the person had

---

29 CA Michaelmas 1764.

30 DRO Easter 1743.

31 DRO Midsummer 1755.

32 CA Q/SO/5 October 1751.

33 CA Q/SO/6 May 1764.

no right to a settlement there, or where a person who had deserted his family was found and sent back, we do not know what happened on arrival. A runaway apprentice passed back as a vagrant was supposed to go back to his master and make up any lost time, but it seems unlikely many did so. Legally the overseers either had to find work for those passed or put them in some institution, but the Proclamation Society certainly believed the failure of overseers to do so was a cause of vagrancy (Proclamation Society 1790, 10). And how many vagrants never reached their destination? There were claims that constables and contractors did not deliver all the vagrants but let them go and pocketed the money, and some vagrants certainly escaped – 2.4 per cent of those conveyed by the Middlesex contractor in the 1770s and 1780s (1821 Vagrancy report 27–30; Eccles 2006, 89). Parish records may well reveal interesting cases, but the numbers will never be known.

Settlement law and parish attitudes

As early as 1742 the downside of settlement and parochial relief was evident: between them they had turned the question of how to provide for the poor into who should provide for them, and so raised 'such a spirit of shifting' that more was spent on getting rid of paupers than on supporting them (Cockburn (1963–66, 507). Burn commented that some parishes farmed their poor by employing 'some obnoxious person of savage disposition for the maintenance of their poor, not with any intention of the poor being better provided for, but to hang over them *in terrorem* if they will not be satisfied with the pittance which the overseers think fit to allow them' (quoted in Scott 1773, 44).

Parish attitudes could be harsh even to settled poor: families might be split up on entering the workhouse, and sometimes the poor preferred to try their luck on the road. Some ran away, others complained to the justices, like Jane Mason, an elderly widow settled in Kirkby Lonsdale, who had been sent away to James Tebay's poor house in the next county, which she said 'is very disagreaball being I was not used to their wicked way of life as I tack a poar house to be nothing but a seen of wickednes', and the town had refused her requests for clothing. It does not appear that the justices intervened, however.[34] Francis Hobler, clerk to the Lord Mayor of London, said all the City parishes farmed their poor, and when asked why they had left the workhouse vagrants would say the places were full of vermin and indecencies, and they could not stand it.[35] It may not always have

34 WRO WQSR 351/5.

35 1815 Mendicity report, 17.

been the overseers who were unsympathetic: Mary Britton, a widow with three children taken up in Manchester, said she had left Tanfield about two months previously 'through the Persuasions of some of the inhabitants of Tanfield'.[36]

Women servants could be turned away if they became pregnant, gaining no settlement, but if the master chose to keep them he became liable for expenses up to one month after the birth and might be under pressure from the parish anxious to avoid the settlement of a woman with a bastard. Two of the women who lay in on the road in Westmorland were servants turned away for pregnancy, and in one case the intention was explicitly stated: Hannah Longfellow was settled in Kendal and then hired in Underbarrow but was turned off before the year on the advice of the curate for fear she should gain a settlement.[37] A similar case in Dorset led to a settlement dispute between the two parishes involved. Susannah Clothier had served six and a half years of her apprenticeship to a yeoman in Long Burton when her master died. Various services followed and lastly she

> hired herself a servant to Robert Norris of Mintern Magna ... for one whole year for which she was to have the sum of 55s but about a month before the expiration of her Year the said Norris turned her away on Account of her being with Child and paid her the wages due to her for the 11 months, and his sister declared that her Brother wou'd not let her stay the other month because she shou'd not be a parishioner in the Parish of Mintern Magna and the Night she reconed with her she ordered her to go away to the Place where she belong'd that same Night.

She had gone back to Long Burton and bore a female bastard there, but Long Burton removed her back to Mintern Magna, which then appealed. The justices however decided in favour of the appellants.[38]

Support for army families with a legitimate settlement could be decidedly grudging. Ann Nicholson's husband was pressed for a soldier in 1745; the overseers refused relief, but the justices ordered 5s weekly for herself and five children under ten. This was whittled down to 3s and then 2s, and eventually in 1749 when Ann was a widow the overseers refused any allowance but offered the family the workhouse.[39]

Robert Yard was taken up in Sherborne and examined 13 December 1752. His was a familiar enough tale: apprenticed by his father to a cordwainer in Bow Devon he served only a year and then went to sea for two years as servant to the master of a privateer. Aged eighteen at the time of his examination, he

---

36 LRO QSP 1870/12–13.

37 WRO WQSR 295/8–9, 15–16

38 DRO Epiphany 1766; QSM 1/9 Epiphany 1766.

39 WRO WQSR 185/2, 188/16, 192/24, 202/6, 209/10, 241/12.

admitted having travelled about begging since his time at sea. The next day William Denning deposed before the same magistrate that Robert Yard had asked at his house for money to pay for lodging, and that he had seen him a few days before at a house where strollers and vagrants lodged. He was committed to Sherborne Bridewell and examined again at Blandford sessions 9 January 1753, then passed.[40]

Settlement law could be particularly hard on children over the age of seven born bastards or whose mothers had remarried, who might be hurried off to a parish where perhaps they knew nobody; and also on increasing numbers, particularly the Irish, who had no settlement. Well over half the male rough sleepers in Middlesex were Irish. Although it was theoretically possible for the Irish to gain a settlement, at least by 1825, very few appear to have gained settlements in the eighteenth century. John Mathews may have done so by hiring and service for seven years to Robert Nugent, Viscount Clare, at his country house in Essex, Goswell Hall; no pass was annexed to his examination, however, which suggests the court had doubts whether this was a settlement.[41]

Burn indeed was doubtful whether an Irishman could gain a settlement on any grounds whatsoever, but by 1825 it seems to have been decided that any natural subject of the king, born anywhere in his dominions, could acquire a settlement, and indeed a national of any country at peace with Britain could do so by renting (Burn 1755 vol. 1, 193–4; Nolan 1825 vol. 2, 150). Probably employers refused to hire Irishmen by the year, and landlords to let property over £10pa to them, aware that they might then become settled. By the nineteenth century the problem of Irish vagrancy had reached such proportions that parliamentary select committees were recommending the abolition of both the 1819 provision for their repatriation and all parish relief to them.[42]

---

40 DRO Epiphany 1753.

41 LMA MJ/SP/1768/04/017.

42 1833 Report on Irish vagrants, 4–5.

Chapter 10

Conclusion

Attention has been drawn in previous chapters to the impact of wars, the exclusion of significant groups from settlement and the poor law, and the failure to make any provision for legitimately travelling poor falling into difficulties. Many of the latter group for whom vagrancy law proved an unintended benefit we met in Chapters 4 and 5. The disadvantaged position of women and children emerges prominently; the eighteenth-century vagrant was far more often female than had been the case in earlier periods or would become the case in the nineteenth century. Poverty, with rising prices and falling real wages in the second half of the century, instability of employment, and low pay especially for unskilled workers were all clearly more widespread than most of the affluent classes acknowledged, although in the late eighteenth century some attempts were made by magistrates to deal with the problem. Probably some of those accused of failing to support their families were unable to earn enough to do so: the household budgets collected by Davies and Eden show how close to destitution most of the labouring poor were (Davies 1795; Eden 1797).

Settlement law and the parish basis of the poor law underlie much vagrancy, leading to the protectionist attitudes of parishes, reluctance to relieve travelling poor in difficulties, and the abuse of parish apprenticeship to shift the settlement of pauper children. Examinations often feature an army or navy background, a succession of insecure unskilled employments, lack of support from family or parish, and in the case of women and children the loss of a male breadwinner. Others, mainly the Irish, had no settlements and were virtually condemned to a life on the margins; nor could they gain a settlement however hard they worked as coal heavers and navvies.

Most contemporary opinion blamed vagrancy and theft on character flaws, voluntary idleness, self-indulgence, luxury, gambling, loose women, alehouses and suchlike, and saw the remedy as strict enforcement of the vagrancy laws preventing the poor starting on the slippery slope to the gallows. Fielding may stand for many when, urging such enforcement, he wrote, ‘Thus if we cannot discover, or will not encourage any Cure for Idleness, we shall at least compel the Poor to starve or beg at home: for there it will be impossible for them to steal or rob, without being presently hanged or transported out of the way’ (Fielding 1751, 71–2).

However, a few writers with more insight highlighted causes outside the control of the poor, such as have emerged from most of the examinations. The eighteenth century had its welfare scroungers, liars and cheats, and its share of socially irresponsible individuals, but they form a minority of those caught up in the vagrancy net.

In 1758 the economist Joseph Massie pointed out some of these involuntary reasons for begging, prostitution and vagrancy in the metropolis. His focus was on preventing females from falling into prostitution, but his analysis applied equally to their risk of becoming vagrants, and some of it equally to men and to the country at large. He pinpointed poverty as the chief cause, and especially the parochial basis of the poor laws leaving non-settled poor without relief. His list of the vulnerable included the dependants of seamen or soldiers, destitute of support and either far from their settlement or ignorant of it, and very young girls without families or neglected by them; he might have added boys in a similar situation. Other causes that applied also to men and boys included those coming from a distance to find employment and not finding any, or losing a former employment, and those unable to work because of accident or illness and not entitled to relief in the metropolis.

Pointing out that there were many circumstances where people needed relief and could not get it, he argued that the knowledge that this was indeed the case both served beggars for plausible excuses and obliged the charitable to help, thus encouraging more begging. His list of beggars' tales included people claiming to be ruined by flood or fire, having had a broken limb and unable to work, belonging to America and unable to afford a passage home, or unemployed and not knowing their settlement; a woman might claim to have a husband gone to sea or enlisted, or to have a cancer in her breast, or to be a widow with several small children (Massie 1758, 18). Every one of these problems was mentioned by at least one vagrant in my study, and might equally well have been genuine reasons for their plight. The Yorkshire magistrate Henry Zouch likewise highlighted the situation of the casual poor (in the sense of those resident in a parish but not settled there) in temporary need, and of discharged military personnel, the Irish and Scots (Zouch 1766, 34). Scott too blamed poor provision for the military and their dependants and thought men with families should be sent home directly at government expense 'however remote from the place of their discharge' (Scott 1773, 104–5).

In 1834 as part of the evidence accumulated in the run-up to the New Poor Law, S.S. Duncan Esq. compiled a memorandum on vagrants and poor travellers in which he listed the chief causes of the problem. The Irish, he said, were motivated by poverty, moving from an area where wages were low to London where they were high. He also blamed vagrancy on

> fluctuations of commerce and manufactures, on our naval and military operations, on our settlement law ... Men of all trades wander for employment. Failures of manufacturers, destruction of machinery, combinations, etc., send many hundreds on the tramp. Soldiers' wives and children are scrambling in all directions after regiments ordered to new stations. Sailors ramble from port to port to find captains for certificates of service, or to find new or old ships, or to pass examinations at public boards for pensions or prize-money etc. Wives are hunting for runaway husbands (rarely the reverse); children for runaway parents. Agricultural labourers are occasional wanderers for employment.[1]

Not much had changed since Massie wrote, except perhaps the share in causing the vagrancy problem of industrial difficulties and Irish immigration, which had both certainly increased. All these factors emerge as causes of vagrancy from the vagrants' examinations.

Featuring prominently is indeed the lack of provision for the military and their dependants, more noticeable in some counties than others: in Westmorland over a quarter of the vagrants had army connections, and a high proportion in Dorset were seamen, who might not all have been serving on men of war. In the eighteenth century there was no strict demarcation between the merchant fleet, the royal navy and privateers – the extra manpower for the royal navy in wartime was supplied by men either pressed or lured by crimps from the merchant service as far as possible, since landsmen were of limited use at sea. Parliament had in the late seventeenth century attempted to make a return to civilian life somewhat easier by permitting veterans to exercise trades without serving an apprenticeship, but there are enough ex-servicemen among the vagrants to suggest this had at best very limited success. The former provision of pensions for maimed soldiers had also lapsed, although Chelsea and Greenwich hospitals and Chatham Chest provided small pensions or residential support for a minority of former soldiers and seamen. Army families, unlike militiamen's families, were not entitled to county support and had to depend on parish relief, which might be decidedly grudging.

Unemployment and the insecurity of workers emerge as significant factors in vagrancy. Hiring and service for one whole year, which provided a fair degree of security and a settlement, was declining, and had only ever been general for servants in husbandry; in the metropolis domestic servants were more often hired and fired as required, although some gained a settlement by long service (Wrightson 2000, 313). Contemporaries disagreed whether there was an oversupply of servants and hence much unemployment, or whether

1 1834 Report on vagrancy, 80E.

servants could take their pick and were therefore becoming demanding and insolent; probably good servants in superior families kept their places and unsatisfactory servants or those working for families who could barely afford a servant constantly changed places (Hecht 1956, 23–4). Hiring and service lay behind many settlement disputes, so much so that in 1828 a parliamentary select committee recommended its abolition as grounds for settlement.[2]

The economic disadvantages of women and their vulnerability when separated from the breadwinner by death, desertion, military service or absence at sea emerge prominently, and were well known to contemporaries. Sir John Fielding commented that widows had only 'the wash-tub, green-stall or barrow' and the needle trades were notoriously low paid (Rule 1986, 200; Morgan and Rushton 1989, 99). The sexual vulnerability of female servants underlay much bastardy and consequent vagrancy, since a pregnant servant was usually dismissed and a bastard bearer was unwelcome to parish ratepayers. Failed apprenticeships were also common in the background of vagrants, especially failed parish apprenticeships, and were similarly fruitful sources of settlement disputes.

The poor sometimes worked as long as they could stand up for little more than a roof and food; a woman apprehended in St Martin in the Fields aged eighty-seven had been hired for two years 'at the Bunch of Grapes a Jelly House in the road to Chelsea' and was still working there for 10s per year; she had thereby gained a settlement in St George Hanover Square.[3]

Disability did not necessarily gain support: a witness to the 1815 mendicity enquiry, describing the difficulty of arresting vagrants with whom the public sympathized, remarked dismissively of a blind beggar, 'he is blind but he is perfectly capable of turning a wheel or anything of that kind'.[4] Parishes would give the disabled a few items to sell and send them on the road without a licence, anything to get them off the poor rate.

It rarely seems to have occurred to the many witnesses complaining to parliamentary enquiries that begging was more profitable than honest labour that the problem was the abysmal wages paid for honest labour; in a decidedly laissez-faire economy such a viewpoint would have been politically incorrect. But it is also hard to know whether vagrants claiming to be seeking work were really doing so as it was a 'respectable' reason for being on the road, increasingly so as industrialization developed. Many economic historians have however noted that most work, especially outdoor work, was weather dependent, seasonal, or fluctuated according to the trade cycle, the vagaries of the fashion

---

2 1828 Report on parochial settlements PP vol. 4, 201.

3 LMA WJ/SP/V/01/007/103–4.

4 1815 Mendicity report, 16.

industry, government policy on imports of foreign fabrics, the overstocking of impoverished trades with pauper apprentices and many such factors, and it is certainly not implausible that many were genuinely unable to find work.

In the nineteenth century tramping became both more common and regarded more cynically by the authorities (1821 Vagrancy report, 21; Hobsbawm 1964, 50; Hunter 2006, 185–6). Almost half the vagrants passing through Bedale in the late 1820s claimed to be seeking employment (Hastings 1981, 157), but G. Henderson Esq. told the 1834 Poor Law enquiry that 'the alleged want of work is a mere pretext for mendicity and a wandering life'.[5]

Historians have differed whether the Old Poor Law was a relatively generous system or provided only a wide-meshed safety net even for those with settlements; probably it varied with time and place. Poor law provision could certainly be inadequate, grudging or refused, at least towards those deemed undeserving. The legal requirement to provide for vagrants passed back to their settlements was largely ignored so that they ended up on the road again (Proclamation Society 1790, 10). Parishes could be harsh in their attitudes to women pregnant with bastards, forcing them to marry men preferably settled elsewhere, who promptly absconded, or to leave the parish for some unknown destination, although if the woman was picked up as a vagrant they would still find the bastard child settled in their parish.

Orphan and bastard children were a particularly unfortunate group, likely to be removed if at all possible and if not to be victims of the frequently abusive parish apprenticeship system, bound to 'any sorry masters that will take them' (Webb and Webb 1927, 198; M.B. Rose 1989) and to end up running away and unable to go back. Institutions such as the workhouse and poorhouse might be so unpleasant, sometimes deliberately so, that the poor preferred to go on the road. Soldiers' families were often removed immediately the men enlisted; others followed the regiment knowing they would receive only meagre relief at best, and that the man might disappear over the horizon leaving the wife with no idea whether she was married or a widow. Any who could not keep up tended to be helped, if at all, by the issue of a vagrant pass.

Few if any of these causes of vagrancy disappeared, or were even much improved under the New Poor Law, and vagrancy remained an intractable and by no means negligible problem late in the nineteenth century and even in the early twentieth (Jones 1982, 182; Hunter 2006).

---

5 1834 Report on vagrancy, 92E.

Appendix: Acts of Parliament

5 Eliz. c. 20 1563: An act for further punishment of vagabonds, calling themselves Egyptians.
14 Eliz. c. 5 1572: An act for the punishment of vagabonds, and for the relief of the poor and impotent.
18 Eliz. c. 3 1576: An act for punishing the parents of bastards, conveying rogues to gaol, setting the poor on work and establishing houses of correction.
39 Eliz. c. 3 1597: An act for the relief of the poor.
39 Eliz. c. 4 1597: An act for the punishment of rogues, vagabonds and sturdy beggars.
43 Eliz. c. 2 1601: An act for the relief of the poor.
1 James I c.7 1604: An act for the continuance and explanation of the statute made in the thirty-ninth year of the reign of the late Queen Elizabeth, intituled, an act for punishment of rogues, vagabonds and sturdy beggars.
7 James I c. 4 1609: An act for the due execution of divers laws and statutes heretofore made against rogues, vagabonds and sturdy beggars, and other lewd and idle persons.
13 & 14 Charles II c. 12 1662: An act for the better relief of the poor of this kingdom (Settlement Act).
3 William & Mary c. 11 s. 29 1691: An act for the better explanation and supplying the defects of the former laws for the settlement of the poor.
9 & 10 William III c. 27 1698: An act for licensing hawkers and pedlars.
11 & 12 William III c. 18 1700: An act for the more effectual punishment of vagrants, and sending them where by law they ought to be sent (Vagrant Removal Costs Act).
1 Anne stat. 2 c. 13 1702: An act for ... reviving and making more effectual an act relating to vagrants.
5 Anne c. 32 1706: An act for the continuance of the laws for the punishment of vagrants, and for making such laws more effectual.
9 Anne c. 14 1710: An act for the better prevention of excessive and deceitful gaming.

12 Anne stat. 2 c. 23 in *Statutes at Large*, 13 Anne c. 26 in *Statutes of the Realm*.: An act for reducing the laws relating to rogues, vagabonds, sturdy beggars and vagrants into one act of parliament; and for the more effectual punishing such ... and sending them where by law they ought to be sent (1714 Vagrant Act). The act came into force 1 August 1714.
5 Geo. I c. 8 1718 An act for the more effectual relief of such wives and children as are left by their husbands and parents upon the charge of the parish.
9 Geo. I c. 22 1723: An act for the more effectual punishing wicked and evil-disposed persons going armed in disguise &c (Waltham Black Act); renewed 1744, made perpetual 1758.
13 Geo. I c. 23 1727: An act for the better regulation of the woollen manufacture.
9 Geo. II c. 5 1735: An act ... for punishing such persons as pretend to exercise or use any kind of witchcraft, sorcery, inchantment, or conjuration (Witchcraft Act).
10 Geo. II c. 22 1737: An act for the better regulating the nightly watch and beadles within the City of London, and the liberties thereof.
10 Geo. II c. 28 1737: An act to explain and amend so much of the 1714 Vagrant Act as related to players of interludes.
12 Geo. II c. 29 1739: An act for the more easy assessing, collecting and levying of county rates (County Rates Act).
13 Geo. II c. 19 1740: An act to restrain and prevent the excessive increase of horse races, and for amending an act for the more effectual preventing of excessive and deceitful gaming.
13 Geo. II c. 24 1740: An act for amending and enforcing the laws relating to rogues, vagabonds, and other idle and disorderly persons (1740 Vagrant Act).
15 Geo. II c. 28 1742: An act for the more effectual preventing the counterfeiting of the current coin of this kingdom, and the uttering and paying of false or counterfeit coin.
17 Geo. II c. 5 1744: An act to amend and make more effectual the laws relating to rogues, vagabonds, and other idle and disorderly persons, and to houses of correction (1744 Vagrant Act).
18 Geo II c. 28 1745: An act to indemnify persons who have been guilty of the unlawful importing, landing, or running of prohibited, uncustomed, or other goods or merchandise.
18 Geo. II c. 34 1745: An act to explain, amend, and make more effectual the laws in being, to prevent excessive and deceitful gaming.
19 Geo. II c. 11 1746: An act for punishing mutiny and desertion (Mutiny Act).
20 Geo. II c. 19 1747: An act for the better adjusting and more easy recovery of wages of certain servants; and for the better regulation of such servants, and of certain apprentices.

24 Geo. II c. 44 1751: An act for rendering justices of the peace more safe in the execution of their office; and for indemnifying constables and others acting in obedience to their warrants.
25 Geo. II c. 29 1752: An act for giving a proper reward to coroners.
25 Geo. II c. 36 1752: An act for ... regulating places of publick entertainment, and punishing persons keeping disorderly houses (Disorderly Houses Act).
26 Geo. II. c. 34 1753: An act to explain, amend and continue several laws more effectually to prevent the spreading of the distemper which now rages among the horned cattle ... and for the more effectual paying the expenses of passing vagrants.
14 Geo. III c. 59 1774: An act for preserving the health of prisoners in gaol, and preventing the gaol distemper.
19 Geo. III c. 10 1779: An act for repealing an act of the last session intituled an act for the more easy and better recruiting of his Majesty's land forces and marines, and for substituting other and more effectual provisions in the place thereof (Press Act).
22 Geo. III c. 64 1782: An act for the amending and rendering more effectual the laws in being relative to houses of correction.
22 Geo. III c. 83 1782: An act for the better relief and employment of the poor.
23 Geo. III c. 51 1783: An act to repeal an act ... for further punishment of vagabonds calling themselves Egyptians.
23 Geo. III c. 88 1783: An act to extend the provisions of an act intituled 'An act to amend and make more effectual the laws relating to rogues, vagabonds, and other idle and disorderly persons, and to houses of correction' to certain cases not therein mentioned.
27 Geo. III c. 1 1787: An act to render more effectual the laws now in being for suppressing unlawful lotteries.
32 Geo. III c. 45 1792: An act to explain and amend an act made in the seventeenth year of his late Majesty King George the Second (1792 Vagrant Act).
32 Geo. III c. 53 1792: An act for the more effectual administration of the office of a justice of the peace in such parts of the counties of Middlesex and Surrey as lie in and near the metropolis (Middlesex Justices Act).
32 Geo. III c. 57 1792: An act for the further regulation of parish apprentices.
33 Geo. III c. 55 1793: An act to authorise justices of the peace to impose fines upon constables, overseers, and other peace or parish officers, for neglect of duty, and on masters of apprentices for ill usage of such their apprentices.
35 Geo. III c. 67 1795: An act for rendering more effectual an act passed in the first year of King James the first, intituled, an act to restrain all persons from marriage until their former wives and former husbands be dead (Bigamy act).
35 Geo. III c. 101 1795: An act to prevent the removal of poor persons until they shall become actually chargeable.

43 Geo. III c. 20 1803: An act for punishing mutiny and desertion; and for the better payment of the army and their quarters.
43 Geo. III c. 61 1803: An act for the relief of soldiers, sailors, and marines, and the wives of soldiers, in the cases therein mentioned, so far as relates to England.
59 Geo. III c. 12 1819: An act to amend the laws for the relief of the poor.
3 Geo. IV c. 40 1822: An act for consolidating into one act and amending the laws relating to idle and disorderly persons, rogues and vagabonds, incorrigible rogues and other vagrants in England (1822 Vagrant Act).
5 Geo. IV c. 83 1824: An act for the punishment of idle and disorderly persons, and rogues and vagabonds, in that part of Great Britain called England (1824 Vagrant Act).
4 & 5 William IV c. 76 1834: An act for the amendment and better administration of the laws relating to the poor in England and Wales (Poor Law Amendment Act).

Select Bibliography

Manuscript sources

The Quarter Sessions records of the following counties have been used:
CA Cambridgeshire Archives (formerly Cambridgeshire County Record Office), Shire Hall, Castle Hill, Cambridge, CB3 0AP
DRO Dorset County Record Office (now Dorset History Centre), Bridport Road, Dorchester, DT1 1RP
HRO Hampshire Record Office, Sussex Street, Winchester, SO23 8TH
LMA London Metropolitan Archives, 40 Northampton Road, London, EC1R 0HB
LRO Lancashire Record Office, Bow Lane, Preston, PR1 2RE
WRO Westmorland Record Office (now Cumbria Record Office), County Offices, Kendal LA9 4RQ
The Dorset and Cambridgeshire Quarter Sessions rolls have not been catalogued; either the sessions or the date of the document is given. In all other cases the record office piece-number is given.

Abbreviations

MB minute book
OB order book
p&e pass and examination
PP *Parliamentary Papers*

Parliamentary Papers

House of Commons Journals (HMSO London) vol. 32
Journals of the House of Commons
Parliamentary Debates
Parliamentary History

First report from the committee appointed to review and consider the several laws which concern the relief and settlement of the poor; and the laws relating to vagrants; and also the state of the several houses of correction, 1775. *House of Commons Sessional Papers* vol. 31.
Second report from the committee to consider the laws which concern the relief and settlement of the poor and the laws relating to vagrants, and also the state of the several houses of correction, 1775. *House of Commons Sessional Papers* vol. 31.
Report from the committee appointed to make enquiries relating to the employment, relief, and maintenance, of the poor; the apprehending and passing of vagrants; and regulating houses of correction, 1776. *House of Commons Sessional Papers* vol. 31.
Second report of the committee appointed to enquire how far the orders of the last session, respecting the poor, had been complied with, 1776. *House of Commons Sessional Papers* vol. 31.
Report from [the] committee on the state of mendicity in the metropolis, 1815. PP vol. 3.
Report from the select committee on the state of mendicity in the metropolis, 1816. PP vol. 3.
Report of the select committee appointed to take into consideration the existing laws relating to vagrants and to report their observations thereupon from time to time to the House, 1821. PP vol. 4.
Report from the select committee on the law of parochial settlements, 1828. PP vol. 4.
Report from the select committee on criminal commitments and convictions, 1828. PP vol. 6.
Report on criminal commitments and convictions, 1828. PP vol. 6.
Report on Irish vagrants, 1833. PP vol. 16.
Report on vagrancy by Harrison Codd Esq., 1834. Appendix E. PP vol. 38.

Primary printed sources

Adolphus, J. (1824), *Observations on the Vagrant Act and on some other statutes ...* (London: John Major).
Alcock, T. (1752), *Observations on the defects of the poor laws* (London: R. Baldwin).
Allen, L.B. (1821), *Brief considerations on the present state of the police of the metropolis: with a few suggestions towards its improvement* (London: J. Butterworth).
Anon. (1742), *Observations upon the Vagrant Laws* (London: T. Cooper).

Anon. (a barrister) (1824), *The Vagrant Act in relation to the liberty of the subject*. 2nd edition (London: John Murray).
Burn, R. (1755), *The justice of the peace, and parish officer* (London: A. Millar, 2 vols).
Burn, R. (1764), *A history of the poor laws: with observations* (London: A. Millar).
Burn, R. (1793), *The justice of the peace, and parish officer*, 18th edition (London: T. Cadell, 4 vols).
Burn, R. (1805), *The justice of the peace, and parish officer*, 18th edition (London T. Cadell and W. Davies, 4 vols).
Colquhoun, P. (1799), *The state of indigence, and the situation of the casual poor* (London: H. Baldwin and son).
Colquhoun, P. (1806) (1), *Treatise on indigence* (London: J. Hatchard).
Colquhoun, P. (1806) (2), *A treatise on the police of the metropolis* (London: J. Mawman).
Davies, D. (1795), *The case of labourers in husbandry* (London: C.G. and J. Robinson).
Eden, Sir F.M. (1797), *The state of the poor* (London, n.p., 3 vols).
Fielding, H. (1751), *An enquiry into the causes of the late increase of robbers* (London: A. Millar).
Gilbert, T. (1781), *A plan for the better relief and employment of the poor; for enforcing and amending the laws respecting houses of correction and vagrants; and for improving the police of this country* (London, n.p.).
Gilbert, T. (1782), *Observations on the Bills for amending and rendering more effectual the Laws relative to Houses of Correction* (London, n.p.).
Giles, J. (1744), *The compleat parish officer* (London: S. Birt and H. Lintot).
Howard, J. (1777), *The state of the prisons* (Warrington: J. Eyres).
Howard, J. (1784), *The state of the prisons*, 2nd edition (Warrington: J. Eyres).
Ilive, J. (1757), *Reasons offered for the reformation of the House of Correction in Clerkenwell* (London: J. Scott).
Ilive, J. (1759), *A Scheme for the employment of all persons sent as disorderly to the House of Correction in Clerkenwell* (London: J. Scott).
Massie, Joseph (1758), *A plan for the establishment of charity-houses for exposed or deserted women and girls* (n.p.).
Nolan, M. (1825), *A treatise of the laws for the relief and settlement of the poor*, 4th edition (London, n.p., 4 vols).
Paley, W. (1814), *The law and practice of summary convictions on penal statutes by justices of the peace* (London, n.p.).
Paterson, D. (1771), *A new and accurate description of all the ... cross roads in Great Britain* (London: T. Carnan)

Paul, Sir G.O. (1784), *Considerations on the defects of prisons* (London: T. Cadell).

Paul, Sir G.O. (1790), *General regulations for ... the houses of correction within the county of Gloucestershire*, presented to B. Cook, British Library RB.23.a.9848 (bound with above).

Proclamation Society (1790), *Resolutions of the magistrates deputed from the several counties in England and Wales assembled at the St Alban's tavern, by desire of the Society for giving effect to his majesty's proclamation against vice and immorality* (London: printed George Stafford).

Saxby, M. (1806), *Memoirs of a female vagrant, written by herself* (London: printed Dunstable).

Scott, J. (1773), *Observations on the present state of the parochial and vagrant poor* (London, n.p.).

Zouch, H. (1766), *Remarks upon the late resolutions of the House of Commons respecting the proposed change of the poor laws etc.* (Leeds, n.p.).

Zouch, H. (1786), *Hints respecting the public police* (London, n.p.).

Secondary printed sources

The literature on many relevant topics is very voluminous. I have here included all those sources from which I have quoted, but not all which form part of the required reading around the subject of eighteenth-century vagrancy.

Anderson, M.S. (1956), 'Great Britain and the Barbary States in the eighteenth century', *Bulletin of the Institute of Historical Research* XXIX, 87–107.

Ashby, A.W. (1912), 'One hundred years of Poor Law administration in a Warwickshire village', *Oxford Studies in Social and Legal History, vol. III* (Oxford: Oxford University Press).

Baker, J.H. (ed.) (1978), *Legal records and the historian* (London: Royal Historical Society).

Beattie, J.M. (1986), *Crime and the courts in England 1660–1800* (Oxford: Oxford University Press).

Beattie, J.M. (2001), *Policing and punishment in London 1660–1750: urban crime and the limits of terror* (Oxford: Oxford University Press).

Beier, A.L. (1985), *Masterless men: the vagrancy problem in England 1560–1640* (London: Methuen).

Brereton, I.M. (1986), *The British soldier: a social history from 1661 to the present day* (London: Bodley Head).

Brewer, J. and Styles, J. (eds) (1980), *An ungovernable people: the English and their law in the seventeenth and eighteenth centuries* (London: Hutchinson).

Bynum, W.F. and Porter, R. (eds) (1991), *Living and dying in London* (London: Wellcome Institute for the History of Medicine).

Chalklin, C. (1998), *English counties and public building, 1650–1830* (London: Hambledon).

Checkland, S.G. and Checkland, E.O.A. (eds) (1974), *The Poor Law Report of 1834* (London: Penguin).

Clark, P. (1979), 'Migration in England 1660–1730', *Past and Present* 83, 57–90.

Cockayne, E. (2007), *Hubbub: filth, noise and stench in England* (New Haven, CT: Yale University Press).

Cockburn, J.S. (1963–66), 'The North Riding justices, 1690–1750: a study in local administration', *Yorkshire Archaeological Journal* 41, 481–515.

Cockburn, J.S. (1978), 'Trial by the book? Fact and theory in the criminal process 1558–1625', in Baker, J.H. (ed.).

Conway, S.R. (1985), 'The recruitment of criminals into the British army, 1775–1781', *Bulletin of the Institute of Historical Research* 58, 46–58.

Curth, L.H. (ed.) (2006), *From physick to pharmacology: five hundred years of British drug retailing* (Aldershot: Ashgate).

DeLacy, M. (1986), *Prison reform in Lancashire 1700–1850* (Manchester: Chetham Society).

Devereaux, S. (2005), 'The promulgation of the statutes', in Lemmings, D. (ed.).

Dobson, M.J. (1997), *Contours of death and disease in early modern England* (Cambridge: Cambridge University Press).

Dyer, C. (ed.) (2006), *The self-contained village? The social history of rural communities 1250–1900* (Hertford: University of Hertfordshire Press).

Eccles, A. (1977), 'Obstetrics in the 17th and 18th centuries and its implications for maternal and infant mortality', *Bulletin of the Society for the Social History of Medicine* 20, 8–11.

Eccles, A. (1982), *Obstetrics and gynaecology in Tudor and Stuart England* (London: Croom Helm).

Eccles, A. (1989), 'Vagrancy in later eighteenth-century Westmorland: a social profile', *Transactions of the Cumberland and Westmorland Antiquarian and Archaeological Society* LXXXIX, 249–61.

Eccles, A. (1990), 'Pain in childbirth before Simpson: perceptions and responses', *Proceedings of the History of Anaesthesia Society* 8a, 36–41.

Eccles, A. (2006), 'The Adams' father and son, vagrant contractors to Middlesex 1757–94', *Transactions of the London and Middlesex Archaeological Society* 57, 83–91.

Eccles, A. (2008), 'A superior kind of vagrant', *Transactions of the London and Middlesex Archaeological Society* 59, 213–20.

Eccles, A (2010) (1), 'Disease and death in Dorset prisons in the eighteenth century', *Proceedings of the Dorset Natural History and Archaeological Society* 131, 29–34.

Eccles, A. (2010) (2), 'Charles Hamilton Mercer – a suspicious vagrant held in Sherborne Bridewell and Dorset Gaol under the 1744 Vagrant Act', *Proceedings of the Dorset Natural History and Archaeological Society* 131, 145–48.

Eccles, A. (2010) (3), 'The eighteenth-century vagrant contractor', *Local Population Studies* 85, 46–63.

Eccles, A. (2011), 'Vagrancy and rising rates in the long eighteenth century', *Southern History* 33, 78–100.

Eccles, A. (2012), '"Pretending to be seafaring men" – vagrancy law and forgery with special reference to eighteenth-century Dorset', *Proceedings of the Dorset Natural History and Archaeological Society* 133 (forthcoming).

Emsley, C. (1996), *Crime and society in England 1750–1900*, 2nd edition (Harlow: Longman).

Floate, S.S. (1999), *My ancestors were gypsies* (London: Society of Genealogists).

Gatrell, V.A.C. et al. (eds) (1980), *Crime and the law: the social history of crime in Western Europe since 1500* (London: Europa).

Hardy, W.D. (ed.) (1905), *Hertford County Records 1581–1698* (Hertford, n.p., 5 vols).

Hastings, R.P. (1981), *Essays in North Riding history 1780–1850* (Northallerton: North Yorkshire County Council).

Hay, D. (2002), 'Dread of the Crown Office: the English magistracy and King's Bench, 1740–1800', in Landau, N. (ed.).

Hecht, J.J. (1956), *The domestic servant class in eighteenth-century England* (London: Routledge).

Henderson, A. (1999), *Disorderly women in eighteenth-century London: prostitution and control in the metropolis 1730–1830* (London: Longman).

Herber, M. (2002), *Criminal London* (Chichester: Phillimore).

Hindle, S. (2004), *On the parish? The micro-politics of poor relief in rural England c. 1550–1750* (Oxford: Oxford University Press).

Hindle, S. (2006), 'Destitution, liminality and belonging: the church porch and the politics of settlement in English rural communities, c.1590–1660', in Dyer, C. (ed.).

Hitchcock, T. (2001), 'The publicity of poverty in early eighteenth-century London', in Merritt, J.F. (ed.)

Hitchcock, T. (2004), *Down and out in eighteenth-century London* (London: Hambledon and London).

Hitchcock, T. and Shoemaker, R. (2006), *Tales from the hanging court* (London: Hodder Arnold).

Hitchcock, T., King, P. and Sharpe, P. (eds) (1997), *Chronicling poverty: the voices and strategies of the English poor, 1640–1840* (London: Macmillan).

Hobsbawm, E.J. (1964), *Labouring men* (London: Weidenfeld and Nicolson).

Hollen-Lees, L. (1998), *The solidarities of strangers: the English poor laws and the people, 1700–1948* (Cambridge: Cambridge University Press).

Houlding, J.A. (1981), *Fit for service: the training of the British Army 1715–1795* (Oxford: Clarendon Press).

Howell, C. and Twomey, R. (eds) (1991), *Jack Tar in history: essays in the history of maritime life and labour* (New Brunswick, NJ: Acadiensis Press).

Hughes, R. (1988), *The fatal shore* (London: Pan Books).

Hunter, R. (2006), 'Vagrancy in the East and West Ridings of Yorkshire during the late Victorian period', *The Local Historian* 36 (August), 185–94.

Ignatieff, M. (1978), *A just measure of pain: the penitentiary in the industrial revolution, 1750–1850* (London: Macmillan).

Innes, J. (1987), 'Prisons for the poor: English bridewells 1555–1800', in Snyder, F. and Hay, D. (eds).

Jones, D. (1982), *Crime, protest, community and police in nineteenth-century Britain* (London: Routledge and Kegan Paul).

Kent, D.A. (1990), '"Gone for a soldier": family breakdown and the demography of desertion in a London parish 1750–91', *Local Population Studies* 45, 27–42.

Kent, J.R. (1981), 'Population mobility and alms: poor migrants in the midlands during the early seventeenth century', *Local Population Studies* 27, 35–51.

Kent, J.R. (1986), *The English village constable 1580–1642* (Oxford: Clarendon Press).

King, P. (1984), 'Decision-makers and decision-making in the English criminal law, 1750–1800', *Historical Journal* 27, 25–59.

King, P. (2000), *Crime, justice, and discretion in England 1740–1820* (Oxford: Oxford University Press).

King, P. (2002), 'War as a judicial resource: press gangs and prosecution rates, 1740–1830', in Landau, N. (ed.).

King, P. (2006), *Crime and law in England, 1750–1840: remaking justice from the margins* (Oxford: Oxford University Press).

King, S. (2000), *Poverty and welfare in England 1700–1850: a regional perspective* (Manchester: Manchester University Press).

King, S. (2004), '"Meer pennies for my baskitt will be enough": women, work and welfare, 1770–1830', in Lane, P. et al. (eds).

King, S. (2006), 'Accessing drugs in the eighteenth-century regions', in Curth, L.H. (ed.).

Kumar, K. (1988), 'From work to employment and unemployment: the English experience', in Pahl, R.E. (ed.).

Landau, N. (1984), *The justices of the peace 1679–1760* (Berkeley, CA, and London: University of California Press).

Landau, N. (ed.) (2002) (1), *Law, crime and English society, 1660–1830* (Cambridge: Cambridge University Press).

Landau, N. (2002) (2), 'The trading justice's trade', in Landau, N. (ed.), 46–70.

Lane, J. (1996), *Apprenticeship in England, 1600–1914* (London: University College London Press).

Lane P. et al. (eds) (2004), *Women, work and wages in England, 1600–1850* (London: Boydell).

Lemmings, D. (ed.) (2005), *The British and their laws in the eighteenth century* (Woodbridge: Boydell).

Leonard, E.M. (1900), *The early history of English poor relief* (Cambridge: Cambridge University Press).

Lieberman, D. (2002) 'Mapping criminal law: Blackstone and the categories of English jurisprudence', in Landau, N. (ed.).

Lightning, R.H. (1966), 'Ealing and the poor: the poor law, the workhouse and poor relief from 1722 to 1800', Ealing Local History Society Members Papers 7.

Linebaugh, P. and Rediker, M. (1991), 'The many-headed hydra: sailors, slaves and the Atlantic working class in the eighteenth century', in Howell, C. and Twomey, R. (eds).

Loudon, I. (1985), 'The nature of provincial medical practice in eighteenth-century England', *Medical History* 29, 1–32.

Malcolmson, R.W. (1973), *Popular recreation in English society 1700–1850* (Cambridge: Cambridge University Press).

Marshall, D. (1926), *The English poor in the eighteenth century* (London: Routledge).

McGowen, R. (2002), 'Making the "bloody code"? Forgery legislation in eighteenth-century England', in Landau, N. (ed.).

McLynn, F.J. (1989), *Crime and punishment in eighteenth-century England* (London: Routledge).

Merritt, J.F. (ed.) (2001), *Imagining early modern London: perceptions and portrayals of the City from Stow to Strype, 1598–1720* (Cambridge: Cambridge University Press).

Morgan, G. and Rushton, P. (1998), *Rogues, thieves and the rule of law: the problem of law enforcement in north-east England 1718–1800* (London: University College London Press).

Neuman, M. (1982), *The Speenhamland county: poverty and the poor laws in Berkshire 1782–1834* (New York: Garland Publishing Inc.).

Oberwittler, D. (1990), 'Crime and authority in eighteenth-century England: law enforcement on a local level', *Historical Social Research* xv, 10–25.

Pahl, R.E. (ed.) (1988), *On work: historical, comparative and theoretical approaches* (Oxford: Blackwell).

Place, G.W. (1985), 'The repatriation of Irish vagrants from Cheshire 1750–1815', *Journal of the Chester Archaeological Society* 68, 125–41.

Radzinowicz, Sir L. (1948–68), *History of criminal law* (London: various publishers, 5 vols).

Richardson, R. (1988), *Death, dissection and the destitute* (London: Penguin).

Rickard, G. (1995), *Vagrants, gypsies and travellers in Kent 1572–1948* (privately published).

Roberts, M.J.D. (1988), 'Public and private in early nineteenth-century London: the Vagrant Act of 1822 and its enforcement', *Social History* 13, 273–94.

Rodger, N.A.M. (1988), *The wooden world: an anatomy of the Georgian navy* (London: Fontana).

Rogers, N. (1991), 'Policing the poor in eighteenth-century London', *Histoire Sociale* (Ottawa) 47, 127–47.

Rogers, N. (1994), 'Vagrancy, impressment and the regulation of labour in eighteenth-century Britain', *Slavery and Abolition* 15:2, 102–13.

Rogers, N. (2002), 'Impressment and the law in eighteenth-century Britain', in Landau, N. (ed.).

Rose, L. (1988), *Rogues and vagabonds* (London: Routledge).

Rose, M.B. (1989), 'Social policy and business: parish apprenticeship and the early factory system 1750–1834', *Business History* 31:4, 5–32.

Rule, J.G. (1981), *The experience of labour in eighteenth-century industry* (London: Croom Helm).

Schwarz, L.D. (1985), 'The standard of living in the long run: London 1700–1860', *Economic History Review* (2nd series) 38:1, 24–41.

Sharpe, J.A. (1997), *Early modern England: a social history 1550–1760*, 2nd edition (London: Arnold).

Sharpe France, R. (1985), *Guide to the Lancashire Record Office* (Preston: Lancashire County Council).

Shoemaker, R.B. (1991), *Prosecution and punishment: petty crime and the law in London and rural Middlesex c.1660–1725* (Cambridge: Cambridge University Press).

Shoemaker, R.B. (2004), *The London mob: violence and disorder in eighteenth-century London* (London and New York: Hambledon and London).
Skelley, A.R. (1977), *The Victorian army at home: the recruitment, terms and conditions of the British regular 1859–1899* (London: Croom Helm).
Slack, P.H. (1974), 'Vagrants and vagrancy in England 1598–1644', *Economic History Review* 27, 360–79.
Smith, J.R (1987), *The speckled monster: smallpox in England 1670–1970 with particular reference to Essex* (Chelmsford: Essex Record Office).
Snell, K.D.M (1985), *Annals of the labouring poor: social change in agrarian England 1660–1900* (Cambridge: Cambridge University Press).
Snell, K.D.M. (1984), 'Parish registration and the study of labour mobility', *Local Population Studies* 33, 29–43.
Snyder, F. and Hay, D. (eds) (1987), *Labour, law and crime: an historical perspective* (London: Tavistock).
Sokoll, T. (1997), 'Old age in poverty: the record of Essex pauper letters, 1780–1834', in Hitchcock, T., King, P. and Sharpe, P. (eds), 127–54.
Stone, L. (1995), *Uncertain unions and broken lives* (Oxford: Oxford University Press).
Styles, J. (1983), 'Sir John Fielding and the problem of criminal investigation in eighteenth-century England', *Transactions of the Royal Historical Society* (5th series) 33, 127–49.
Sweeney, T. (1985), *The extension and practice of summary justice in England 1790–1860* (Cambridge, Ph.D. thesis).
Taylor, J.S. (1989), *Poverty, migration and settlement in the industrial revolution* (Palo Alto, CA: The Society for the Promotion of Science and Scholarship).
Taylor, J.S. (1997), 'Voices in the crowd: the Kirkby Lonsdale township letters, 1809–36', in Hitchcock, T., King, P. and Sharpe, P. (eds), 109–26.
Thompson, E.P. (1975), *Whigs and hunters: the origin of the Black Act* (London: Allen Lane).
Tollit, S.S. (1953), 'The first house of correction for the county of Lancaster', *Historical Society of Lancashire and Cheshire* 105, 69–90.
Trustram, M. (1984), *Women of the regiment: marriage and the Victorian army* (Cambridge: Cambridge University Press).
Wear, A. (1991), 'Caring for the sick poor in St Bartholomew's Exchange 1580–1676', in Bynum, W.F. and Porter, R. (eds).
Webb, S. and Webb, B. (1906, reprinted 1963), *The Parish and the County* (London: Longman).
Wells, R. (1993), 'Migration, the law, and parochial policy in eighteenth- and nineteenth-century southern England', *Southern History* 16, 87–139.

Western, J.R. (1965), *The English militia in the eighteenth century: the story of a political issue 1660–1802* (London: Routledge and Kegan Paul).
Wrightson, K. (2000), *Earthly necessities: economic lives in early modern Britain, 1470–1750* (London: Penguin Books).

Index

For Product Safety Concerns and Information please contact our EU representative GPSR@taylorandfrancis.com Taylor & Francis Verlag GmbH, Kaufingerstraße 24, 80331 München, Germany